RENAISSANCE DRAMA

New Series XXX   1999–2001

Renaissance Drama

New Series XXX

Institutions of the Text

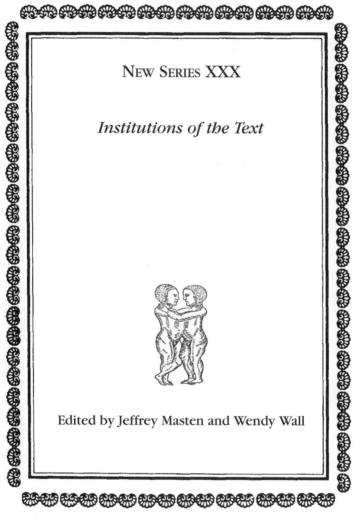

Edited by Jeffrey Masten and Wendy Wall

Northwestern University Press

Evanston 2001

Contents

Editorial Note

R ENAISSANCE DRAMA, an annual and interdisciplinary publication, invites submissions that investigate traditional canons of drama as well as the significance of performance, broadly construed, to early modern culture. We particularly welcome essays that examine the impact of new forms of interpretation on the study of Renaissance plays, theater, and performance. There are no fixed chronological or geographical limits.

Volume XXX, "Institutions of the Text," includes essays that examine playtexts in their relationship to a structure or structures shaping early modern culture: the printing industry, the marketplace of texts and of fashions, theatrical companies, manuscript culture and circulation, authorship, the family and paternity. As this list begins to suggest, the essays range widely across the terrain of early modern culture and display a variety of methodologies and interests. But at the same time that these essays shed light on the institutions and shaping ideologies of early modern culture, they are also remarkably attuned to the language of the playtexts they analyze within the world that produced them. Some essays focus on the materiality of the text and therefore speak to the stakes of editorial practice: what rests on discerning a single word in manuscript or in print? How does a phrase on a title page shape concepts of literary property or reveal the terms by which literary ambition was expressed? What happens to the meaning of these playtexts in their manifestation as modern performance and/or as text? Other essays locate plays within/as part of the linguistic structures that shaped conceptions of gender, sexuality, family, and nation.

What conceptions of masculinity and paternity were available in the period, how did they circulate, and in what terms? What other aspects of culture were at stake in definitions of paternity? Using distinct approaches to discern the meaning and cultural capital of a wide range of Renaissance playtexts and performances, these essays thus raise critical questions about the texts and textures of early modern institutions.

❀❀❀

Beginning in 2002, *Renaissance Drama* will conform to the stylistic conventions outlined in *The Chicago Manual of Style* (14th edition). Scholars preparing manuscripts for submission should refer to this book. Manuscripts should be submitted in triplicate; those accompanied by a stamped, self-addressed envelope will be returned. Submissions and inquiries regarding future volumes should be addressed to: *Renaissance Drama,* Department of English, 215 University Hall, Northwestern University, Evanston, IL 60208, USA.

Jeffrey Masten and Wendy Wall
Editors

RENAISSANCE DRAMA

New Series XXX   1999–2001

Tennis Balls: Henry V *and Testicular Masculinity, or, According to the* OED, *Shakespeare Doesn't Have Any Balls*

REBECCA ANN BACH

T HE ALTERNATIVE TITLE of this essay is a lie, at least in the literal sense. The *Oxford English Dictionary* does, of course, refer its readers to Shakespeare for many uses of the word "balls." The dictionary tells us that "ball" occurs in *Richard II,* meaning earth: "From under this Terrestrial Ball" (3.2.41). It also cites *Henry V,* the subject of this essay, for the ball as "the golden 'orb' borne together with the scepter as the emblem of sovereignty" and as "a globular body to play with, which is thrown, kicked, knocked or batted about in various games." The *OED* uses Shakespeare again for the meaning of "ball" as ball of the eye and for "a globular rounded mass of any substance." There are balls in Shakespeare, then, but no balls in the sense that my prospective title would have implied. In fact, the first citation of "balls" with the sense of "Courage, determination; (manly) power or strength; masculinity" that the *OED* gives is from D. H. Lawrence's 1928 *Lady Chatterly's Lover;* and the dictionary characterizes that definition as "*slang* (chiefly U.S.)." For its usages as "golden 'orb,'" as a thing to throw, as a round body used in games, and as a "missile . . . projected from an engine of war," the dictionary cites Shakespeare's *Henry V.* The *OED* can reach into that play repeatedly for its "balls" because, of the ten Shakespeare plays with "balls," *Henry V* uses the word six times, while the other nine plays (including *Love's Labour's Lost,* whose "balls" are enclosed in the compound word "pitch-balls") each use the word only once.

3

Henry V has all of these "balls" because the play dramatizes the historical incident of the French Dauphin's—or as the English wrote it, Dolphin's— gift to the king of "a tun" of tennis balls. Shakespeare could have taken the incident from a number of chronicle and popular sources. In 1586, Holinshed's *Chronicles* records the story as:

Whilest in the Lent season the king laie at Killingwoth, there came to him from Charles Dolphin of France certaine ambassadors, that brought with them a barrell of Paris balles, which from their master they presented to him for a token that was taken in verie ill part, as sent in scorne, to signifie, that it was more meet for the king to passe the time with such childesh exercise, than to attempt any worthie exploit. Wherefore the King wrote to him, that yer ought long, he would tosse him some London Balles that purchance should shake the walles of the best court in France. (64)

Hall's chronicle history dismisses the story, telling its readers:

Here I ouerpasse howe some writers saie that the Dolphyn thynking kyng Henry to be geuen still to such plaies and light folies as he exercised & vsed before the tyme that he was exalted to the croune sent to hym a tunne of tennis balles to plaie with, as who said that he could better skil of tennis then of warre, and was more expert in light games than marciall pollicy. (57)

As well as Holinshed's and Hall's versions of the story, Shakespeare may have seen William Caxton's printing of Brut's *Chronicles,* in which the king "lete make tenys balles for the dolphyn in al the hast that they myght be made, and they were harde and grete gunne-stones for the Dolphyn to playe with-alle," because Shakespeare employs the term "Gun-stones" in the king's dialogue with the French ambassador (Bullough 352). Henry tells the Dauphin's ambassadors that "this Mocke of his / Hath turn'd his balles to Gun-stones, and his soule / Shall stand sore charged, for the wastefull vengeance / That shall flye with them" (TLN 431–34, 1.2.281–84).[1]

In his 1982 Oxford edition of the play, Gary Taylor notes the wordplay here. His note says, "balls: tennis balls, but probably also punning on 'testicles.'" Taylor, who seems to be alone among editors in venturing beyond the *OED*'s coyness, gives a Shakespearean reference for the sense of "ball" as testicle in the period: *Henry VIII*'s dialogue between Anne and the Old Lady; in that dialogue, when Anne disclaims her desire to be queen, the lady answers her, "In faith, for little England / You'd venture an emballing" (2.3.46–47). Taylor also cites an unmistakable reference from

Middleton's *Women Beware Women* (3.3.85): "*Ward.* 'Why, can you catch a ball well?' *Isabella.* 'I have catched two in my lap at one game.'" Taylor argues that "the pun [in the *Henry V* dialogue] is somewhat irrational, but the defiant and contemptuous tone with which 'balls' is spoken makes it hard to avoid" (1.2.282n.)[2] Actually, Shakespeare's use of "gun-stones" in the dialogue points directly at the pun on "balls" since "stones" was the most common familiar term for testicles in the sixteenth and seventeenth centuries.[3]

In this essay, I argue that the pun is wholly rational and indeed is a key lexical moment in a play that repeatedly shows its audience an embodied English masculinity. Peter Erickson perceptively remarks of *Henry V* that it "portrays a sharp contrast between the English and the French, a contrast turning on manliness and the lack of it" (55).[4] The English masculinity portrayed in *Henry V* is located in early modern notions of the body as well as in ideology, or, better, the ideology of the body in early modern England informs and is inseparable from an early modern ideology of masculinity.[5] Shakespeare takes the story of Henry's rejection of the tennis balls and writes it as a story of the potent, masculine, English warrior body. This is an English body with balls, the organs that guarantee a conjunction of reproductive and warrior potency. In this story, when the Dauphin's ambassadors hand over their "treasure" of tennis balls, they unwittingly geld themselves, and Henry is not only supplying the English with "stones" for their guns, he is increasing England's virility. Although this version of masculinity sounds familiar to the late-twentieth-century or early-twenty-first-century reader, that virility is distinctly not modern. *Henry V*'s story of England and Henry's masculine warrior body—what I will be calling testicular masculinity—is specific to the culture that produced the play because it is a notion of male bodily power that values breeding for itself and not for the sexual act.

That is, *Henry V*'s testicular masculinity, unlike late-twentieth-century American masculinity, does not esteem the sexual act in itself, but only in its realized potential to create male children. That testicular masculinity sees "semen as that which is passed to women to insure procreation and (ideally, [Francis Bacon] would say) to maintain patrilineal descent" (Breitenberg 30). This is a masculinity that excludes women, that sees women as emasculating even as they become the receptacles within which more men are bred. *Henry V* tells the story of a testicular masculinity scornful of sexual play, a masculinity in which balls are gun-stones in war and the producers of male seed which breeds more men. The play defines masculinity in terms associated with breeding, and it establishes it in contrast to the emasculated woman-loving French and to the woman-identified Pistol, a parody of testicular masculinity—his "cock is up."

When we hear the puns on balls and stones in the king's dialogue with the French ambassador, we can also hear the full range of meaning of the word "treasure," which can signify semen as well as precious jewels, as shown in Emilia's complaint in *Othello* about husbands who "powre our Treasures into forraigne laps" (TLN 3061, 4.3.91). The "tun of treasure" that the French ambassador offers Henry will be shown in the course of the play to have expended the French soldiers' "spirit" (in the sense used in sonnet 129), as the French display themselves without luster on the battlefield and effeminized in their dialogues with each other. The French impoverish their masculinity by pouring out their "treasure," but Henry's arousal will unbreed the French as it proves him a son of an Englishman, a nephew of an Englishman, and a father of a son. The paranomasia on the game of tennis in Henry's long speech to the ambassadors is accompanied by wordplay in the realm of male sexual potency and breeding. Henry demonstrates that potency in his response that England and Henry will "rowse [him] in [his] Throne of France," will show his "sayle of Greatnesse" and "will rise there with so full a glorie" (TLN 425, 424, 428, 1.2.275, 274, 278). And that arousal will direly affect France's breeding potential, making widows, destroying French male progeny, "mock[ing] mothers from their sonnes" and, like some early modern thalidomide, maiming the future of the "vngotten and vnborne" (TLN 436–37, 1.2.286–87).

Early modern anatomies demonstrate the power of the balls and their status as distillers of treasure. One mid-sixteenth-century English anatomy text shares the *OED*'s coyness, declaring as it reaches the groin, "Nowe I have descrybed all the partes of the lowest bellye, so well as I coulde, sauyng the priuy partes both of man and woman, whyche for dyvers causes I wylle omytte at thys tyme, fyrste because I wyll gyve no occasion to youth of wantones, and then that I wyll offende no honeste eares in descrybynge them playnlye" (Langton fol.xli.verso). But most anatomy books from the Tudor and Stuart era are explicit about the primacy of the stones. N. Udall's 1553 translation of Thomas Gemini's *Compendiosa Totius Anatomie Delineatio,* following Galen, insists that although the testicles are "numbred amongst the generative membres, yet it is a pryncipal membre, for withoute it is no generation" (A.v.). Helkiah Crooke declares that "the testicles are esteemed the prime instruments of generation, and also by some, principall parts of the body"; they are "the first and immediate organs of generation" (207, 282). They act in the early-seventeenth-century sense of "immediate," without an intermediary, as the sole font of life (*OED* "immediate"). Crooke says that he must describe the details of generation, for "The whole body is the Epitomie of the world, containing therein whatsoeuer is in the large viniuerse; [and] Seede is the Epitomy of the body, hauing in it the power and immediate possibility of all the parts" (197). The *OED* offers only literary or abstract examples of "epitome" used as Crooke employs it here; but Crooke means the word to signify materially as "something that forms a condensed record or representation 'in minature' " (*OED* "epitome"). The seed is made of "fierie & aery substances wandering and coursing about the whole bodye [which] doe containe in themselues the Idea or forme of the particular parts" (278); these substances which are "the second matter of the seed" record the body's every facet so that, after the seed is concocted in the testicles, it can reproduce the body perfectly.

Seed is the source of life, and seed reaches its full potential in the testicles: "prolificall seede such as is apt for generation" attains "his forme and perfection" "onely in and about the Testicles" (Crooke 57). According to Thomas Vicary's much reprinted *Englishemans Treasure,* "the Brayne, Sinewes . . . the Heart Arteirs . . . and the Liuer Ueynes" bring the testicles "both feeling and stirring, life, and spirit, and nutrimentall blood, and the most purest blood of all other members of the body, whereof is made the Sparme by the labour of the Testicles" (52). Vicary attributes to the testicles the job of producing life-giving spirit, without which the fetus would presumably be inert, unable to feel and stir. Crooke agrees that the blood as well as the fiery spirits are perfected in the testicles: "the nearer [blood] approacheth to these Testicles, the better is it still laboured, till in the end it receyue from them his vtmost perfection both in the color, consistence, and prolificall vertue" (198). The stones distill the blood with the spirits, producing blood's "final concoction," which in the humoral patriarchal system is solely responsible for life (Paster, *Body Embarrassed* 71).

Crooke cites all of the classical authorities who agree that the seed formed in the stones creates new life, and he extends their arguments to prove that semen provides the material of life as well as its enlivening spirit. Although the womb is a necessary vehicle and the mother's blood nourishes the fetus, the seed provides the original material—which constitutes the "spermatical parts": the "bones, gristle, nerves, veins, arteries"—and the essential spirit. According to Galen, Crooke says, the seed is "aboundantly stored" with "fierie" spirits. These spirits are "the instruments of the soule, by which that noble architect formeth her mansion or habitation out of the seede, working and forming it into parts conuenient. These are called forming spirits, and in respect of these, the seed is sayd to be *artifex,* a workman, and carrieth the nature of an Efficient cause" (58). Although Crooke gives the soul its customary feminine designation, his account of generation casts the male seed as prime mover; the seed is the workman and within it is what is "efficient" in that word's dominant seventeenth-century sense: "that [which] makes (a thing) to be what it is" (*OED* "efficient"). Thus Crooke's Renaissance physiology accepts without question the ancients' premise that only male seed contributes the vital spirit and asserts that, in addition, male seed creates the body's material frame. The testicles are therefore primarily responsible for the production of new men.

The testicles are the source of male potency in war as well as in reproduction. John Banister's *Historie of man, sucked from the sappe of the most approved Anathomistes* asserts that the force of the stones "is the cause of strength and manhode" (Bbiij verso). Banister equates manliness with physical strength and attributes both to the power of the testicles. Crooke agrees:

Surely the power and vertue of the Testicles is very great & incredible, not onely to make the body fruitfull, but also in the alteration of the temperament, the habit, the proper substance of the body, yea & of the maners themselves . . . Hence it is, that the Egyptians in their Hieroglyphickes doe paint *Typhon* gelt, signifying thereby his power and soueraignty to be abolished and decayed. (241)

Crooke argues that the testicles not only enable reproduction but also alter the body's "temperament," "habit," and "substance." He thereby attributes to them the vital function of regulating the male humoral body. In sixteenth- and seventeenth-century physiology, "temperament" could signify "the combination of the four cardinal humours of the body, by the relative proportion of which the physical and mental constitution were held to be determined"; "habit" denoted "bodily condition or constitution" and also "mental constitution, disposition, character," which were intimately related, since one's humoral condition determined one's character; and "substance" could signify both "the material of which a body is formed and in virtue of which it possesses certain properties" and "that which constitutes the essence of a thing; the essential part" (*OED* "temperament," "habit," "substance"). Because the testicles alter the "temperament," "habit," and "substance" of the body, they are the cause of male power—they provide men with the courage and strength to dominate in war. Crooke cites Galen, who argued, Crooke says, that "The Testicles are another Fountaine or Well-spring of in-bred heate; the Feu-place or Fire-hearth, where the *Lares* or houshold-Gods of the body do solace and disport themselues: from hence the whole body receyueth an encrease of heate, and by that meanes not onely fecundity, but also a great alteration of the temper" (45). Heat differentiates men from "dull and sluggish" women, and the testicles are responsible for keeping the male body hot (Crooke 204).[6] For Crooke, the testicles govern and determine the essential humoral balance that makes a man a man: the bodily heat without which a man loses his power and domination.

Since the testicles determined the physical strength of masculinity, as well as ensuring generation, gelding could undo masculinity completely. Crooke observes that "the testicles being taken away . . . there presently followeth a change from a hot to a cold temper" and "the voice and the very forme becommeth womanish" (241, 242). Alexander Read's *Manuall of the Anatomy or dissection of the body of man* concurs with Crooke's *Microcosmographia* on this point, noting that "the second [use of the stones] is, they adde heat, strength and courage to the body, as gelding doth manifest, by the which all these are empaired" (208–09). Ambrose Parey also adduces this link between the testicles and warrior power through observation of men deprived of the organ: "the action of the testicles is . . . by a certaine manly irradiation to breed or encrease a true masculine courage. This you may know by Eunuches or such as are Gelt, who are of a womanish nature, and are oftentimes more tender and weake than weomen" (120). Male courage and martial power stem from the action of the stones on the body. Therefore, loss of the testicles can make men even less powerful than women. The seed produced in the testicles made male fetuses, and it also guaranteed male physical strength, courage, and, crucially, male dominance. The stones both differentiated men from women and assured their power over women.

As Thomas Laqueur argues, Galenic medicine also asserted that women produced seed in the act of orgasm and that women's orgasm was essential for procreation.[7] Until its final scene, *Henry V,* however, with its concentration on male seed and male power, elides the connection between female seed and reproduction. The play assents to Crooke's disempowerment of female seed. *Henry V* insists upon the conjunction of male martial power and the ability to produce potent seed, as it insists upon English men's differentiation from women. In a play concerned with conjuring an English nation of gentlemen from a collection of Irish, Welsh, and English men,[8] the French king claims his descent from a man while the English must, by force of their history, claim the throne of France through a woman. In the gendered logic of early modern England, this situation threatens to devalue English masculinity. The play solves this problem by having the French castrate themselves in the first act in their gift of the "Paris-Balls." After their initial defeats at the hands of the newly empowered English, the French acknowledge that their madams are declaring that Frenchmen's "Mettell is bred out" (TLN 1408, 3.5.29). The Constable's wonder and lament at the English's superior "mettell" in this scene is couched in what Gail Paster has shown is the ubiquitous early modern language of the humoral body:

> *Dieu de Batailes,* where haue they this mettell?
> Is not their Clymate foggy, raw, and dull?
> On whom, as in despight the Sunne lookes pale,
> Killing their Fruit with frownes? Can sodden Water,
> A Drench for sur-reyn'd Iades, their Barly broth,
> Decoct their cold blood to such valiant heat?
> And shall our quick blood, spirited with Wine,
> Seeme frostie?
> > (TLN 1394–1401, 3.5.15–22)

Unexpectedly hotter than the French, the English soldiers have revealed their heat in their "mettell" or "ardent or spirited temperament; spirit, courage" (*OED* "mettle"). In contrast, the French soldiers' defeats make manifest their cold blood, which, since it makes them weak and womanish, has ensured their military defeats. The word "mettle," which occurs more often in this play than elsewhere in Shakespeare, is also a term in the vocabulary of breeding. Macbeth declares to Lady Macbeth, "Bring forth Men-Children onely / For thy vndaunted Mettle should compose / Nothing but males" (TLN 554–56, 1.7.73–75). Parey describes those men with cold testicles as unable to "beget many children, and those they get are rather female than male" (120). With the gift of the balls, the French have lost their masculine heat: both their courage and their power to breed. They are suddenly cold and wet like women, even though their English enemies, by virtue of their climate, should be the wetter men.

As often happens in Shakespeare's plays, an enemy or subordinate will acknowledge and reify the dominant group or person's power. For example, Vernon's epideitic speeches about the young Henry make his superhuman transformation real (*1H4* TLN 2335-41, 4.1.104-10; TLN 2837-54, 5.2.51-68). Likewise in the later play, the French acknowledge England's superior breeding prowess; they also continually speak of their own madams and mistresses and, as critics of the play have noted, *Henry V* continually stages French women. The Dauphin even measures French masculinity by what the French "Madames" are saying about French men. Paradoxically (in modern terms), French male talk of mistresses and madams defines the French characters as "effeminate" in one of its sixteenth-century senses. As a nation, then, the French are identified on stage as attending to women and including both women and men who are sexually interested in women. A twentieth-century ideology of virility would include this boasting about heterosexual feats, but in this play virility is defined, as Coppélia Kahn has noted, by "other men" and against involvement with women (79). The play has the French point to the effeminacy of their leader, when Orléans swears of the Dauphin, "By the white Hand of my Lady, hee's a gallant Prince" (TLN 1719-20, 3.7.93-94). The Dauphin's courage is attested to by the marker of pure femininity: "the white hand" of sonnet mistresses.[9] Like Orléans's oath, the ensuing discussion of the Dauphin marks his effeminacy in its early modern terms:[10]

CONSTABLE: Sweare by her Foot, that she may tread out the Oath.
ORLÉANS: He is simply the most actiue Gentleman of France.
CONSTABLE: Doing is actiuitie, and he will still be doing.
ORLÉANS: He neuer did harme, that I heard of.
CONSTABLE: Nor will doe none tomorrow.
(TLN 1721-27, 3.7.95-101)

Rather than killing on the battlefield, the Dauphin expends his energy with women—he is active, but he does no harm. In fact, his sexual activity has weakened him to the point of martial disability, as the anatomy texts warn: for "the great expence of Seede wasteth the bodye fortie times so much as the expence or the losse of blood, if the losse of them both bee proportionable" (Crooke 280). The Dauphin's active doing has wasted his body so that he has neither the strength nor the courage to do battle in the field.

Because it violates the modern understanding of effeminacy, which connects womanly behavior with lack of heterosexual vigor, the sexual innuendo in this dialogue has worried readers. Both of the play's Arden editors see the Dauphin as effeminate, noting that he loves his "palfrey," which they gloss as a "lady's horse." But J. H. Walter, the play's first Arden editor, does not gloss the sexual language in this dialogue—although as Eric Partridge notes, both "treading" and "doing" signify as copulating in the period (Partridge 103, 208). And the comments of *Henry V*'s second Arden editor, T. W. Craik, on "doing" in the dialogue show how the play's portrait of the Dauphin's effeminacy troubles a modern notion of effeminacy. Craik asserts that doing "here is often taken to mean 'copulating' . . . but there is nothing in the dialogue to support this view of the Dauphin's character" (l. 3.7.99n.). Craik acknowledges the possible signification of "doing" in this scene but takes pains to defend the Dauphin from a charge that would obviate his effeminacy—would mark him as a modern manly man. Actually the dialogue *is* about the Dauphin's proclivity for copulation with women. It is precisely this proclivity that makes the Dauphin effeminate; he is what late-twentieth-century slang would call a stud, and this makes him a pathetic warrior. The anatomists understood basic male physiology as discouraging sexual desire. According to Crooke, the testicles "hang out vnder the belly at the rootes of the yarde, partely to abate lustfull desires" (204). But the lustful Dauphin lacks the testicular masculinity that would defend him from lust and make him a potent warrior.

Erickson calls the Dauphin "a travesty of masculinity" and claims that "his laughable presence diverts and exorcizes fears of effeminacy: the English tenderness imaged by York and Suffolk must be virile because the French—epitomized by the Dauphin—are so patently effete" (55–56). His choice of "effete" is especially apposite in the word's early modern sense—according to the *OED*, "effete" was coined in 1660—because in the play the French are "effete" in the 1660 sense of an animal "that has ceased to bring forth offspring" (*OED*); they will not be breeding men. But it is less accurate to contrast the York and Suffolk tableau with the Dauphin's lack of vigor. York and Suffolk's potent homoerotic death in one another's arms is the picture of virility in the play, although, as Jean Howard brilliantly shows, it has the potential to induce homosexual panic in modern production. Although York's amorous death with Suffolk is so beautiful that it threatens to emasculate its narrator temporarily by inducing tears, the tableau itself is described as the height of warrior masculinity. York lies, "braue Soldier," with Suffolk, "Yoake-fellow to his honour-owing-wounds." They die together, " As in this glorious and well-foughten field / [They] kept together in [their] Chiualrie." And before York dies kissing Suffolk, he asks Exeter to commend his "seruice to [his] Soueraigne" (TLN 2491, 2493, 2502–03, 2507, 4.6.7, 9, 18–19, 23). In early modern terms this is excessively beautiful masculinity. The death of such a noble pair of male lovers brings sorrow, but their love inspires only admiration. In contrast, the Dauphin is effeminate precisely because of what a modern audience would read as his heterosexual vigor.

After the treading scene in the French camp, the chorus introduces the contrast between the French and English fighting forces as between "the poore condemned English" and "the confident and ouer-lustie French" (TLN 1811, 1807, 4.0.22, 18). The note in David Bevington's edition of the *Complete Works* glosses "overlusty" as "overly merry," but the word also signifies as too lusty in the sense of too "full of lust or sexual desire" (*OED* "lusty"), as the *OED*'s citation from Golding's 1583 translation of Calvin shows: "That fancie of theirs caryeth them into so fond or rather furious overlustinesse" (*OED* "overlusty"). And this portrait of excessively desirous Frenchmen is exactly what the previous scene draws. The French prince and nobles condemn the English as outnumbered while implicitly condemning themselves as "overlusty." The French are weak in battle because they are too "full of lust or sexual desire" for women.

Even in their condemnation of the English, though, the French acknowledge English male power when Rambures admits that "That Iland of England breedes very valiant Creatures; their Mastiffes are of vnmatchable courage" (TLN 1768–70, 3.7.140–41). England's testicular power, then, is indicated as much by French tribute as by English boasting, although the play certainly does not stint on English hubris. But it is the French king who connects Henry most powerfully to his male heritage:

> Thinke we King *Harry* strong; . . .
> The Kindred of him hath beene flesht vpon vs:
> And he is bred out of that bloodie straine,
> That haunted vs in our familiar Pathes:
> Witnesse our too much memorable shame,
> When Cressy Battell fatally was strucke,
> And all our Princes captiu'd by the hand
> Of that black Name, *Edward*, black Prince of Wales:

> Whiles that his Mountaine Sire, on Mountaine standing
> Vp in the Ayre, crown'd with the Golden Sunne,
> Saw his Heroicall Seed, and smil'd to see him
> Mangle the Worke of Nature, and deface
> The Patternes, that by God and by French Fathers
> Had twentie yeeres been made. This is a Stem
> Of that Victorious Stock; and let vs fear
> The Natiue mightinesse and fate of him.
>   (TLN 938–54, 2.4.48–64)

The French king's tribute is replete with the language of testicular masculinity. Henry's strength, this speech insists, is "bred" into him, derived from his male "kindred," the memory of whose flesh is imprinted on the French. Henry's blood comes from his great-uncle who has shed French blood. The French king connects Edward to his father, who both "sire[d]" Edward and admired the result of his "seed." "Seed" here certainly signifies as "offspring, progeny" (*OED*), but the word is as often used in the period, as it is throughout anatomy texts, to denote "semen," which in early modern terms is the sole cause of sons. The king's picture of Edward's father "on Mountaine standing / Vp in the Ayre, crown'd with the Golden Sunne" (TLN 947–48, 57–58) reprises Henry's earlier speech to the ambassadors, linking Henry's earlier vow to "rowse" himself in war to the arousal of his male ancestors. And that arousal will destroy French paternal legacies. The words "stem" and "stock" also signify in the language of breeding, connecting Henry only and strongly to his male ancestry: Henry is a "descendant of a particular ancestor" (*OED*) who is "*the* progenitor of a family" (*OED*, my emphasis).

Like the French king, Henry and the play's other representative Englishmen speak only of fathers. The French king's speech only embellishes the vision of Henry's masculine heritage that tellingly ends Canterbury's speech about Henry's ability to claim through a woman. Canterbury must immediately put the woman under erasure to dwell on the martial power of Henry's great-uncle and "his most mightie Father" (TLN 255, 1.2.108). As Alan Sinfield and Jonathan Dollimore note, the English "dependance upon female influence over inheritance, legitimacy and the state produces so much anxiety that the English can hardly bring themselves to name it . . . Henry's *male* lineage . . . is repeatedly asserted" (129).

The king's speech before Harfleur constructs an English warrior masculinity based in male breeding:

for my manly heart doth erne" (TLN 826, 2.3.3). His name indicates that
he should be full of gun-stones, and the play reminds us of that name's
significance: "*Pistols* cocke is vp, and flashing fire will follow," he says
to Nym (TLN 554-55, 2.1.53-54).[11] But the play devalues Pistol's version
of masculinity by displaying both his cowardice and his love of women;
Pistol's masculinity is the inverse of testicular masculinity.

Like the effeminate French Dauphin, Pistol loves "doing" with women.
Pistol's command to Nym to "rowse [his] vaunting Veines" (TLN 826, 2.3.4)
appears in a scene where his wife, the Hostess, has the majority of the
lines. Crucially, Pistol enters this play with his wife, who calls him her
"honey sweet Husband" (TLN 823, 2.3.1); and the audience sees him obey
Quickly's command to attend Falstaff's deathbed, which she phrases as,
"Good Husband, come home presently" (TLN 587-88, 2.1.88-89). When
Quickly returns to Pistol and his crew, she begs, "As euer you come of
women, come in quickly to Sir *Iohn* . . . Sweet men, come to him" (TLN
615-18, 2.1.117-20). In a play that buries the fact that its king comes of
a woman, the Hostess's conditional clause, "As ever you come of women,"
and her husband's obedience to it undercut all of Pistol's masculine claims.
Likewise his command to his wife to "Let Huswiferie appeare" (TLN 882,
2.3.60) demonstrates his effeminate interest in women's affairs. Although
Pistol will not fight for his country, hanging back and singing at Harfleur,
he gets his dander up and draws his sword on Nym over his woman (TLN
598, 2.1.62). The audience is meant to understand Pistol's association with
women and his concern with women's affairs and sex with women as
emasculating, as analogous to the mistress-talk of the "effeminate" French.

In case the audience has missed the point—that Pistol's overblown
masculinity is distant from Henry's, the real article—the play teaches us that
lesson three times. The Boy in soliloquy tells us, "As young as I am, I haue
obseru'd these three Swashers [Nym, Bardolph, and Pistol]: I am Boy to
them all three, but all they three, though they would serue me, could not be
Man to me" (TLN 1145-47, 3.2.27-29). Even were the "swashers" demoted
to the rank of servants, they would not deserve the term "man." Gower
exposes Pistol as an imitation, an actor, who in the costume and beard-cut
of a soldier will fool drunks "among foming Bottles" (TLN 1525, 3.6.78).
Disabused of his respect for Pistol by Gower, Fluellen responds, "I doe per-
ceiue hee is not the man that hee would gladly make shew to the World hee
is" (TLN 1529-31, 82-84). Although Pistol displays himself like a man with
balls, he is only a display. And Gower and Fluellen deflate him with anatom-

ical precision: "*Gower.* 'Why heere hee comes, swelling like a Turky-cock.' *Fluellen.* "Tis no matter for his swellings, nor his Turky-cocks' " (TLN 2912–15, 5.1.15–17). The English nation has real balls; Pistol has the debased animal imitation. Sandwiched between French effeminacy and Pistol's parodic masculinity, both predicated on association with women and both impotent, Henry's testicular masculinity looks authentic and powerful.

Although the wooing scene in the fifth act of *Henry V* is often viewed as an afterthought, divorced from the overbearing action of the rest of the play, if we read the play through its embodiment of English testicular masculinity, that scene is also the denouement of the play's story of male potency. After all, to finally demonstrate the breeding power of balls, one needs a woman. But for all that the play couches that need in talk of love, Katherine is explicitly the conduit for English virility between man and man. In her astute reading of the play against both the Olivier and the Branagh film versions, Jean Howard notes that in order to produce a masculinity that is acceptable to the late-twentieth-century audience, Branagh had to excise the homoerotic elements of the play from his film: she specifically points to Henry's elegiac speech on his "bedfellow" Scroop and to the tableau of the dead warrior-lovers York and Suffolk. Branagh also chose to remove from his script most of the folio dialogue of the "love scene" that ends the play. The excision that is most telling for this testicular reading is Henry's speech:

> If euer thou beest mine, *Kate,* as I haue a sauing Faith within me tells me thou shalt; I get thee with skambling, and thou must therefore needes proue a good Souldier-breeder: Shall not thou and I, betweene Saint *Dennis* and Saint *George,* compound a Boy, halfe French, halfe English, that shall goe to Constantinople, and take the Turke by the Beard . . . doe but now promise *Kate,* you will endeauour for your French part of such a Boy; and for my English moytie, take the Word of a King, and a Batcheler." (TLN 3190–97, 3201–03, 5.2.204–10, 214–16)

Important critical attention has been paid to this image of a "scrambling" king,[12] but the vocabulary of this speech also once again stresses the play's primary interest in a breeding masculinity. The first four acts have demonstrated that England has the balls to defeat France martially. The wooing scene assures us that Henry can also generate a son. The image of "Kate" as "soldier-breeder" indicates the play's focus on a testicular masculinity; it also demonstrates once again the distance of this masculinity from an acceptable twentieth- or twenty-first-century version of heterosexuality.

Emma Thompson can look like an attractive sexual partner for the rugged king; but audiences today are less likely to enjoy the image of her as a breeding receptacle. However, the folio version of the play, with its deflating final chorus, also shows the precariousness of this testicular power, just as the eunuchs that continually accompany early modern anatomists' description of testicles show the dangers of locating masculinity in this body part. What Phyllis Rackin calls "the indispensable female ground of patriarchal authority" rears her pretty head in this scene, and the folio's chorus reveals that Henry's seed will be anything but potent (168).[13]

Thus the folio version of *Henry V*, which long-standing critical disagreements have shown is finally equivocal on the question of Henry's character as king,[14] is also equivocal on testicular masculinity. The folio *Henry V* both elaborates that masculinity's terms and finally deflates its power. The choruses, which appear for the first time in the folio, envision a fighting force focused on martial power to the exclusion of all effeminate pursuits: "Now all the Youth of England are on fire, / And silken Dalliance in the Wardrobe lyes" (TLN 462-63, (2.0.1-2). "Dalliance" certainly signifies here as "idle pleasure,"[15] but the *OED* finds the word denoting "wanton toying" with women as early as 1400 (*OED* "dalliance"). In *The Life and Death of King John*, Shakespeare has the patriotic Bastard condemn the French Dauphin as "a beardlesse boy, / A cockred-silken wanton" (TLN 2238-39, 5.1.69-70). *Henry V*'s chorus depicts English warriors who are real men, leaving boyish and womanish sexual pleasures behind. The chorus also declares that those warriors are physically marked as masculine: "For who is he, whose Chin is but enrich't / With one appearing Hayre, that will not follow / These cull'd and choyce-drawne Caualiers to France?" (TLN 1066-68, 3.0.22-24). The production of hair, the anatomy texts insist, is a function of the testicles; therefore "Eunuches . . . become fatter and smooth without haires" (Crooke 242). Although the 1600 quarto, *The Cronicle History of Henry the fift*, contains the essential backbone of testicular masculinity, that masculinity is elaborated in the folio in its choruses and in long speeches such as TLN 938-54 (2.4.38-64) and TLN 1100-11 (3.1.17-28). The folio's initial choruses and its developed speeches insist on Henry and England's testicular masculinity, but the folio's final chorus undercuts the very masculinity its earlier choruses developed.

Modern masculinity developed unevenly over the last four hundred years. The hegemonic masculinity that we live with today which, as Breitenberg points out, limits men as well as women in myriad ways, partakes of the "discourse of biological sexual difference, the supposedly instinctive desire of men to rape and the assumed physical vulnerability of women to be raped" (Howard and Rackin 215). Howard and Rackin's analysis of *Henry V*'s rape imagery shows that the play approves a masculinity that includes the threat of rape. But despite its affinities to modern masculinity, the testicular masculinity in *Henry V* is more related to medieval models than it is to today's hegemonic masculinity. One of the most powerful mainstays of today's masculinity—heterosexual desire—is absent from the approved masculinity in the play. The play denigrates rather than lauds that desire, attributing it to the effeminate French and the parodic Pistol. In *Henry V*, "A man's desire for a woman, now coded as a mark of masculinity" still "constituted a double degradation, the enslavement of a man's higher reason by his base bodily appetites and the subjection of the superior sex to the inferior one" (Howard and Rackin 193–94). And the play's testicular masculinity is biological, but not in modern terms. When they illustrate the reproductive organs, the early modern anatomies cited in this essay depict women's ovaries as testicles inside the body.[16] But as the anatomists' commentaries on testicular power and their discussions of eunuchs show, early modern gendered bodies were essentially differentiated by their relative temperatures and potency. As Paster has indisputably demonstrated, early modern bodies may have had one sex, but they were powerfully gendered by their humoral conditions (*Body Embarrassed* and "Unbearable"). According to Shakespeare's play, Henry V has balls: balls full of "valiant heat," balls he has inherited from his dominant warrior ancestors. *Henry V*'s story of testicular masculinity pits the gun-stones of a hot heroic England against the frosty, woman-loving French. The result is the killing field of Agincourt and the seed that will, albeit temporarily, give England a legitimate male heir.

As Howard and Rackin suggest, however, the play also contains intimations of masculinities that will cohere into dominance in the coming years; since modern masculinities developed unevenly, we can see continuities between the testicular masculinity in *Henry V* and more modern masculinities. The eighteenth and nineteenth centuries would bring ever-increasing nationalism that encouraged English writers to differentiate England from France xenophobically. And as in *Henry V*, English writers used gendered insults to degrade the French and tout the superior masculinity of the English. Defending Shakespeare's art against Voltaire's

criticism, Elizabeth Montagu accuses French dramatists of approving of
weakness and womanish manners: In French drama, she says, "Theseus
is made a mere sighing swain. Many of the greatest men of antiquity, and
even the roughest heroes among the Goths and Vandals, are exhibited
in this effeminate form" (viii). In the eighteenth century, French "effeminacy" continued to function as a foil for English masculinity, even as that
dominant masculinity began to change form; even as it moved away from
what Carole Pateman calls "classic patriarchalism [that] declares women
to be procreatively and politically irrelevant" (87) and began to include
features of what we now see as heterosexuality.[17] But the gendered behavior of the uxorious Pistol, the other foil for Henry's testicular masculinity,
would become valued rather than denigrated in the coming centuries.
With the rise of the individual private family, Pistol's desire to "earn"
rather than to fight becomes valued along with his condition as a "honey
sweet" husband. And it is Pistol's verbal swelling that is invaluable to a
twentieth century that approves of sales rather than physical strength in
its dominant men. In the male executive with a body pumped only in
and for gym display and a "trophy wife" to demonstrate his heterosexual
vigor, we find the parody of testicular masculinity—only today *he* is the
"real man."[18]

Notes

1. All quotations of *Henry V* follow the first folio with through line numbering (TLN) from
The Norton Facsimile. For ease of reference, the through line numbers (TLN) are followed
by act-scene-line numbers from *The Complete Works of Shakespeare*, edited by Bevington.

2. Partridge does not gloss "balls" as testicles, although he does gloss an incidence
of "bawl" (*Henry IV*, 1) this way. Onions, likewise, omits this significance of "ball," as
does, surprisingly, Rubinstein. Colman notes the "probable quibble" (183) and offers the
same references as Taylor. Williams's comprehensive three-volume *A Dictionary of Sexual
Language and Imagery in Shakespearean and Stuart Literature* provides an inferential
reference from *Eastward Hoe* as well as the *Henry VIII* example and many seventeenth-
century references; see his entry "ball" and also "tennis."

3. See Williams, "ball" and "stone."

4. See especially Kahn.

5. There is, of course, more than one "masculinity" in early modern England. For a
historical discussion, see Amussen. Breitenberg makes a similar point. Also see Paster, *Body
Embarrassed* 16.

6. For the central place of heat in the system that distinguished men from women, see
Paster, "The Unbearable Coldness of Female Being."

7. For Shakespearean implications of this theory, see Traub 141 and Greenblatt 66–93.

8. See Cairns and Richards, 8–12.

9. See K. Hall for the racial implications of this trope.

10. See Traub 134–36. See also Spear. Even Spear's seminal reading of effeminacy in *Troilus and Cressida*, which insists on "specifying the distance between our modern concepts of patriarchy, gender, masculinity, and sexuality and those of early modern England" (412), and succeeds brilliantly at just that, at times falls prey to today's hegemonic understandings of "effeminacy." So, for example, Spear states that "the term could name phenomena as widely divergent as male physical weakness, love of excessive pleasure (especially sexual pleasure with women), or an antiheroic military ethos" (411). But these are not "divergent" phenomena; rather they are all features of the metaphorically gelded body, all the antithesis of testicular masculinity. Also, although Spear is clearly not a homophobic reader, he states that the "model of masculinity" that he describes is "endowed with explicit homoerotic overtones that always shadow even the most seamless performance of virility with images of effeminacy, emasculation, and sodomy" (419). I would argue, in contrast, that this connection between homoeroticism and "effeminacy, emasculation, and sodomy" is part of the common sense of our heterosexual imaginary, not of the homosocial imaginary of early modern England. See Bach.

11. Erickson notes that the play "had a sexual current from the start in the challenge presented by tennis balls. One does not need the conflict between the clowns—'Pistol's cock is up' (2.1.52)—to alert us to the phallic implication of the king's conversion of balls to gun-stones" (60).

12. See Kahn 81.

13. In numerous discussions of Henry's character, critics have noted the deflation in this final chorus. On the two texts of *Henry V,* see Taylor. Also see Patterson.

14. For the classic statement on the play's equivocal nature, see Rabkin.

15. See the note in the Bevington *Complete Works.*

16. See Laqueur.

17. Pateman offers an analysis of the political theory that accompanied and contributed to the emergence of a modern masculinity.

18. Like all pieces of hegemonic formations, gender ideologies are always in process. Just as we can see residual traces of the humoral understanding of sex for men in athletic coaches' pregame advice to refrain from sex, so emerging and competing notions of masculinity exist alongside the triumphant masculinity I am postulating in the pumped hyper-heterosexual businessman. In 1999 a series of beer commercials from different companies celebrated men who preferred beer to women; in one commercial, a man dreams of Michelob beer and asks the beautiful negligee-clad woman leaving him in anger to bring him a beer. As these commercials show, gender is always inflected by race and class, and codes of gender and sexuality always exist in complicated relationship to one another. On this latter relationship and the dangers of conflating gender and sexuality, see Traub. One fascinating thing about the coupled emergence of dominant modern masculinity and heterosexuality is how once-denigrated sexual behavior associated with men of low status has become a feature of a dominant masculinity associated with upper-class men.

Works Cited

Amussen, Susan Dwyer. "'The Part of a Christian Man': The Cultural Politics of Manhood in Early Modern England." *Political Culture and Cultural Politics in Early Modern England.* Ed. Susan D. Amussen and Mark A. Kishlansky. Manchester: Manchester University Press, 1995.

Bach, Rebecca Ann. "The Homosocial Imaginary of *A Woman Killed With Kindness.*" *Textual Practice* 12.3 (1998): 503–24.

Banister, John. *The Historie of Man, Sucked from the Sappe of the Most Approued Anathomistes.* London, 1578. STC 1359.

Breitenberg, Mark. *Anxious Masculinity in Early Modern England.* Cambridge: Cambridge University Press, 1996.

Bullough, Geoffrey. *Narrative and Dramatic Sources of Shakespeare.* Vol. 4. New York: Columbia University Press, 1966.

Cairns, David, and Shaun Richards. *Writing Ireland: Colonialism, Nationalism and Culture.* Manchester: Manchester University Press, 1988.

Colman, E. A. M. *The Dramatic Use of Bawdy in Shakespeare.* London: Longman, 1974.

Crooke, Helkiah. *MIΙΚΡΟΚΟΣΜΟΓΡΑΦΙΑ: A Description of the Body of Man.* London, 1615. STC 6062.

Elshtain, Jean Bethke. *Public Man, Private Woman: Women in Social and Political Thought.* Princeton: Princeton University Press, 1981.

Erickson, Peter. *Patriarchal Structures in Shakespeare's Drama.* Berkeley: University of California Press, 1985.

Gemini, Thomas. *Compendiosa Totius Anatomie Delineatio.* Trans. N. Udall. London, 1553. STC 11716.

Greenblatt, Stephen. *Shakespearean Negotiations.* Berkeley: University of California Press, 1988.

Hall, Edward. *Hall's Chronicle; Containing the History of England, During the Reign of Henry IV and the Succeeding Monarchs, to the End of the Reign of Henry VIII.* [1548.] 1809. New York: AMS Press, 1965.

Hall, Kim F. *Things of Darkness: Economies of Race and Gender in Early Modern England.* Ithaca: Cornell University Press, 1995.

Holinshed's Chronicles of England, Scotland, and Ireland. [1586.] 1808. Vol. 3. New York: AMS Press, 1976.

Howard, Jean E. "The English History Play; Now" World Shakespeare Cong., Biltmore Hotel, Los Angeles. April 9, 1996.

Howard, Jean E., and Phyllis Rackin. *Engendering a Nation: A Feminist Account of Shakespeare's English Histories.* London and New York: Routledge, 1997.

Kahn, Coppélia. *Man's Estate: Masculine Identity in Shakespeare.* Berkeley: University of California Press, 1981.

Langton, Christopher. *An Introduction into Phisycke, wyth an vniuersal dyet.* London, [1545?]. STC 15204.

Laqueur, Thomas. *Making Sex: Body and Gender from the Greeks to Freud.* Cambridge: Harvard University Press, 1990.

Montagu, Elizabeth. *An Essay on the Writings and Genius of Shakespeare.* 1769. 6th ed. London, 1810.

Onions, C. T. *A Shakespeare Glossary.* Oxford: Clarendon, 1986.

Oxford English Dictionary. Ed. J. A. Simpson and E. S. C. Weiner. 2nd ed. Oxford: Clarendon Press, 1989.

Parey, Ambrose. *The Workes of that Famous Chirurgion Ambrose Parey.* Trans. fr. Latin and compared with French by Th. Johnson. London, 1634.

Partridge, Eric. *Shakespeare's Bawdy.* London: Routledge, 1991.

Paster, Gail Kern. *The Body Embarrassed: Drama and the Disciplines of Shame in Early Modern England.* Ithaca: Cornell University Press, 1993.

————. "The Unbearable Coldness of Female Being: Women's Imperfection and the Humoral Economy." *English Literary Renaissance* 28.3 (1998): 416–40.

Pateman, Carole. *The Sexual Contract.* Stanford: Stanford University Press, 1988.

Patterson, Annabel. "Back by Popular Demand: The Two Versions of *Henry V.*" *Renaissance Drama* 19 (1988): 29–62.

Rabkin, Norman. "Rabbits, Ducks, and *Henry V.*" *Shakespeare Quarterly* 28.3 (1977): 279–96.

Rackin, Phyllis. *Stages of History: Shakespeare's English Chronicles.* Ithaca: Cornell University Press, 1990.

Read, Alexander. *The Manuall of the Anatomy or Dissection of the Body of Man.* London, 1638. STC 20784.

Rubinstein, Frankie. *A Dictionary of Shakespeare's Sexual Puns and Their Significance.* New York: St. Martin's, 1989.

Shakespeare, William. *The Complete Works of Shakespeare.* Ed. David Bevington. New York: Addison Wesley, 1997.

————. *Henry V.* Ed. Gary Taylor. Oxford: Clarendon, 1982.

————. *King Henry V.* Ed. T. W. Craik. Arden Shakespeare. London: Routledge, 1995.

————. *King Henry V.* Ed. J. H. Walter. Arden Shakespeare. London: Methuen, 1967.

————. *The Norton Facsimile.* New York: Norton, 1996.

Sinfield, Alan, and Jonathan Dollimore. "History and Ideology, Masculinity and Miscegenation: The Instance of *Henry V.*" *Faultlines: Cultural Materialism and the Politics of Dissident Reading.* Ed. Alan Sinfield. Berkeley: University of California Press, 1992.

Spear, Gary. "Shakespeare's 'Manly' Parts: Masculinity and Effeminacy in *Troilus and Cressida.*" *Shakespeare Quarterly* 44 (1993): 409–22.

Taylor, Gary, with Stanley Wells. *The Text of Henry V: Three Studies. Modernizing Shakespeare's Spelling.* Oxford: Clarendon, 1979.

Traub, Valerie. *Desire and Anxiety: Circulations of Sexuality in Shakespearean Drama.* London: Routledge, 1992.

Vicary, Thomas. *The Englishemans Treasure with the True Anatomie of Mans Bodie.* London, 1587. STC 24708.

Williams, Gordon. *A Dictionary of Sexual Language and Imagery in Shakespearean and Stuart Literature.* 3 vols. London: Athlone, 1994.

(see figure 1), which includes a sword, feathers, a scarf, roses on his shoes, a pipe, and a yellow band (collar). Taylor ironically praises Mary Frith, the eponymous heroine of Middleton and Dekker's *The Roaring Girl,* who was known for her literally hermaphroditic mode of attire: "a doublet and a petticoat."[2] Her garb was, according to Taylor, at least, consistent, while Sack's variety and excesses of dress are the "fit patterne" of the times. "Unfashion'd fashions," a misrule governing sumptuary demeanor, characterizes what Taylor sees among the English women and men of his time. Women were dressing in masculine garments, men were adopting effeminate fashions, and players on the stage crossed lines of both class and gender in their costumes. Stephen Orgel points out the vexed nature of the legal attempts to regulate what one wore in this period: "The [sumptuary] statutes were finally acknowledged to be unenforceable in the civil law, and were repealed in 1604, but this only complicated matters further: it did not mean that there were no longer any sumptuary regulations, it only transferred the jurisdiction over questions of appropriate dress, as an issue of public morality, from the criminal courts to the ecclesiastical ones, where the guidelines were much less clear."[3] Philip Massinger's *The City Madam* (1632)[4] presents London as a city in social flux, an instability realized in the characters' dress: the wife and daughters of a London merchant dress themselves as court ladies; a prostitute attires herself in satin and velvet, which she receives from one of her clients as payment for her services; and a country gentleman apes the fashions of city aristocrats. This play is populated by a newly knighted merchant, impoverished aristocrats, gentlemen apprentices, a prostitute who wants garments rather than money, city women who desire the habits of court ladies, an astrologer, and visiting "Indians" from Virginia in search of female victims for their ritual sacrifice to the devil. In this setting, the play presents a battle between characters regarding what clothes are appropriate for which characters to wear; even more crucially, at issue is what clothing means and what it does to the person who wears it. The play, in its characters and their costumes, stages contests between ideas about clothing, particularly the "tension" in this period, identified by Ann Rosalind Jones and Peter Stallybrass, between "fashion-as-change" and "fashion as 'deep' making."[5] While these struggles take place along lines of both class and gender, the resolution of the play attempts to restore order to a London society that has seemingly become Taylor's "meere bable *Babell* of confusion." Massinger's play suggests that control of what women wear is ultimately the decision that counts. While men can dress

Figure 1. Title page of *Muld Sacke: or The Apologie of Hic Mulier,* 1620 (by permission of the Huntington Library).

in ways that cross lines of class and race, the female characters must finally be "put in their place": the Lady Frugal and her daughters must don the garb of commoners—attire suited for their allotted social status—and the prostitute must appear in prison garb, not in a robe made of satin or velvet.

The City Madam is, perhaps, unfamiliar to most readers, so let me begin with a summary of the plot. The recently knighted merchant Sir John Frugal is plagued by the demands of his wife and two daughters, Anne and Mary, who wish to be attired and equipped with the clothing and trappings of court ladies. Anne and Mary ruin their chances for advantageous marriages to the noble, but financially strapped, Sir Maurice Lacie and the wealthy, if lowborn, "country gentleman" Plenty, respectively. Sir John wants his daughters to marry "up"—Anne will get a title, and Mary will get money. However, Anne and Mary insist that their future husbands be their servants rather than their masters, and the appalled suitors declare that they will take a three-year sea voyage to rid themselves of the scandal of having pursued such untoward women. Meanwhile, Frugal's brother, Luke, who has recently been released from debtors' prison and resides in the Frugal household, serving ignominiously as a servant to Lady Frugal and her daughters, advises Frugal's apprentices, Goldwire and Tradewell, both the only sons of gentlemen, to cheat their master by withholding some of his merchandise for themselves.

Sir John sends word to his wife through Lord Lacie, Sir Maurice's father, that his frustration with her extravagant ways has led him to quit England and to retire to a monastery in Belgium. The ways of his wife and daughters are enough to send Sir John into celibacy and Catholicism. Sir John leaves his estate in the hands of Luke, whose first command is to amend the dress of Lady Frugal and her daughters. Luke, who has previously been portrayed as a miser, unexpectedly declares that these women deserve even finer clothes than those they presently wear: dress, he argues, should reflect one's wealth, not one's status by birth. He instructs the women to remove their clothes at bedtime, and he will provide them with goddesslike array. When the women awake the next day, they find that Luke has left them with "buffin gowns, and green aprons" (4.4.26), clothing that returns them to their common origins.

At this point in the play, three "Indians" from Virginia arrive, presumably sent by Sir John, whose final request to Luke is that he convert them to Christianity; the "Indians" are, in fact, Sir John, Sir Maurice, and Plenty in disguise. The "Indians" convince Luke that they have no interest in religious conversion and have come to England to find two virgins and a matron for a blood sacrifice to the devil. If Luke can provide such women, they offer him untold wealth in exchange; the enterprising Luke realizes that Lady Frugal and her daughters fit the description and that sending them off to their doom in the New World means that he will not have to worry about providing dowries for Anne and Mary. In a phantasmagoric denouement, which suggests the end of *The Winter's Tale* grafted onto *Scream*, Sir John, still in disguise, presents the banqueting Luke with three theatrical spectacles. In the first, Orpheus plays to Cerberus and Charon, and his music moves them so that they allow him to enter Hades. Luke, however, declares that he is completely unmoved by this scene. Sir John then presents those whom Luke has had arrested for various debts to him, as well as those who have committed other infractions against him, imprisoned. This group features about half the characters in the play: Massinger includes the larcenous apprentices Goldwire and Tradewell; the "decaied"[6] merchants and gentlemen Fortune and Hoyst; the impoverished gentlemen Old Goldwire and Old Tradewell; Lady Frugal's maid Milliscent and the fraudulent astrologer Stargaze; the procurers Dingem and Secret; and the whore Shavem. Luke laughs in triumph at this spectacle. Finally, Anne and Mary enter to bid farewell to the statues of their lovers, which Sir John has had placed in the room, and express their regret for their untoward behavior to these suitors. The statues come to life, and Sir John reveals his identity. Luke's avarice and double-dealing are exposed. The two pairs of lovers and the husband and wife reconcile. When Sir John advises Luke to "Pack to *Virginia*, and repent" (5.3.144), Lady Frugal requests that Luke be shown mercy, "Because his cruelty to me, and mine, / Did good upon us" (5.3.148–49).

The play initially appears to be Massinger's version of *Volpone*, with the hypocrite Luke and his machinations occupying center stage—Luke first urging Goldwire and Tradewell to cheat Sir John and then having them arrested when he becomes master of the estate; Luke pleading with Sir John to be lenient with the debtors Hoyst, Fortune, and Penury and then having them thrown in prison as well; Luke's sartorial double-dealing with Lady Frugal and her daughters. After Sir John reveals himself, Luke has two short speeches, but neither demonstrates clear repentance on Luke's part: Luke says, "I am lost. / Guilt strikes me dumb" (5.3.110–11), and "I care not where I go, what's done, with words / Cannot be undone" (5.3.146–47); Luke sounds about as contrite as does Antonio at the end of

The Tempest. However, the Frugal women, Lady Frugal and Anne and Mary, attempt to undo their wrongs "with words," via speeches which explicitly reveal their faults: Anne speaks of her "contempt," "foolish pride," and "insolence" (5.3.86–87) in her behavior toward Lacie; Mary declares herself "unworthy" (5.3.90) of Plenty; Lady Frugal admits the "disobedience" (5.3.92) which drove Sir John to the monastery and her current "penitence" (5.3.94). These confessions allow for the reconciliation of Sir John and Lady Frugal, Anne and Lacie, Mary and Plenty. In this respect, the ending of *The City Madam* looks more like Shakespeare's *The Taming of the Shrew* than *Volpone,* with Mary's vow "to shew my self / When I am married, an humble wife, / Not a commanding mistris" (5.3.120–22) and Anne's declaration, "I am another creature, / Not what I was" (5.3.119–20). Anne, Mary, and Lady Frugal are "other creatures" than they were at the beginning of the play: not only do their speeches reveal their newfound humility, but their clothing—the buffin gowns and green aprons assigned to them by Luke— also transforms them from the gaudy, haughty creatures who appear in the first scene of *The City Madam.*

The play begins with a conversation between Goldwire and Tradewell in which Goldwire reports that Frugal's household is "grown a little Court, in bravery, / Variety of fashions, and those rich ones: / There are few great Ladies going to a Masque / That do out-shine ours in their every-day habits" (1.1.24–27). Beyond the desire of the Frugal women for dress above their station, their taste for Continental fashions marks them for particular criticism: when Luke describes Lady Frugal's "monstrous Metamorphosis" (4.4.92) from modest wife to clotheshorse, he notes, "No English workman then could please your fancy; / The French and Tuscan dresse your whole discourse" (4.4.93–94), as well as her favoring of Hungarian and Spanish items of clothing. Massinger's depiction of Lady Frugal and her daughters, who insist upon Spanish shoes and French and Italian chefs, reinforces the notion that their fault is not merely a desire for novelty, but an anti-English Europhilia. This desire for things non-English is emphasized when Luke gives the women "buffin gowns" (4.4.26): "buffin" is defined in the *OED* as an obsolete term for "A coarse cloth in use for gowns of the middle class in the time of Elizabeth," and the significance of this fabric lies in its status not only as a class marker, but also its Englishness and ties to the English past.

Luke describes to Lady Frugal, in exacting terms, her former, appropriate attire:

> [Sir John] made a Knight,
> And your sweet mistris-ship Ladyfi'd, you wore
> Sattin on solemn days, a chain of gold,
> A Velvet hood, rich borders, and somtimes
> A dainty Miniver cap, a silver pin
> Headed with pearl worth three-pence, and thus far
> You were priviledg'd, and no man envi'd it,
> It being for the Cities honour, that
> There should be a distinction between
> The Wife of a Patritian, and Plebean.
>
> (4.4.72–81)

Her dress on these occasions was correct because it served to maintain the distinction between "The Wife of a Patritian, and Plebean," the dress of women serving to mark them as belonging not only to a certain class, but, more particularly, to men of a certain class.

In their current mode of attire, Lady Frugal, Anne, and Mary could be, and desire to be, mistaken for women of a higher class standing; as such, they would not be recognizable as the wife and daughters of, the property of, Sir John Frugal. Further, Luke's detailing of the fabrics that Lady Frugal wore, her garments and accessories, down to the "three-pence" cost of her "silver pin / Headed with pearl," recalls the language of the civil sumptuary laws with their strict injunction: "None shall wear any . . . Except."[7] Luke's speech evokes a nostalgia for a time when "Sattin" and "a chain of gold" could mark class distinction and when women knew on what occasions such attire was fitting. The "Velvet hood" and "Miniver cap" to which Luke refers are items of clothing that are anachronisms for Massinger's audience, but, significantly, they were worn by "grave Matrons" of bygone times.[8] Like the buffin cloth, which denoted class for Elizabethans, these items suggest clothing with a history, and a history specific to England; such clothing, as Peter Stallybrass notes, is "a means of incorporation, the marking of a body so as to associate it with a specific institution"[9]; and it, "unlike money, powerfully inscribed *memory.*"[10] In rejecting these English clothes which make identifiable a woman's class and marital status, Lady Frugal replaces the native with the foreign, convention with innovation, history with "fashion." While the merchant Frugal has made his fortune by trafficking in fabrics—"Cloth of Bodkin, / Tissue, Gold, Silver, Velvets, Sattins, Taffaties" (2.1.71–72)—Lady Frugal, Anne, and Mary threaten to bankrupt him by their refusal to recognize that these items should be

seen as goods that are translatable into the cash that has enabled Sir
John to raise the status of the family and which will further enrich them,
not items for their consumption. In addition, while Sir John deals in the
materials themselves, his wife and daughters crave products made from
them, particularly those that come from abroad: gowns and ornaments.
Hence, these women are being economically spendthrift insofar as they
are spending more (for materials plus labor plus whatever additional cost
is appended for "fashionable" and foreign goods) than Sir John is making
in the traffic of the raw materials. The women's second fault, therefore,
is their failure to understand the economics of Sir John's trade; they are
literally not living up to the family name of Frugal.

At the same time, the threat posed by Lady Frugal and her daughters
is that they reduce the significance of clothing to its mere cash value. In
the rejection of objects that have "intrinsic" and national meaning, like
buffin and the Miniver hat, in favor of items from Spain, France, Italy,
and Hungary, these women embrace the notion of attire as something
that continually varies. The specific foreign country of origin is ultimately
not the real issue. For Lady Frugal and her daughters, what is fashionable
is always dictated from someplace else, whether it be the Court or the
Continent: these women do not set styles; they merely ape them. In this
economy, fashion takes on the modern meaning of the term, the implied
sense that what today is "in fashion" will at some point be "out of fashion";
hence, clothing becomes something meant to be discarded because it
denotes contemporary and ever-changing taste rather than "powerfully
inscribed *memory.*" Fashionable items have a built-in obsolescence: the
obsolescence into which the Miniver cap and sober matron's hood had
fallen and from which the play, in a sense, seeks to redeem them. Further,
this built-in obsolescence ensures that followers of fashion will be continual
consumers, for they will always desire what is fashionable. When clothing
becomes simply what is in style at the moment, it comes to signify only
one thing: that one has the means to purchase it.

While Lady Frugal and her daughters in their all-consuming consumerism
appear to be the most modern of characters, close relations to the Beverly
Hills teens in the film *Clueless,* their behavior when they wear their finery
seems to be an illustration of the warnings issued by early modern English
moralists like Stubbes, who denounces women who wear "male clothing":
he claims that such women "degenerate from godly, sober women in
wearing this wanton lewd kind of attire, proper only to man."[11] However,

not only the style of women's clothes is vexing but also the fabrics with which they have been made, or inlaid: Stubbes's Philoponus comments that even "if the whole gown be not silk or velvet, then the same shall be laid with lace, two or three fingers broad, all over the gown or else the most part."[12] In Massinger's play, we see the (negative) transformative effects of clothing: attire that alters the behavior of women who don it. While some of Lady Frugal's actions appear to be self-conscious affectation—Luke accuses her of feigning illness in order "That [her] night rayls [dressing gowns] of forty pounds a piece / Might be seen with envy of the visitants" (4.4.111-12) and of "going / To Church not for devotion, but to shew/ [her] pomp" (4.4.115-17)—she actually seems to believe that her dress has caused her to appear younger, taking as fitting praise the gross flattery of her maid Milliscent, who claims that if Lady Frugal were not known to be the mother of Anne and Mary, she "might passe / For a Virgin of fifteen" (1.1.82-83).

When Anne and Mary meet their suitors, Sir Maurice and Plenty, respectively, they make demands and dictate the terms upon which they will live as wife and husband rather than hearing and acquiescing to the men's wishes. Anne tells Lacie she will have "[her] will / In all things whatsoever, and that will / To be obey'd, not argu'd" (2.2.104-05). The scene becomes a comical inversion of the love test in *King Lear*. After Anne's speech, Lady Frugal then desires to hear her younger daughter Mary speak, and she begins, "In some part / My Sister hath spoke well . . . [but I] must say / Under correction in her demands / She was too modest" (2.2.133-37), these lines echoing Regan's "In my true heart / I find [Goneril] names my very deed of love; / Only she comes too short" (1.1.70-72).[13] The parody of Shakespeare continues as Mary tells an indignant Plenty, "I know my value and prize it to the worth; / My youth, my beauty" (2.2.139-40). Shakespeare's Regan claims, "I am made of that self metal as my sister, / And prize me at her worth" (1.1.69-70). Mary declares her "worth" to be qualities that she possesses, her "youth" and "beauty"; these things constitute her value, not the sizable dowry Plenty hopes for from Sir John.

The disregard by women for patriarchal authority further links *The City Madam* to *King Lear*. However, while Goneril is provoked by her husband's military meekness to "give the distaff / Into [his] hands" (4.2.17-18), and she and Regan must wait until Lear has handed his power to them before exercising control over him and their households, Anne and Mary Frugal make clear from the outset who will ply the distaff in their marriages: their husbands. Anne and Mary believe that their appearances

Anne's requirement of "fresh habit," along with the demands of the Frugal women for the latest fashions, links them with the other major female figure in the play: the whore Shavem. Shavem reveals to her bawd Secret that she continues to see Goldwire because he "Maintains [her] in cloaths" (3.1.7). In the play's first scene, Luke tells Goldwire that he has been with "The *Lady*, and delivered her the Sattin / For her Gown, and Velvet for her Petticote; / This night She vows Shee'l pay you" (1.1.136–38). As the Frugal women seek clothing beyond their social station, so a prostitute craves the satin and velvet that are allotted for women above her rank, and as Anne and Mary negotiate with Sir Maurice and Plenty to become wives in exchange for "fresh habit," so does Shavem keep Goldwire as a client because he can supply her with "cloaths."

Shavem decides to dress herself finely for a banquet given by the newly wealthy Luke in order to seduce him; Luke, however, is the one who has instructed Shavem to appear "in her best trim" (4.1.49) for this event. Luke, again, reveals the way in which the women in this play equate sartorial elegance with power; he tempts Shavem to dress beyond her station in the same way that he beguiles Lady Frugal, Anne, and Mary to divest themselves of their clothes with the promise of richer garments. Shavem, attiring herself for the banquet, becomes a parodic imitation of Lady Frugal, who runs her household with an emphasis upon ostentatious dress and an insistence upon copious amounts of the finest foods, with which she is, typically, unsatisfied; as the Frugal's steward Holdfast reports:

> though
> The dishes were rais'd one upon another
> As woodmongers do billets, for the first,
> The second, and the third course, and most of the shopps
> Of the best confectioners in *London* ransack'd
> To furnish out a banquet, yet my Lady
> Call'd me penurious rascall, and cri'd out,
> There was nothing worth the eating.
>
> (2.1.17–24)

The play thus links the desire of Lady Frugal and her daughters with the desires of whores, suggesting that the desire for clothing above one's given status is itself a kind of whoredom. However, in *The City Madam,* the female characters do not make up the sole group who commit violations centered around clothing. Goldwire steals from Sir John to provide Shavem with satin and velvet, and Plenty, the country gentleman, appears to be as much of a sumptuary upstart as Lady Frugal; Sir Maurice's Page reports of him: "he is transform'd / And grown a gallant of the last edition; / More rich then gaudie in his habit" (1.2.2–4). When Sir Maurice and Plenty confront one another, they argue about Plenty's right to wear the clothing that he does. When the aristocrat Lacie asserts that Plenty is simply a boor made fine by a good suit of clothes—"What a fine man / Hath your Taylor made you!" (1.2.43–44)—Plenty retorts with a claim that Sir Maurice cannot deny:

> 'Tis quite contrary,
> I have made my Taylor, for my cloaths are pai'd for
> Assoon as put on, a sin your man of title
> Is seldom guiltie of, but Heaven forgive it.
> (1.2.44–47)

Plenty asserts that while Sir Maurice may be able to assert his authority via a hereditary title, what counts is the ability to pay cash for the clothing one purchases, something Sir Maurice and most aristocrats are unable to do. Similarly, Luke informs Lord Lacie, when he declares that he will provide the Frugal women with even richer attire than that which they currently wear, "Since all the titles, honours, long descents / Borrow their gloss from wealth, the rich with reason / May challenge their prerogatives" (3.2.157–59). That Luke can make this argument to Lord Lacie and then criticize Lady Frugal's dress with the claim that Court ladies' "high titles / And pedegrees of long descent, give warrant / For their superfluous braverie" (4.4.44–46) may be an indicator of Luke's character as a complete hypocrite, but the articulation of these positions makes clear that clothing is not merely superficial ornamentation but one of the fields upon which contesting ideologies about social identity—birth versus wealth—wage their struggle.

The society depicted in Massinger's play seems to be one in which male characters like Sir John Frugal, Sir Maurice Lacie, Old Goldwire, Old Treadwell, and Master Plenty want a return to the supposedly stable values of an earlier, class-based society. However, the characters who possess actual wealth in this play are the merchant Frugal and nouveau riche Plenty, whose genealogy Sir Maurice lays out in less than flattering terms:

> thy great grandfather was a Butcher,
> And his son a Grasier, thy sire Constable
> Of the hundred, and thou the first of your dunghill,
> Created gentleman.
>
> (1.2. 67–70)

Frugal's apprentices, Goldwire and Tradewell, are the sons of gentlemen, and while the apprenticing of the younger sons of gentlemen was becoming increasingly common in this period, that Goldwire and Tradewell are "onely sons" (5.2.10) reveals upon what hard times these families have fallen. Sir Maurice's courting of Anne is, on his side, a necessity brought on by financial hardship; as Goldwire assesses the situation, the "lovers" are actually making a business transaction: "the Lord *Lacie* . . . needs my Masters money, / As his daughter does his honour" (1.1.54–55). Even Lord Lacie, the father of Sir Maurice, who appears to be the most morally unwavering and upright of the characters, the voice of stable aristocratic values, is discovered to have pawned his estate to Sir John and is threatened with ruin by Luke when Luke assumes control of Sir John's holdings.

Paradoxically, Sir John wishes to maintain a fantasy of stable, hierarchical relations between aristocrats and nonaristocrats, family members, husbands and wives, masters and servants, though these values are crumbling in the face of an overwhelming desire for money and the commodities one can purchase with it, and Sir John himself has acquired his title because of the wealth that he has accrued. Luke's misfortune, we learn, was caused by a breech of the law of primogeniture when Sir John's father, out of "fondnesse" (1.3.139) for the younger son Luke, left Luke his inheritance, which he immediately squandered, ending up in prison for debt. Lady Frugal holds the reins in her household as Anne and Mary intend to do in theirs. Goldwire and Tradewell cheat their master. Luke is willing to send off his sister-in-law and nieces to become human sacrifices in exchange for wealth. The world of this play is one in which truly everything is for sale: clothing, titles, sex, spouses, human lives. Sir John appears to embody the desire to return to a system of morals based upon patriarchy and primogeniture rather than cash and female power, but Massinger undoes his stabilizing presence in the conclusion of the play.

Although the Frugal women, Luke, and Plenty all at some point in the play espouse the view that money bestows upon one the right to buy and wear whatever one wishes, the play's ending focuses upon returning women to clothing which is deemed appropriate, according to their familial, marital,

or class standing. Significantly, in the world of *The City Madam,* there are
no soft-spoken Cordelias or modest Celias: there are the clothes-hungry
Lady Frugal, Anne, Mary, and Shavem, and two servants, Milliscent, who
serves Lady Frugal, and Secret, Shavem's bawd; the two servants serve as
mirrors, parasites who gain from their mistresses' misdeeds, with Secret's
occupation as bawd reinforcing the connection between the behavior of
the city ladies and that of the whore. In the final scene, Plenty is allowed
to appear as an aesthetically perfected version of himself, as a statue, along
with the statue of Sir Maurice, while the sartorially humbled Anne and
Mary express their contrition to them. Sir John, in a slightly zany revision
of the climax of *The Winter's Tale,* brings these statues to life, and it is to
the point that Massinger reverses the genders of the figures in Shakespeare:
the "magical" powers of Paulina are transferred to Sir John; the idealized
object is not Hermione but the suitors; the awed and repentant spectators
are Anne and Mary rather than Leontes.

   Throughout the play, women have attempted to turn themselves into
"shews" in which they act as author, lead actor, and costumer, whether
it be Lady Frugal's feigning illness to display her expensive nightwear,
Anne's fantasy of becoming the true spectacle at the playhouse, or Shavem's
appearance at her banquet as a "*Cleopatra*" (4.2.39). By the end of the play,
the finery in which these women have attired themselves has been replaced
by clothing placed upon them and which designates their "proper" place
in the social order. In the tableau vivant of the people whom Luke has
had imprisoned, presented to him by Sir John disguised as an Indian,
of the dozen or so characters who appear, the stage directions give a
specific indication of only one of the characters' dress: "Shavem *in a
blew gown*" (5.3.59 s.d.), her garb being the uniform worn by prisoners at
Bridewell. Likewise, from 4.4 to the conclusion of the play, Lady Frugal
and her daughters wear the buffin gowns and green aprons given to
them by Luke; in these garments the Frugal women will serve "[a]s fair
examples for our proud City dames, / And their proud brood to imitate"
(4.4.58–59), spectacles "to fright / Others by [their] example" (4.4.134–
35). These women have again been made into "shews," and these "shews"
are not, as previously imagined, of their devising nor are the costumes
of their choosing. Legal and male authority has replaced female decisions
regarding dress: Shavem is a convict; Lady Frugal, Anne, and Mary are a
city wife and daughters. Fittingly, when Luke ejects Milliscent from the
Frugal household, he allows her to take "Not a rag" (4.4.139); without the

patronage of Lady Frugal, Milliscent basically becomes nothing, a being without an identity.

Mary has one final "shew" to perform; she tells Plenty, "I vow to shew my self / When I am married, an humble wife, / Not a commanding mistris" (5.3.120-22). As Court fashions seemingly caused Lady Frugal and her daughters to act as if they were Court ladies, so the buffin gowns and green aprons appear to have worked their countermagic, reversing the spell, so to speak, by transforming impudent women into obedient wives: Goneril has transformed herself into Katherina. As Luke says to the women when they first enter in these garments, "now shew you like your selvs / In your own naturall shapes" (4.4.49-50), and he claims that he seeks to "reduce [them] to / [Their] naturall forms" (4.4.132-33). Luke's speech posits the power of clothing not to conceal but to reveal, that clothing serves to make visible the true self, one's "naturall form."

As the merchant who traffics in fine cloths and as a middle-class citizen who has acquired a title, Sir John might be seen as the most problematic character in the play, perhaps as the problem in the play: his goods are what the characters, particularly, though not exclusively, the female ones, crave; it is his rise in social status via financial success that the other characters emulate. However, he is given the final speech of the play, an address to Lady Frugal:

> Make you good
> Your promis'd reformation, and instruct
> Our City dames, whom wealth makes proud, to move
> In their own spheres, and willingly to confesse
> In their habits, manners, and their highest port,
> A distance 'twixt the City, and the Court.
>
> (5.2.150-55)

Like Luke's speech to Lady Frugal concerning the decorum involved maintaining "a distinction between / The Wife of a Patritian, and Plebean" (4.4.80-81), Sir John's speech makes social distinctions the grounds for social order, and the maintenance of that order is the responsibility of the wife as well as the husband. The wives' "habits"—"habit" meaning dress as well as behavior[14]—will "confesse" the "distance 'twixt the City, and the Court": clothing here not only shows, but also speaks. However, while the play suggests the reinstatement of stability to the "babble *Babell*" that was London at the beginning, the theatrical presentation of the scene undercuts this notion: Sir John is, after all, still in his disguise as an Indian from Virginia, and the buffin-gowned wife whom he advises is a boy.

As the Indian from Virginia, Sir John proposes a lurid scenario of blood sacrifice, which, instead, is transformed into (almost) the most benign of family reunions with the reconciliation of husband and wife and the promised union of daughters with the husbands of their father's choice. Lady Frugal, Anne, and Mary are united with their "correct" partners rather than being butchered. While Lady Frugal and her daughters are made to repent for their slavish devotion to Court and Continental fashion, Sir John's disguise as a Virginian Indian facilitates the comic ending of the play. At the same time that Massinger's play concludes with a return to an imagined restoration of social values in which the father controls his wife and daughters, Sir John's appearance as an Indian from Virginia suggests two points. First, Lady Frugal and her daughters were wrong in looking to the Continent for style. Sir John, dressed as a New World Indian, points the way in which the English should look; perhaps, Native American garments and pigment are the "dress-for-success" look. Likewise, for all the confessions of sartorial transgression that Lady Frugal expresses, she is still a male actor; her attire—whether buffin gown or fine attire—determines who "she" is for the audience. The costume of the actor—as an Indian or a woman— makes the audience see this player as a commoner or an aristocrat, a Native American or a Continental pretender, a man or a woman.

Notes

A version of this essay was originally presented in a seminar, "Borrowed Robes: Clothes and the Renaissance Theatre," at the meeting of the Shakespeare Association of America in Washington, DC, in March 1997, led by Ann Rosalind Jones and Peter Stallybrass. I would like to thank them for allowing me to use their recently published work and, along with Stephen Orgel, for being invaluable contributors to the argument and ideas in this piece. I would also like to acknowledge the part Ann McEntee played in the development of this article; her interest in costume in early modern English theater opened an avenue of inquiry that I had not previously considered.

1. John Taylor, "The Water Cormorant," *All the Workes of Iohn Taylor the Water-Poet* (London, 1630) 3 vols., 2nd sig. Aaa, 4.

2. *The Life and Death of Mistress Mary Frith, Commonly Called Moll Cutpurse,* ed. Randall S. Nakayama (1662; New York: Garland, 1993) 33. In *The Roaring Girl,* Middleton and Dekker likewise have Moll Cutpurse making her entrance in a jerkin and a petticoat.

3. Stephen Orgel, *Impersonations: The Performance of Gender in Shakespeare's England* (Cambridge: Cambridge University Press, 1996) 98. Many other works deal with the

issues of costume in the early modern English theater: see Jonathan V. Crewe, "The Theater of the Idols: Marlowe, Rankins, and Theatrical Images," *Theatre Journal* 36 (1984): 321–33; and Peter Stallybrass, "Worn Worlds: Clothes and Identity on the Renaissance Stage," *Subject and Object in Renaissance Culture,* ed. Magreta de Grazia, Maureen Quilligan, and Peter Stallybrass (Cambridge: Cambridge University Press, 1996) 289–320. Issues of dressing across lines of gender and class are addressed in Lisa Jardine, *Still Harping on Daughters: Women and Drama in the Age of Shakespeare* (New York: Columbia University Press, 1989), esp. ch. 5, and *Worldly Goods* (New York: Doubleday, 1996); Laura Levine, *Men in Women's Clothing: Antitheatricality and Effeminization, 1579–1642* (Cambridge: Cambridge University Press, 1994); and Linda Woodbridge, *Women and the English Renaissance: Literature and the Nature of Womankind, 1540–1620* (Urbana: University of Illinois Press, 1984).

4. Citations from *The City Madam* and notes for the play are taken from Philip Massinger, *The Plays and Poems of Philip Massinger,* vols. 4 and 5, ed. Philip Edwards and Colin Gibson (Oxford: Clarendon, 1976). For the dating of *The City Madam,* see Massinger 4: 1–3.

5. Ann Rosalind Jones and Peter Stallybrass, "Introduction: Fashion, Fetishism, and Memory in Early Modern England," *Renaissance Clothing and the Materials of Memory* (Cambridge: Cambridge University Press, 2000) 5.

6. See Massinger's descriptions of these characters in "The Actors Names," Massinger, 4: 18.

7. This legislation is cited in Jardine, *Still Harping on Daughters,* 143–44.

8. For glosses regarding the wearers of velvet hoods and Miniver caps and the outdatedness in Massinger's time, see Massinger 5: 240, n. for 4.4.75–76.

9. Stallybrass 290.

10. Stallybrass 304.

11. Phillip Stubbes, *The Anatomie of Abuses,* ed. Arthur Freeman (New York: Garland, 1973) F5v.

12. Stubbes F6r.

13. Quotations from *King Lear* are from the Arden Shakespeare, ed. Kenneth Muir (London: Methuen, 1952).

14. See Jones and Stallybrass regarding the meanings of this term, 6; see also 267, 327 n. 74.

Bastards and Broadsides
in The Winter's Tale

AARON KITCH

I N ACT 2 OF *The Winter's Tale,* Paulina boldly appears before King Leontes and his court with the newborn Perdita in her arms. Her self-appointed mission is to convince them that the infant she carries is legitimate. Imploring the assembled to observe the babe's physical features and be assured of its true paternity, she employs the language of print:

> Behold, my lords,
> Although the print be little, the whole matter
> And copy [are] of the father—eye, nose, lip,
> The trick of's frown, his forehead, nay the valley,
> The pretty dimples of his chin and cheek, his smiles,
> The very mould and frame of hand, nail, finger.
> (2.3.97–102)[1]

Although the word "print" had multiple meanings in early modern England, including handwriting, stamping an image, and imprinting a seal, its combination in this passage with "matter" and "copy"—and especially with the technical terms "mould" and "frame"—alludes to the printing press specifically.[2] Paulina lists the infant's body parts individually as ocular proof of the legitimacy of the royal offspring, though it requires both Apollo's oracle and the deaths of Mamillius and (supposedly) Hermione in act 3 to convince Leontes that Hermione is faithful and the "innocent babe truly begotten" (3.2.132). Leontes rejects Paulina's argument, at least initially,

43

but he absorbs its logic. After an extended period of contrition and his eventual submission to Paulina's will, the king uses the same language in 5.1 when he tells Prince Florizel that his mother "was most true to wedlock . . . / For she did print your royal father off, / Conceiving you" (5.1.123–25). Both passages imagine the press as a tool for measuring the legitimacy of paternal relations. This repeated figuration, I would like to suggest, offers an important perspective from which to evaluate the central but paradoxical structure of paternity and its anxieties in the play, the threat of bastardy as a form of material debasement, the function of Autolycus and the early modern print practices he stands for, and the play's own hybrid generic status as a "mongrel" tragicomedy.

The printing press is not an obvious institution for a Jacobean playwright (and this Jacobean playwright in particular) to invest with authority and legitimacy. If technical language of the printing trade seems out of place in pre-Christian Sicilia, where ultimate judicial authority is vested in Apollo's oracle, it would also have been counterintuitive as a model of validity to early modern viewers. Shakespeare's own ambivalence toward the press perhaps reinforces what many of his contemporaries considered to be the dubious status of print as degraded and unauthorized because made common, a stigma which early modern authors frequently acknowledged and used to negotiate the category of authorship in their own printed works.[3] But the model of paternal control based on print as it functions in *The Winter's Tale* must be understood in relation to other formulations in the play, including Leontes's misogynistic polemic against the word of women who "will say anything" (1.2.130), bastardy as a threat to the linguistic polity of Sicilia, and the dangerous ballads of Autolycus that appropriate codes of print-oriented authority in order to spread lies. These ballads also embody anxieties of uncontrolled reproduction manifested within the Stationers' Company itself, exposing the material dialectic of print and paternity as it functioned both in the drama and in society more generally.[4] One specific broadside genre alluded to by the play, the monstrous-birth ballad, functioned for early modern print producers as a way to displace anxieties of reproduction about the press as a cultural institution.

The shared anxieties of paternity and print in the play inscribe broader cultural anxieties about printing as a shift in modes of material production. The press offers a more complex and conflicted model of paternal authority than the traditional "imprint" model traced by several contemporary critics and found, for instance, in Shakespeare's Sonnet 11: "[Nature] carved thee for her seal, and meant thereby / Thou shouldst print more, not let that copy die" (lines 13–14). The print/paternity dialectic provides a cultural context from which to analyze plot, character, and generic status in a way that is unique to *The Winter's Tale,* with its multiple investments in forms of print—not only the source text in Robert Greene's romance *Pandosto* but also the broadside ballad as a competing commercial commodity. But I argue that the play ultimately resolves this dialectic in the statue scene, from which a feminine aesthetic of "living sculpture" emerges that can both accommodate the marks of time and mediate between fixed forms and diachronic change.

In an influential account of the relations between Elizabethan structures of gender and power, Louis Montrose identifies paternity as a "shaping fantasy," an act of imprinting, drawing on Theseus's speech in *A Midsummer Night's Dream* depicting the father as a "god" to his malleable daughter, who should be "but as a form in wax / By him imprinted, and within his power / To leave the figure or disfigure it" (1.1.47, 49–51). The paternal relation for Montrose becomes a "fantasy of male parthenogenesis" that entails complete patriarchal control (40). Margreta de Grazia examines the "imprint" metaphor as it is used by Plato, Aristotle, Descartes, and Shakespeare to understand "reproductive bodies and minds . . . [and] the conception and generation of ideas and children" (90). She traces the cultural semantics of the imprint in sealing wax, stamping, coining, and ultimately printed texts, which she sees as an extension of the signet/wax model. While the printed press in *The Winter's Tale* can be situated within these accounts of paternity as acts of masculine imprinting, it also problematizes the notion of the paternal imprint because it is a more complex and collaborative form of labor that alters the structure of paternity modeled around it. The "imprint" model which Montrose finds in *Midsummer* constructs the father as a "demiurge or *homo faber*" (40), where paternity shapes formless matter like the God who breathes the first human life out of clay. The fantasy of the printing press elaborated by *The Winter's Tale,* however, situates the labor of parenting on a wholly different level—what Marx specifies as an early form of alienated and disembodied labor in industries that depend on machines.[5] By linking the mechanical labor of print with the human labor of childbirth, the play demonstrates a cultural link between the fantasies of authentic paternity and identical printed copies but also stages the defeat of both models by exposing the flaw of print as an authorizing institution: the structure of authority imbedded within print as an ideal of fixity unravels through the circulation of identical copies whose appearance seems to buttress their truth value while their iterability actually transforms the authoritative structure they enact. The promise of uniformity and centralization of textual production inherent in the press succumbs in the play, through its alliance with paternity as a category, to the inability to control multiple copies and to anxieties of hybridity and illegitimate form that pervade discourses of early modern printing.

Traditional accounts of paternity from Aristotle to St. Thomas Aquinas identify the masculine seed as more perfect than the female ovum, a seed that the poet Statius in Dante extols as the "perfect blood. . . . that's never drunk / . . . [but] acquires, within the heart, formative powers / to build the members of the human shape."[6] By this model, paternity imposes spiritual form on maternal matter in reproducing the child. James I famously defined his absolutist monarchy in terms of being a father to England, and patriarchalism as the direct justification of social and political obligations also pervaded seventeenth-century institutions. In the Anglican Church, catechistical instruction drew on the Fifth Commandment to vest in fathers, magistrates, masters, and teachers the authority of the original Father, while in political discourse Robert Filmer offered the fullest example of patriarchalism as a defense of divine-right monarchy (based on God's original bequest to Adam) in his *Patriarcha,* a book and an argument against which Locke notoriously positioned his contractual theory of government.[7] Yet the paternal bond as a biological function is inherently unstable, dependent for its legitimization on an external material or narrative source traditionally associated with the mother.[8] When Leontes seizes on Paulina's metaphor of the printing press as a potential method of authentification, he supplants the word of the mother as the traditional guarantee for paternal legitimacy with a mechanical process of "labor," replacing the woman's reproductive organs with a machine that was in Shakespeare's day overseen primarily by men.[9]

This intervention in the biological process of reproduction occurs in the context of one of Shakespeare's most sustained and complex explorations of paternal relations.[10] Beyond the frequency of references to fathers and sons in the play and the importance of paternal bonds to the plot, there are moments like Antigonus's offer to spay his daughters and "glib" (emasculate) himself if the charges against Hermione prove true that register the play's obsession with models of paternity and legitimate "issue" (2.1.144-49). In the opening dialogue we learn from Archidamus and Camillo that the young prince Mamillius, a "gentleman of the greatest promise," "physics the subject, makes old hearts fresh," and heals "they that went on crutches ere he was born" (1.1.34, 36-37). Much like the kingdom of James, the political stability of Sicilia rests on the shoulders of a healthy male heir.[11] But the positive sentiment voiced here is undermined by the unequal relation between the two courtiers, who speak of the "great difference" between themselves and a corresponding inability of Bohemia to live up to the "magnificence" which Sicilia has bestowed (1.1.3, 11). The promise of the son exposes cracks in the diplomatic relations between Sicilia and Bohemia reflected eventually in the split between Leontes and Polixenes. When Hermione in 1.2 attempts to convince Polixenes to extend his stay in Sicilia, she suggests that the only excuse that would justify Polixenes's return to Bohemia is his desire to see his son: "To tell he longs to see his son were strong; / But let him say so then, and let him go; / But let him swear so and he shall not stay— / We'll thwack him hence with distaffs" (1.2.34-37). Hermione here suggests that the paternal bond should be allowed to trump the codes of hospitality and international diplomacy that might otherwise keep Polixenes in Sicilia. But using the paternal bond as a way to justify the separation of the two kings anticipates how Leontes and Polixenes will find in paternity a sign of their deteriorating relationship. After feeling the first pangs of jealous suspicion against his wife, Leontes asks his "brother" Polixenes if he is as "fond" of his son as Leontes is of Mamillius, to which Polixenes replies:

> If at home, sir,
> He's all my exercise, my mirth, my matter;
> Now my sworn friend and then mine enemy;
> My parasite, my soldier, statesman, all.
> He makes a July's day short as December,
> And with his varying childness cures in me
> Thoughts that would thick my blood.
> (1.2.163-69)

Post-Freudian readers may recognize in this confession an element of excessive libidinal investment in the filial object. Florizel fulfills many roles at once for his father—parasite, soldier, statesman, friend, enemy—in ways that seem to preclude the healthy functioning of the state and of the king himself by concentrating all necessary actors into one person, and a person of "varying childness" at that. This element of excess in Polixenes's reply to what is on the surface a straightforward question indeed mirrors the psychological state of Leontes himself at this moment in the play, since he asks the question as a way of disguising his own *"tremor cordis"* that has overcome him after witnessing his queen and Polixenes arm in arm (1.2.109). The fraternal bond implied by Leontes's many references to Polixenes as a "brother" and reciprocated in Polixenes's "twinned lambs" speech (1.2.66) begins to "branch" (1.1.23) not just around the issue of the fall into sexual activity that Hermione identifies (1.2.79-85), but also around the question of paternity—that vertical relation of biological heredity within a family that puts strain on the horizontal bonds of identification between them.

Polixenes himself contributes, however subconsciously, to the onset of Leontes's jealous furor by lacing his language in the early part of the scene with words of conception and procreation. This language also introduces the conjunction of sexual reproduction and print to the play:

> Nine changes of the watery star hath been
> The shepherd's note since we have left our throne
> Without a burden. Time as long again
> Would be filled up, my brother, with our thanks,
> And yet we should for perpetuity
> Go hence in debt. And therefore, like a cipher,
> Yet standing in rich place, I multiply
> With one "we thank you" many thousands more
> That go before it.
>
>   (1.2.1-9)

When Polixenes describes himself as "standing in [a] rich place," he invokes the womb, as in Titania's reference in *A Midsummer Night's Dream* to her pregnant serving woman, "rich with my young squire" (2.1.131). His procreative imagery continues in his use of words like "breed" ("I am questioned by my fears of what may chance / Or breed upon our absence" [1.2.11-12]) and provides a sexual subtext in his language that proves damaging to the fragile mental state of Leontes. Polixenes describes himself as a "cipher" in the sense of a character or number of no value in itself that multiplies other characters by virtue of its relative position, deriving from the Arabic word for "zero" (*çifr*). This is how the passage is typically glossed.[12] But another definition of the word common to early modern

England was a "secret or disguised manner of writing" that required a code for interpretation (*OED* 5.a). This second level of meaning, with specific reference to writing, aligns procreation in the womb with making "many thousands" of copies, a process most readily associated with the printing press by Jacobean viewers. This "rich" womb has a copiousness that eclipses the capacity of biological reproduction in humans and imagines a fecundity of reproduction found only in the mechanical world of print.

Leontes's initial test of his suspicions against Hermione is to inspect Mamillius for signs of resemblance to himself. "What, hast smutched thy nose? / They say it is a copy out of mine . . . / yet they say we are / Almost as like as eggs—women say so, / That will say anything" (1.2.120-21, 128-30). Paternity must be secured through examination of a textual "copy" that will reveal the supposed evidence of the mother's truthfulness (or her sins), a text whose physical similarity to its originating father is a guarantee of paternal legitimacy.[13] Though this "copy" is not explicitly printed in the context of the speech, its relation to Polixenes's earlier "cipher" speech and foreshadowing of Paulina's explicit reference to print in act 2 make its association with print consistent with the logic of the play. Leontes elevates the supposed fixity of the printed copy over the untrustworthy word of women, who will "say anything" and are as "false / As o'er-dyed blacks, as wind, as waters" (1.2.130-31), a metaphor taken from the early modern practice of mixing two or more dyes together to make colored cloth. Where print ideally fixes words on paper through punches and standardized letters that control the flow of ink, the "o'er-dyed blacks" represent uncontrolled and unstructured dissemination of vitriolic dye that makes the resulting fabric weak. Paulina appropriates the metaphor when she says with regard to Hermione's imprisonment, "Here's such ado to make no stain a stain / As passes colouring" (2.2.18-19), suggesting that it is Leontes himself who is guilty of making something out of nothing, of groundless excess in his baseless accusations. But her appropriation nevertheless subscribes to the logic of the structure of paternity as a textual mark whose uncertainties demand something like the machine of the press for standardization.

Leontes carries the figure still further when responding to Camillo's doubts about his accusations against Hermione:

> Dost think I am so muddy, so unsettled,
> To appoint myself in this vexation? Sully
> The purity and whiteness of my sheets—

> Which to preserve is sleep, which being spotted
> Is goads, thorns, nettles, tails of wasps—
> Give scandal to the blood o'th'prince, my son
> Who I do think is mine and love as mine,
> Without ripe moving to't?
>
> (1.2.322-29)

The preservation of manly honor and peace of mind is aligned with textual imprints through the image of adulterated white sheets whose original purity is like a piece of paper before it is sullied by ink. The king's peace of mind is imagined as a clean sheet, a blank page for which the threat of adultery is a stain. Both the method of verifying the truth of paternity using textual and/or printed signs as well as the image of mental and social equilibrium imagined as a blank sheet are male qualities. The orderly impression of color or letters is equated with legitimate paternity, while the amorphous stain, the illegible excess of ink, connotes bastardy.

Leontes concludes from his examination of his son and his speculations about his wife that his newborn daughter is a bastard, a word which becomes a virtual mantra in 2.3—used five times by Leontes in the space of ninety lines (73, 139, 154, 160 [twice])—and which does a significant amount of work in the play as a register of the dangers of adulteration, hybridity, and illegitimacy. The bastard in early modern England was a cultural and political exile, a potentially subversive force connected with the failure to control discourse as well as with illicit sexual union.[14] But the word also had ramifications for material production in print and cloth making, since it could mean a mixed cloth of low quality or unusual size (*OED* I.5.a), a print typeface, and, starting in the seventeenth century, an incomplete page before the full title page of a printed book (*OED* I.6.d and I.11). Richard Huloet's 1552 dictionary defines the word as a style of handwriting, the *litera adulterina*.[15] And in printing the *batârde* typeface imitated cursive handwriting to combine mechanical print with the human hand.[16]

Bastardy, of course, also had quite tangible political consequences in early modern society, threatening not only monarchy as an institution based on authentic and pure bloodlines (Elizabeth and James were both subject to political challenges based on their heredity),[17] but also primogeniture as the primary institution for transferring wealth and property—a legal institution built around paternal bonds.[18] *The Winter's Tale* frames the threat of bastardy as a threat to the legitimacy of language systems in such a way that opens up the space for a model of paternity based on print. When Leontes sees his wife holding hands with Polixenes and says "Too hot, too hot! / To mingle friendship far is mingling bloods," his fear of mixing categories of relationship shades easily into a fear of hybridized or bastardized bloodlines (1.2.107–8). The stability and well-being of the state, not to mention Leontes's own psychological condition, depends on the purity of language and its use within a social system. In accusing Hermione of allowing Polixenes to impregnate her, Leontes draws on his wife's supposed transgression to construct a theory of linguistic polity:

> O thou thing,
> Which I'll not call a creature of thy place
> Lest barbarism, marking me the precedent,
> Should a like language use to all degrees,
> And mannerly distinguishment leave out
> Betwixt the prince and beggar. I have said
> She's an adultress, I have said with whom.
> (2.1.82–88)

Leontes imagines social order as founded on language, where words both constitute and enforce social status; he fears that his use of a vulgar word might tear down the system of social difference, leaving the distinction between "prince and beggar" no longer valid. Language for Leontes both defines the speaker's class identity and, in certain cases, undermines the structure of oppositions between classes itself. Because it lies at the very foundation of society, language must be constantly surveyed and policed in its connection to social difference. Leontes, who sees himself at the center of this order, is driven to relate sexual reproduction with this linguistic order, which includes, as we have seen, both the oral register of women's talk and the textual register of Mamillius as a "copy" of the father. This relationship anticipates the need for a machine that might regulate and fix textual production as a way to secure proper sexual reproduction and thus retain fixity and order within his linguistic polity.

But the press that might contain this disorder by extending the pen/ paper or signet/wax model of paternal reproduction also alters the model of paternity it adopts. *The Winter's Tale* demonstrates how the printing press complicates the "imprint" model of paternity in which the father shapes the child as a signet impresses wax. That is, both the press and paternity are legitimating structures (of texts and children, respectively) whose weak link is in the reproducibility of that structure through the production of multiple copies. Shakespeare shows the double-edged capacity of printed texts to authorize the written word in the same way that a true father authorizes his child, but also to make that authenticity dependent on reproducible signs that are easily appropriated and redirected in ways that challenge the entire structure of authority itself.

The dissemination of printed materials in the late sixteenth century to a broader and more diverse reading public than ever before produced new social arrangements that brought with them new anxieties about forms of representation and their cultural and political impact.[19] The act of printing was often figured by printers and authors in early modern England in biological terms, whether in the naming of the parts of the press or in the representation of authors as fathers to their texts and printers as stepfathers to abandoned textual children.[20] Early modern authors themselves were often conscious of the alteration to existing structures of cultural authority that print introduced. Henry Chettle, for instance, describes in his *Kind-Hartes Dreame* how print produces visible signs that create a false sense of authority. Through the persona of the balladeer Anthony Now Now, Chettle complains about ballad sellers who "sweare" that their wares "are published by Authoritie: and people farre off thinke nothing is printed but what is lawfully tollerated" (60). The act of printing overcomes the distance between the central site of authorization and the periphery, but in bridging this gap, it also usurps the original proximity or immediate presence on which authority depends; its authoritative structure is weakened by the reproducibility of the signs of that authority. The broadside ballad in particular exemplifies this dual nature of the press in relation to cultural authority: on the one hand, its seeming uniformity and centralized mode of production create an aura of fixity and legitimacy, making possible the differentiation between good and bad forms of textuality, but on the other, it is part of an explosion of printed texts in which classifications and hierarchies of authority were becoming dependent on their forms of expression, rather than resting in existing nontextual sources.[21]

In *The Winter's Tale,* Autolycus is associated with printed ballads and bastardy alike.[22] Alluding to Ovid's account of Chione's double rape by Apollo and Mercury, resulting in the birth of the twins Autolycus and Philamon (Ovid 11.345–402), Autolycus claims to be "littered under Mercury" (4.3.25) and thus aligns himself with a pagan mythology fitting for Bohemia and the play's other mythical sources in the Prosperina and Pygmalion stories. But in his connection to the printed broadside and the London print industry, he also signifies his contemporaneity with the audience. Vagabond, petty thief, con artist, impersonator, peddler, and court exile, Autolycus traffics in stolen "sheets" that echo Leontes's references to the stained purity of his marriage sheets. He also sells linens, ribbons, gloves, and other trinkets ("inkles, caddises, cambrics, lawns" [4.4.209]), "bastard" remainders of the textile industry that were sewn into other garments to complement an outfit, emphasizing his connection with a mobile marketplace and with fragments rather than wholes. His versatility and status as a "snapper-up of unconsidered trifles" (4.3.25–26) connect him with new market economies and the expansion of capitalism rather than traditional rural agricultural economies such as Bohemia.[23] His own impersonations, first as a beggar who has been robbed, then as a courtier in the borrowed garb of Florizel when the latter elopes with Perdita, align him with forces of malleability. He decenters the play, yet the play cannot do without him, in the sense that he cheats the simple peasants out of their money by fictionalizing himself but is at the center of the sheepshearing in Bohemia because his fictional ballads are a prime source of the festive energy of the country ritual.

Autolycus sells a specific form of printed broadside that was new to the sixteenth century, a type of ballad that appropriated traditional oral ballads for commercial printers. For a penny, consumers could purchase these broadsides depicting religious primers, verse libels, political "flytings," epitaphs, and bawdy songs.[24] Autolycus sells ballads like the one about a "fish that appeared upon the coast on Wednesday the fourscore of April forty thousand fathom above water, and sung . . . against the hard hearts of maids" (4.4.273–76), and another, "how a usurer's wife was brought to bed of twenty money-bags at a burden" (4.4.260–62). The latter ballad refers to an actual genre of broadsides that first achieved popularity in the 1560s and feature an explicit conjunction of print and paternity in early modern culture. An examination of this genre of monstrous-birth ballads reveals how it provided a format within a nascent print marketplace for producers of print to navigate the murky waters of their own cultural authority (see figures 1 and 2).

It is no coincidence that Anthony Now Now invokes the ballad specifically as a problem of the authority of print. The mobility and cheapness of the ballad as a printed sheet, part of its function as one of the earliest

The true description of two monsterous children,

lawfully begotten betwene George Steuens and Margerie his wyfe, and borne in the parish of Swanburne in Buckyngham shyre, the .iiij. of Aprill. Anno Domini. 1566. the two children hauing both their belies fast ioyned together, and imbracyng one another with their armes : which children wer both a lyue by the space of half an hower, and wer baptized, and named the one John, and the other Joan.

I Read how Affrique land was fraught
for their most filthie life,
With mōstrous shapes, confusedly
that therin wer full rife.

But England now pursues their vyle
and detestable path,
Embracyng eke all mischéefs great
that moues Gods mightie wrath.

As these vnnaturall shapes & formes,
thus brought forth in our dayes :
Are tokens true and manifest,
how God by dyuers wayes :

Doth styrre vs to amendment of
our vyle and cankred lyfe :
Which how to to much abused is,
in man, in chylde, and wyfe.

We wallow so in filthie sin,
and naught at all regarde :
Nor wyll we feare the threats of God
tyll we for iust rewarde :

Be ouerwhelmd withmischéefs great,
which ready bent for vs
Full long a go decreed wer,
as Scriptures doth discus.

Both tender babes & she baytc beastes,
in shape disfourmed bée :
Full manie wayes he plagues the earth,
(as dayly we may sée)

Thus mightie Ioue, to pearce our harts
these tokens straunge doth send,
To call vs from our filthie lyfe
our wicked wayes t'amend.

And thus by these two children here,
forewarnes both man and wyfe :
How both estates ought to bewaple,
their vile and wretched lyfe.

For sure we all may be agast,
to sée these shapes vnkynd :
And trēblyng feare may pearce our harts
our God to haue in mynd.

For yf we printed in our brest,
these signes and tokens straunge :
Wold make vs from our sinnes to shrike
our lives a new to chaunge.

But some proude boastyng Pharisie,
the parents wyll detest :
And iudge with heapes of bglie vice
their lives to be infest.

No, but lessons for vs all,
which dayly & se offend :
Yea more perhaps, then hath the frends,
whom God this birth did lend.

For yf you wyll with single eye,
note well and view the text :
And marke our Sauiours aunswer eke,
that thereto is annext :

Where his disciples askcd him,
to know therein his mynd :
Yf greatter wer the parents sinnes,
or his that was borne blynd.

To whom Christ aunswered in a bréef,
that neither bée, nor they :
Deserued had that croked fate,
although they sin each day.

But to the end Gods glorie great,
and miracles diuine :
Might on the earth apparaunt be,
his workes for to define.

Such lyke examples moued me,
in these forgetfull dayes :
To rue our state that vs a mong,
vice beares such swings and swayes.

Wherein the gwdnesse great of God
we may and set so light :
By such examples callyng vs,
from sin both day and night.

Where we doe runne at randon wyde,
our selues flatteryng styll :
And blazyng others faults and crimes,
yet we our selues most pll.

But if we doe consider right,
and in euen balaunce way :
The ruine great of hartie loue,
among vs at this day :

And well behold with inward eyes,
th'embracyng of these Twinnes :
That God by them vpbraides vs for
our false discemblyng sinnes.

We would with Niniuie repent
our former passed yeares,
Bewaylyng eke our secret sinnes
in sacke cloth and in teares.

Therfore in time amend your state,
and call to God for grace :
Bewaile your former lyfe and sinnes,
while you haue time and space.

FINIS. ⸿ Iohn Mellys Nor.

Imprinted at London by Alexander Lacy, for William Lewes : dwellyng in Cow lane aboue Holborne cundit, ouer against the signe of the Plough.

FIGURE 1. John Mellys, *The True Description of Two Monsterous Children* (London: Alexander Lacy, 1566; STC 17803).

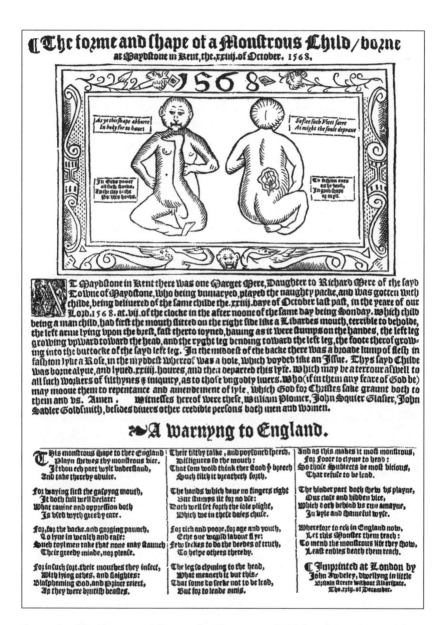

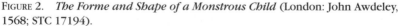

FIGURE 2. *The Forme and Shape of a Monstrous Child* (London: John Awdeley, 1568; STC 17194).

mass-produced commodities, was also a mark of potential degradation. Henry Fitzgeffrey, for instance, seems to have the monstrous-birth broadsides specifically in mind when he fulminates in 1617, "Let Natures causes (which are too profound / For every blockish sottish *Pate* to sound.) / Produce some *monster:* some rare *spectacle* . . . / Bee it a worke of nere so sleight a waight, / It is recorded up in *Metre* straight, / And counted purchase of no small renowne, / To heare the *Praise* sung in a Market-towne" (sig. A7v). Fitzgeffrey scoffs at the lowly reduction of profound matter and denounces the association of "Nature's causes" with the marketplace, where a matter of "so sleight a waight" achieves "purchase."

The monstrous-birth ballads can be read in the context of the nascent print industry of England that fostered their formal and generic possibility. Their obsession with aberrations of natural form represented by the figure of the monstrous child—the potentially endless deviations from the norm that the human body can take—occurs at a time when the broadside format itself became a target of reform within the Stationers' Company as a bastardized type of print commodity. A majority of the ballads were produced during an important period of increasing regulation in the printing trade, including the 1551 proclamation of Edward VI requiring all printed matter to secure approval in advance, the formal charter of the Stationers' Company in 1557, Queen Elizabeth's injunctions of 1559, and the 1566 Star Chamber decree expanding the powers of search and seizure of printers in their policing of illegally printed materials.[25] The commercial trade in ballads was especially hard to regulate due to its small size and quick printing time; printers of ballads were repeatedly fined in the book of records kept by the wardens of the company for "disorderly printing," meaning either piracy or failure to register a group of ballads that they had sold. The single-sheet broadside was relatively cheap and easy to produce. It was also sold primarily in wholesale until well into the seventeenth century, mostly to itinerant chapmen. Where the English and Latin stock institutionalized entire classes of books as valuable commodities that secured financial reward for many printers, no ballad stock was ever established.[26]

To compensate for anxiety about its form of production, the monstrous-birth ballad associates its own form with the amendment of the illegitimate birth it depicts as a way of displacing its own anxieties of inauthenticity, using the trope of uncontrolled and illegitimate sexual production. It assimilates the event of the deformed birth into a providential framework by which it is understood to be one of many wondrous natural portents that signify God's omnipotence and warnings of his forthcoming judgment against sinners. Such a gesture places the genre within the tradition of Protestant "providence" tales that documented God's presence on earth through unnatural events unexplained by natural laws and in such a way that would prove the superiority of reformed religion to Catholicism.[27] The genre can also be understood as a problem of knowledge in the early modern period, denoting for scholars like Jean Céard, Lorraine Daston, and Katherine Park a shift in thinking about preternatural phenomenon as religious signification ("portents") to scientific fact ("evidence").[28] Prodigies like monstrous births provide ways to transcend established systems of thought, whether classical accounts by Aristotle, Cicero, and Pliny, or Christian interpretations by Augustine and Aquinas, in favor of new disciplines of fact-based inquiry into the natural world.

The English monstrous-birth ballad was overtly concerned with theological meaning and thus justified its own representation of highly sensational and potentially transgressive content, including explicit pictures, by reinscribing this disorder within the Christian salvation myth. What seems like a breach in nature thus becomes part of God's will; the pain and suffering of the innocent child forms a necessary prelude to the reader's deliverance from the evil it represents. As one writer suggests, "Wherein the goodnesse great of God / we way and set so light: / by such examples callyng us, / from sin both day and night."[29] As miraculous and unnatural signs, the ballads fulfill Christian providence, as described by an author calling himself John D.: "The heathen could forese and saye / That when suche wonders were, / It did foreshew to them alwaye / That some yll hap drew nere. / The scripture sayth, before the ende / Of all things shall appeare, / God will wounders straunge thinges sende, / as some is sene this yeare." The specific act of printing broadsides, which could be construed as commercial exploitation of suffering on the part of printers and balladeers, becomes an act justified and even demanded by God. Indeed, printing can uniquely perform God's work, as John D. argues:

> No carver can, nor paynter maye,
> The same so ougly make,
> As doeth itself shewe at this day,
> A sight to make the[e] quake!
>
> But here thou haste, by printing arte,
> a signe thereof to se;

> Let eche man saye within his harte,—
> It preacheth now to me."

The printing press performs what painting and sculpture cannot. Representing the printed ballad as a minister that "preacheth" to each reader individually, according to his or her conscience, the press invokes the authority of the church to buttress its own insecure claims to legitimacy. This appropriation of the institutional authority of the pulpit for the fledgling institution of print is one method by which to reauthorize the institution of print, one that not incidentally draws on a model of divine authority overtly invested in the metaphorics of the Father, and shows how it mediates its own uncertain cultural status by displacing its anxieties of illegitimate print production onto the topos of the monstrously deformed birth.

Shakespeare incorporates the monstrous-birth broadside in part to parody the naive association of print with truth by the peasant class,[30] but also, echoing the sentiments voiced by Anthony Now Now in Chettle's *Kind-Harte's Dreame,* to stage exactly the kind of threat to established structures of authority that print undermines through its processes of reproduction and distribution:

MOPSA: Pray now, buy some. I love a ballad in print, a-life, for then we are sure they are true.

AUTOLYCUS: Here's one to a very doleful tune, how a usurer's wife was brought to bed of twenty money-bags at a burden, and how she longed to eat adders' heads and toads carbonadoed.

MOPSA: Is it true, think you?

AUTOLYCUS: Very true, and but a month old.

DORCAS: Bless me from marrying a usurer!

AUTOLYCUS: Here's the midwife's name to't, one Mistress Taleporter, and five or six honest wives that were present. Why should I carry lies abroad?

(4.4.258–69)

The monstrous-birth ballad here conflates unnatural birth with the unnatural breeding of money in usury, both instances of reproduction out of control.[31] Typical of many "wondrous" accounts found in broadsides that Shakespeare himself might have seen, this one has eyewitnesses who vouch for its truth value. Moreover, as Maurice Hunt notes with relation to the concept of labor in the play, the midwife's name puns on the process of birthing and publishing ("Taleporter/Tailporter," 355). The midwife is a "tale" porter in the sense of one who spreads gossip orally, with associations again of an untrustworthy feminine oral network. Autolycus appeals to this Mistress Taleporter as an oral authorization of the truth of his printed ballad, suggesting within the logic of the play (and of course through the satire of the scene) that the printed broadside, like the child as "copy," needs an authorizing structure but that this structure itself—the word of woman—is woefully inadequate to guarantee the truth of its printed content, figured here explicitly as the offspring brought to the print marketplace by a midwife.

The introduction of a different commercial genre like the monstrous-birth broadside into Shakespeare's play implitcitly raises questions about the play's own generic status. When these broadsides depict monstrous births and midwives in the process of making "tales," they draw specifically on a connection between biological and mechanical modes of production, between the worlds of nature and of art. It is indeed not surprising that *The Winter's Tale* filters the question of its own generic status through the concepts of bastardy and hybridity during the debate between Perdita and Polixenes in act 4 about the "gillyvor" flower, or "nature's bastard." Perdita doesn't allow the gillyvor in her rustic garden because of its dangerous hybridity, vowing that she will "not put / The dibble [spade] in the earth to set one slip of them; / No more than, were I painted, I would wish / This youth [Florizel] should say 'twere well, and only therefore / Desire to breed by me" (4.4.99–103). She equates hybridity with deceptive artifice of a sort that is inappropriate for a pure pastoral heroine like herself, though this disdain entails a certain amount of irony in the context of Perdita's and Florizel's double disguises—Perdita's ignorance of her own parentage and Florizel's disguise of his, plus their costumed impersonations of Flora and Doricles, respectively. Polixenes, however, defends the "pied" gillyvor flower, arguing that:

> nature is made better by no mean
> But nature makes that mean; so over that art
> Which you say adds to nature, is an art
> That nature makes. You see, sweet maid, we marry
> A gentler scion to the wildest stock,
> And make conceive a bark of baser kind
> By bud of nobler race.
> . . . .
> Then make your garden rich in gillyvors,
> And do not call them bastards.
>
> (4.4.89–95, 98–99)

Polixenes's language of genetic engineering celebrates what he himself will soon reject—the discovery of his own noble son's wish to "marry" Perdita, a member of that "wildest stock." According to Polixenes, the gillyvor provides a positive model of hybridity, not one that deserves denigration as a bastard. But the language of bastardy in this exchange clearly echoes the high tragic consequences of bastardy in the first three acts, filtered here through the lens of the humanist *débat* tradition. The exchange between Perdita and Polixenes uses bastardy to evaluate artistic form, echoing (as Harold Wilson and others have noted) a passage from George Puttenham's *Arte of English Poesie* (1589) that uses the gillyvor flower as a way of illustrating his version of the art/nature interaction where the artist is like a gardener.[32] Polixenes becomes an apologist for the mixing of categories by deconstructing the art/nature binary.

The "gillyvor" speech is a self-conscious attempt in the play to question the purity or impurity of art. The "pied" mixing of categories here reverses the paradigm in *Hamlet* where art holds up a mirror to nature, suggesting that Shakespeare is conscious of occupying a different aesthetic register in this later play. Within contemporary debates on the subject, Philip Sidney provides the most useful terms for understanding the relation of mixed categories to generic form in his *Apology*, where he downgrades drama that takes abundant liberties with conventions of representational reality. Sidney scorns a play that can stage "three ladies walk[ing] to gather flowers and then [asks us to] believe the stage to be a garden" before abruptly representing a "shipwreck in the same place." His criticism of drama engaged in the "mingling of clowns and kings" would perhaps extend to most of Shakespeare's plays, but he singles out for criticism the genre of "mongrel tragicomedies" that "match hornpipes and funerals," interestingly using the same language of crossbreeding that Shakespeare uses in act 4 to discuss the hybridity or bastardy of artistic form.[33] The logic of the "gillyvor" analogy in Shakespeare, then, equates tragedy with the "bud of nobler race" and more mixed comedy with the "wildest stock." The pastoral mode of the sheepshearing festival, highlighted by the presence of the shepherd and the costumed youths Flora and Doricles, is the genre of mediation between the two, an appropriate role for a genre regarded by Renaissance theorists as the earliest literary type from which its "offspring" tragedy and comedy emerged.[34]

But if the pastoral mode at the heart of *The Winter's Tale* cites the Edenic origins of drama itself, this space is haunted by the figure of Autolycus as a figure of contamination of the pastoral, not least through his printed broadsides. He is aligned with the new potential of print to undermine existing authoritative structures, and the printed broadside he introduces troubles the authenticity of pastoral as the original father of the genre and challenges the ideology of closure offered by Leontes and Paulina in proposing the press as an instrument of regulation of sexual reproduction. This highlights the importance of print and the question of its status as labor—whether it can be considered as an artistic technique or merely a machine. The presence of the dialectical model of print and paternity in the play depends, that is, on historically determined conditions of seventeenth-century England, including the increased circulation of printed matter in everyday life, technological innovation that makes possible new kinds of knowledge, and the role of mechanized labor as a mode of production associated by Marx with the increasing reification and rationalization of the external world.

The play's generic status as a tragicomedy, perhaps the only true tragi-comedy in Shakespeare's plays,[35] can be seen in part as a function of the intersection of print and paternity we have been tracing. This relation might be understood as a change in modes of production (the printing press) that reifies natural relations (sexual procreation) in a process that Fredric Jameson describes as the "analytical dismantling of the various traditional" unities into their constituent parts in order to reorganize them "into more efficient systems which function according to an instrumental" logic (227). The press itself, considered as a social force of reification, not only opens up the possibility for imagining biological reproduction through the lens of the mechanical labor of print, but also anticipates the divisions and structural fragmentation of the play. The structure of mutual anxiety in the relationship between print and paternity, in this sense, exposes the ideal of technological rationalization of natural reproductive relations as a newly available cultural fantasy of Jacobean society that demands new forms of cultural expression.

At the time when Shakespeare composed *The Winter's Tale,* tragicomedy was the dominant genre on the London stage, spurred by John Fletcher's rewriting of Guarini's *Il Pastor Fido* in *The Faithful Shepherdess.* Fletcher's English defense of the genre picks up the classical definition of depicting both "familiar people" and the gods, adding that "tragicomedy is not so called in respect of mirth and killing, but in respect it wants deaths, which is enough to make it no tragedy, yet brings some near it, which is enough to make it no comedy."[36] In staging two real deaths, *The Winter's Tale* perhaps favors Sidney's definition over Fletcher's, by emphasizing a "mongrel" form of construction as a tragicomedy through the appearance of figures like Time and the bear that eats Antigonus, as well as in the relative autonomy of its constituent parts.[37] The multiple genres of the play appear as a series of separate and relatively distinct modes, so that the tragic ethos of Sicilia, for instance, contains only one brief exchange that could be considered tangential comic relief (2.1.1–32), and the spectacle of Hermione's reanimation achieves the status of an autonomous theatrical set piece, a status emphasized by nineteenth-century directors who staged it separately as an interlude.

The final two scenes exemplify this fragmentation in modes of representation, contrasting the highly mediated narrative mode of 5.2 with the direct revelation of the play's final, visual-oriented interlude. Shakespeare in 5.2 stages the recognition scene between Leontes and Perdita indirectly as a mediated narration by Autolycus and a series of courtiers who rush in and out with breathless excitement about the scene they have been privileged enough to witness. Their language is peppered with words like "amazedness" and "wonder," and they deliberately construct their "news" of the paternal reunion between Perdita and Leontes in relation to the generic mode of the broadside ballad, explaining the otherwise inexplicable presence of Autolycus in the scene: "such a deal of wonder is broken out within this hour that ballad-makers cannot be able to express it" (5.2.23–25). "This news, which is called true, is so like an old tale that the verity of it is in strong suspicion," another courtier adds (5.2.27–29). Shakespeare acknowledges the affinities of his own "tale" in *The Winter's Tale* with the "old tales" of yore and as more "wondrous" than the very ballads that Autolycus has just offered for sale several scenes earlier.[38] But the mode of narration depicts, as the Third Gentleman says, something that "cannot be spoken of" (5.2.43)—that is, a scene beyond the powers of language to describe even though description remains the only means of expression available. With the introduction of the commercialized and exaggerated pathos of the printed ballads, which Shakespeare simultaneously acknowledges and distances himself from in the play, the most emotionally charged scene of human interaction must be staged as inaccessible. The numerous references by the narrators in the scene to the world of "wonder" and the ballad also remind the audience that what they are witnessing is a highly mediated form of representation.

Scene 5.2 achieves the most important reunions of the play: Leontes discovers that the strange but beautiful girl who has arrived in Sicilia is actually his daughter; Polixenes and Leontes heal their sixteen-year rift; Florizel is reconciled to his father as well as to Leontes; Camillo is welcomed back to Sicilia; and missing details of events, such as the story of Antigonus and the storm, are discovered. Even more than the final scene of the play, which actually leaves certain threads unraveled (Leontes and Hermione, for instance, never actually speak to each other), 5.2 provides the comic reunion and recuperation from the potential tragic loss introduced in the first three acts. Most importantly for our purposes, it is the moment of the recuperation and reunion of father with child. Because Shakespeare stages the scene in such a highly mediated fashion, however, he ironizes the paternal fantasy of authenticity based on print by using a print-related frame to represent the return to paternal fullness. Where Mamillius in act 2 provides a means of direct examination of the "copy" under the lens of paternal authentication and legitimization, here the father-and-child relation can be realized only through mediated stage narration by hitherto unknown characters and one (Autolycus) whose authority and legitimacy are tainted by print. The genre of the broadside challenges the dramatic representative mode at the moment that the play successfully reunites father and daughter and brings unity to its central plotline.

The final scene, in which the statue of Hermione is awakened through the reanimation of Leontes's faith (and a touch of music), moves in exactly the opposite direction of 5.2, as if to reexamine the potential of unmediated dramatic representation in the wake of the disturbance to the play by the printed broadside at the level of genre. Shakespeare returns to a directly visual theater, though the scene also announces itself as a source of "marvel" and "wonder" (5.3.68). Here, however, it is "silence" as opposed to forms of print that expresses such wonder (5.3.21). Paulina, as if in direct response to the previous scene, explains why she chooses to stage the statue scene in the way she does: "That she is living, / Were it but told you, should be hooted at / Like an old tale" (5.3.115–17). The fictional spectacle of the statue coming to life again, staged through the visual mode of sculpture, allows for apprehension as truth in a way that narratives— specifically those of Autolycus—cannot. But, of course, the play *is* an old tale, and Paulina's comments draw attention to the need for a specific mode of visual dramatic representation in order to ring true and to achieve authority.

The statue scene defines this authority against the inauthentic wonder of
the broadside ballad by retelling the Pygmalion myth, as Leonard Barkan has
masterfully explained. But where Ovid depicts a masterful sculptor who
can tap into the potential life of stone and thus animate his creation, here
the sculpture of Hermione is nonidealized and "wrinkled" (5.3.28). Paulina
justifies the wrinkles as products of the "carver's excellence" (5.3.30),
redefining artistic value in terms of mimetic authenticity rather than, as in
Ovid, as an idealized form that is so unspoiled in its purity that Pygmalion
fears that "sum blacke or broosed print / Should come by touching over
hard."[39] Such a gesture says something about the fantasy of print-based
paternity that Paulina herself introduces into the play, since Hermione's
statue is a fixed form that can accommodate change over time and that
"rebuke[s]" Leontes as "more stone than it" (5.3.37-38). The scene's focus
on the feminine aspects of reanimation that resemble a new birth, overseen
by the midwife figure of Paulina and allowing the reunion of mother and
daughter, emphasizes what Janet Adelman and others have noted as the
maternal force of recuperation in the play.[40]

But the feminine forces of recuperation still depend on Leontes as the
representative of law to legitimize the "spell" of Paulina, whose defense of
her magic raises the specter of its illegitimacy (5.3.104-106). By proclaim-
ing, "If this be magic, let it be an art / Lawful as eating," Leontes legitimizes
the spectacle of the statue's awakening (5.3.110-11). This "lawful magic"
is also the space of generic negotiation between the illegitimate and the
formal which pushes the play finally beyond the fantasy of printing as a
legitimating device for paternal production. Its feminine strength reappro-
priates the positive valences of motherhood from the inhuman printing
press itself, but the model of the wrinkled statue also accommodates
the fixed form of representation (whose highest art is sculpture) with
the synchronic change that can register the deformative hand of time.
Hermione's rebirth is not monstrous, but it is a birth in which youthful
features have been stretched and marked up. As sculpted by the Italian
sculptor Giuilo Romano (one of the few contemporary persons named
in Shakespeare), she is also an imported artifact from that most cutting-
edge nation of formal literary innovation, Italy. Her youthful/aged hybridity
and defiance of theatrical conventions (where characters who die stay
dead) justify the hybridity of tragicomedy as a mode of theater, gesturing
beyond the anxiety-producing dialectic of print and paternity associated
with Leontes and the court's attempt to regulate both sexual and textual

reproduction. Hermione represents the triumph of live theater, present and in the flesh on stage, over the cheap miracles of the popular broadsides. In this triumph, the court's misplaced desire to use the printing press as a guarantee of paternal legitimacy is safely returned to the institution of the theater itself.

Notes

For their helpful criticism on earlier versions of this essay, I would like to thank David Bevington, Douglas Brooks, Zachary Cannon, Janel Mueller, Michael Murrin, Sarah Rivett, Josh Scodel, Richard Strier, and the members of the 1999 Renaissance Workshop at the University of Chicago. The two anonymous readers at *Renaissance Drama* also offered valuable observations and suggestions.

1. Shakespeare, *Winter's Tale,* ed. Orgel. All subsequent citations are to this edition. Citations of other texts by Shakespeare refer to Shakespeare, *Complete Works.*

2. The "mould" was an iron device into which molten lead was poured to make letters. The "frame" was a wooden storage unit for sets of matrices (pieces of type) and punches (steel dies) which the compositor used in setting pages of typeface. Both terms are explained in Moxon 134-42 and 30-33, 401, respectively. Moxon cites "matter" as a technical printing term (347), and the *Oxford English Dictionary* (*OED*) gives examples of "copy" (s.v. 9a) as related to print practices in the sixteenth century.

3. See, for example, Saunders 139-64. For an account of how authors "reproduced this stigma in published works as a way of safeguarding class distinctions and at the same time displaced it onto sexual ideologies that reinforced the writers' masculine authority," see Wall 17.

4. Jeffrey Masten provides an influential account of this dialectic in tracing the emergence of authorship as inextricably bound with discourses of paternity and political authority in early modern England; see Masten.

5. The printing industry exemplifies for Marx the problem of the division of labor, since in gradually dissolving the guild trade in which apprentices advanced through the ranks to higher positions, the printing machine creates positions for young boys who are largely illiterate to spread sheets of paper under the machine, never progressing to a better-paying job. See Marx 615.

6. Dante, *The Divine Comedy,* Vol. 2, *Purgatory,* trans. Mark Musa (Harmondsworth: Penguin, 1981), 270. Quoted in Andréoli 17.

7. For James I's statements about paternity as a principle of government, see James I 65. The domestication of absolutist claims through the family in Stuart England is discussed in Goldberg. On Filmer and patriarchalism within the context of seventeenth-century English political theory, see Schochet.

8. See, for example, Kahn.

9. According to Cyprian Blagden, the first female wasn't apprenticed to the printers' guild until 1666, though it was a common practice for women to inherit print shops from their husbands. See Blagden 162. On the gendered division of labor in the printing shop,

see de Grazia 87–90. For accounts of women's participation in the print trade before the Restoration, see Orgel 72–73 and Bell.

10. B. J. Sokol has found, for instance, that the word "father" appears 57 times and is the most common substantive in the play, excluding pronouns and proper names, followed in rank by "time" (49), "son" (40), "daughter" (32), "brother" (20), and "mother" (13) (Sokol 42). Peter Erickson devotes an essay to "patriarchal structures" in *The Winter's Tale,* arguing that the play refashions a "brutal, crude, tyrannical" concept of patriarchy into a more "benign" one modeled on feminine nurture and natural bounty (819). His reading is accurate, up to a point, but it depends on a model of paternity as a cohesive force that is disrupted and then revived by an essentializing feminine nature (based on ideas of nature, harmony, and nurturing motherhood), rather than one that employs specific strategies in order to define paternal relations from the start. See Erickson.

11. Interestingly, both James's England and Sicilia experience the death of the first-born male. Shakespeare wrote his play before Prince Henry died of typhoid fever in 1612, but it was performed as part of the celebration of Princess Elizabeth's betrothal to Frederick in late 1612 or 1613.

12. See Shakespeare, *Winter's Tale,* ed. Orgel, 95; Shakespeare, *Winter's Tale,* ed. Greenblatt, 2884; and Shakespeare, *Winter's Tale,* ed. Schanazer, 162. For more on the relationship between the history of arabic numerals, accounting practices, printing, and bookmaking in early modern Europe, see Jaffe.

13. For other accounts of the copy metaphor in the play, see Barkan's analysis of the play's investment in the rivalry between the arts and Hunt's allusion to "copy" as a means of aligning the labor of childbirth with that of writing.

14. See, for instance, Findlay.

15. Huloet [unpaginated], "bastarde hande" entry.

16. The *batârde* typeface elicited criticism even in the twentieth century for its "extremely untidy" appearance (Isaac 29). See also Isaac xii–xiii, 10, 29, and 31, and plates 13, 22, 24, 29, 30, and 58.

17. Elizabeth was technically considered a bastard, according to Henry VIII's 1536 Succession Act, and James I was subject to the rumors that he was son to his mother's secretary, David Riccio, rather than Mary's husband.

18. Stephen Orgel provides commentary on the political allegory of Hermione's trial in Shakespeare, *Winter's Tale,* ed. Orgel, 29–31.

19. One account of these changes in the material conditions of authorship (including print) with relation to the legitimacy of the theater itself as an institution is Murray, esp. 16, 35–37, 57–63, and 147–53.

20. For a discussion of the gender connotations of the naming of the parts of the press by Moxon, see de Grazia 82–86. An example of representing printed texts as abandoned children is given by the printer Walter Burre, who describes the text of Beaumont and Fletcher's *The Knight of the Burning Pestle* as an "unfortunate child . . . begot and born, soon after was by his parents . . . exposed to the wide world, who . . . utterly rejected it" (Beaumont and Fletcher 3). For a discussion of this passage in the context of collaborative authorship, see Masten 21–26.

21. The evolution of authority as a function of representation itself, rather than of classical tradition, is traced in Weimann; Müller argues that numerous institutions were required with

the advent of print for the selection and maintenance of texts to ensure their endurance and cultural effectiveness (32-44).

22. Subsequent collections of ballads, such as Rollins, associate the name Autolycus with the printed ballad and with the specific kind of topic with which he is associated.

23. See Agnew 21.

24. See Livingston for a catalog of extant sixteenth-century printed ballads.

25. Reprints of the 1557, 1559, and 1566 documents can be found in Arber 1:xxvii-xxxii, 1:xxxviii-xxxix, and 1:322, respectively. For the 1551 document and an account of the development of the Stationers' Company in the sixteenth century, see Clegg 14-65. See also Blagden 38-46.

26. For a discussion of the ballad partners and the failure of the regulation of trade in ballads, see Jackson xii-xiv.

27. Popular examples of these providence tales include Anthony Munday's *A View of Sundry Examples* (1580) and Phillip Stubbes's *Anatomie of Abuses* (1583), as well as parts of John Foxe's *Acts and Monuments* (1563). For a historical account of the providence tale genre, see Hartman 1-3, 18-25, 39-63.

28. Céard; Daston and Park; and Daston. See also D. Wilson. For a discussion of the monstrous-birth genre as a problem of truth, see Cressy.

29. Mellys. The same sentiment can be found in other examples, including Fulwood; Elderton; and three anonymous accounts: "True Description," "True Discription," and "Forme and Shape."

30. Achinstein discusses the exclusion of the ballads in the Elizabethan and Jacobean process of defining literature and discusses the scene of Autolycus and the peasants as a "dramatization of fears about authors of unacceptable literature" (314).

31. For more on the association between breeding and usury, see Fisher.

32. H. Wilson. Frank Kermode discusses the horticultural analogy of gardens and nature, with reference to *The Winter's Tale*, in his introduction to the Arden *Tempest* (xxxv-xxxvi).

33. Sidney 174-75. For an analysis of the play as a response to Sidney, see Frye 56-57.

34. J. C. Scaliger in his *Poetices libri septem* (1581) describes pastoral as the "most ancient" form of dramatic art, compared with the most recent forms "comedy and its *offspring,* tragedy" (emphasis added). Quoted in Herrick 125.

35. For consideration of *The Winter's Tale* as the only authentic tragicomedy of Shakespeare, see Herrick 258-60.

36. Fletcher, preface. On Plautus's influence, see Herrick 1-15.

37. For accounts of the association of the bear with generic classification, see Clubb; Bristol.

38. For examinations of Robert Greene's *Pandosto* as a popular printed wonder book of the day, of mass production of print as a form of abstraction of human labor to make the printed commodity a "social thing," and of *The Winter's Tale* as a rejection of its own origins in popular fiction "but with an insistence that tends to emphasize its own fictiveness," see Newcomb 753-81, quotation at 772.

39. Ovid 256 [10.278-79]. Leonard Barkan reads the statue scene as a triumph of Renaissance artistry and the fulfillment of Pygmalion's art of releasing the potential life from stone, though he acknowledges in the final paragraph of his essay that the wrinkled statue suggests

AARON KITCH

the victory of Nature over Art in its power of verisimilitude. Nevertheless, he concludes by observing how the scene represents the "ability to crystallize a true essence." See Barkan 664.

40. The feminine source of positive transformation and recuperation in the play is noted in Barber and Erickson. Carol Thomas Neely argues that the play concludes with "an extended acknowledgement of [women's] power and centrality" (182). Janet Adelman suggests that the play dramatizes the "return of a masculine authority grounded in a benignly generative maternal presence" (194).

Works Cited

Achinstein, Sharon. "Audiences and Authors: Ballads and the Making of English Renaissance Literary Culture." *Journal of Medieval and Renaissance Studies* 22 (1992): 311-26.
Adelman, Janet. *Suffocating Mothers: Fantasies of Maternal Origin in Shakespeare's Plays, "Hamlet" to "The Tempest."* New York: Routledge, 1992.
Agnew, Jean-Christophe. *Worlds Apart: The Market and the Theater in Anglo-American Thought, 1550-1750.* Cambridge: Cambridge University Press, 1986.
Andréoli, Max. "Heredity and Paternity." *Paternity and Fatherhood: Myths and Realities.* Ed. Lieve Spaas. New York: St. Martin's, 1998. 15-26.
Arber, Edward, ed. *A Transcript of the Registers of the Company of Stationers of London; 1554-1640* A.D.. 5 vols. London: privately printed, 1875.
Barber, C.L. " 'Thou that beget'st him that did thee beget': Transformation in *Pericles* and *The Winter's Tale.*" *Shakespeare Survey* 22 (1969): 59-67.
Barkan, Leonard. " 'Living Sculptures': Ovid, Michelangelo, and *The Winter's Tale.*" *ELH* 48.4 (Winter 1981): 639-67.
Beaumont, Francis, and John Fletcher. *The Knight of the Burning Pestle. Beaumont and Fletcher Select Plays.* Ed. M. C. Bradbrook. London: Dent, 1962.
Bell, Maureen. "Women in the Book Trade." Topic Essays. Renaissance Women Online. *Women Writers Project, Brown University.* 29 Feb. 2000 (*http://www.wwp.brown.edu*).
Blagden, Cyprian. *The Stationers' Company: A History, 1403-1959.* London: Allen, 1960.
Bristol, Michael D. "In Search of the Bear: Spatiotemporal Form and the Heterogeneity of Economies in *The Winter's Tale.*" *Shakespeare Quarterly* 42.2 (1991): 145-67.
Céard, Jean. *La nature et les prodiges: L'insolite au XVIe siècle, en France.* Geneva: Droz, 1977.
Chettle, Henry. *Kind-Hartes Dreame. "Kind-Hartes Dreame": 1592. William Kemp, "Nine Daies Wonder": 1600.* Ed. G. B. Harrison. London: Bodley Head, 1923. 5-65.
Clegg, Cyndia Susan. *Press Censorship in Elizabethan England.* Cambridge: Cambridge University Press, 1997.
Clubb, Louise George. "The Tragicomic Bear." *Comparative Literature Studies* 9 (1972): 17-30.
Cressy, David. "Monstrous Births and Credible Reports: Portents, Texts, and Testimonies." *Travesties and Transgressions in Tudor and Stuart England: Tales of Discord and Dissension.* Oxford: Oxford University Press, 2000. 29-50.
Daston, Lorraine. "Marvelous Facts and Miraculous Evidence in Early Modern Europe." *Critical Inquiry* 18 (1991): 93-124.

Daston, Lorraine, and Katharine Park. "Unnatural Conceptions: The Study of Monsters in Sixteenth- and Seventeenth-Century France and England." *Past and Present* 92 (1981): 20–54.

de Grazia, Margreta. "Imprints: Shakespeare, Gutenberg, and Descartes." In *Alternative Shakespeare*. Vol. 2. Ed. Terrence Hawkes. London: Routledge, 1996. 63–94.

D., John. "A Discription of a Monstrous Chylde, Borne at Chychester in Sussex." London, 1562. STC 6177.

Elderton, William. "The True Fourme and Shape of a Monsterous Chyld." London, 1565. STC 7565.

Erickson, Peter B. "Patriarchal Structures in *The Winter's Tale*." *PMLA* 97 (1982): 819–29.

Findlay, Alison. *Illegitimate Power: Bastards in Renaissance Drama*. Manchester: Manchester University Press, 1994.

Fisher, Will. "Queer Money." *ELH* 66.1 (1999): 1–23.

Fitzgeffrey, Henry. *Satyres and Satyricall Epigrams*. London, 1617.

Fletcher, John. *The Faithful Shepherdess. Beaumont and Fletcher Select Plays*. Ed. M. C. Bradbrook. London: Dent, 1962.

"The Forme and Shape of a Monstrous Child Born at Maydstone in Kent." London, 1568. STC 17194.

Frye, Northrop. *A Natural Perspective: The Development of Shakespearean Comedy and Romance*. New York: Columbia University Press, 1965.

Fulwood, William. "The Shape of II Monsters." London, 1562. STC 11485.

Goldberg, Jonathan. "Fatherly Authority: The Politics of Stuart Family Images." In *Rewriting the Renaissance: The Discourses of Sexual Difference in Early Modern Europe*. Ed. Margaret Ferguson, Maureen Quilligan, and Nancy Vickers. Chicago: University of Chicago Press, 1986. 3–32.

Hartman, James D. *Providence Tales and the Birth of American Literature*. Baltimore: Johns Hopkins University Press, 1999.

Herrick, Marvin T. *Tragicomedy: Its Origin and Development in Italy, France, and England*. Illinois Studies in Language and Literature 39. Urbana: University of Illinois Press, 1955.

Huloet, Richard. *Abecedarium Anglico-Latinum*. 1552. Facsim. ed. 208. Ed. R. C. Alston. Menston, Eng.: Scolar, 1970.

Hunt, Maurice. "The Labor of *The Winter's Tale*." *"The Winter's Tale": Critical Essays*. Ed. Hunt. New York: Garland, 1995. 335–60.

Isaac, Frank. *English Printers' Types of the Sixteenth Century*. Oxford: Oxford University Press, 1936.

Jackson, William A., ed. *Records of the Court of the Stationers' Company, 1602 to 1640*. London: Bibliographical Soc., 1957.

Jaffe, Michele. *The Story of O: Prostitutes and Other Good-for-Nothings in the Renaissance*. Cambridge: Harvard University Press, 1999.

James I. *The Trew Law of Free Monarchies*. 1598. *King James VI and I: Political Writings*. Ed. Johann P. Sommerville. Cambridge: Cambridge University Press, 1994.

Jameson, Fredric. *The Political Unconscious: Narrative as a Socially Symbolic Act*. Ithaca: Cornell University Press, 1981.

Kahn, Coppélia. *Man's Estate: Masculine Identity in Shakespeare*. Berkeley: University of California Press, 1981.

Kermode, Frank, ed. *The Tempest.* By William Shakespeare. London: Arden-Routledge, 1987.

Livingston, Carole Rose. *British Broadside Ballads of the Sixteenth Century: A Catalogue of the Extant Sheets and an Essay.* New York: Garland, 1991.

Marx, Karl. *Capital: A Critique of Political Economy.* Vol. 1. Trans. Ben Fowkes. New York: Penguin, 1976.

Masten, Jeffrey. *Textual Intercourse: Collaboration, Authorship, and Sexualities in Renaissance Drama.* Cambridge: Cambridge University Press, 1997.

McDowell, Paula. *The Women of Grub Street: Press, Politics, and Gender in the London Literary Marketplace, 1678-1730.* Oxford: Clarendon, 1998.

Mellys, John. "The True Description of Two Monsterous Children." London, 1566. STC 17803.

Montrose, Louis. " 'Shaping Fantasies': Figurations of Gender and Power in Elizabethan Culture." *Representing the English Renaissance.* Ed. Stephen Greenblatt. Berkeley: University of California Press, 1988.

Moxon, Joseph. *Mechanick Exercises on the Whole Art of Printing.* 1683-84. Ed. Herbert Davis and Harry Carter. London: Oxford University Press, 1958.

Müller, Jan-Dirk. "The Body of the Book: The Media Transition from Manuscript to Book." *Materialities of Communications.* Ed. Hans Ulrich Gumbrecht and K. Ludwig Pfeiffer. Trans. William Whobrey. Stanford: Stanford University Press, 1994. 32-44.

Murray, Timothy. *Theatrical Legitimation: Allegories of Genius in Seventeenth-Century England and France.* New York: Oxford University Press, 1987.

Neely, Carol Thomas. "Women and Issue in *The Winter's Tale.*" *Philological Quarterly* 57.2 (1978): 181-94.

Newcomb, Lori Humphrey. " 'Social Things': The Production of Popular Culture in the Reception of Robert Greene's *Pandosto.*" *ELH* 61.4 (1994): 753-81.

Orgel, Stephen. *Impersonations: The Performance of Gender in Shakespeare's England.* Cambridge: Cambridge University Press, 1996.

Ovid. *Metamorphoses.* 1567. Trans. Arthur Golding. Ed. John Frederick Nims. New York: Macmillan, 1965.

Oxford English Dictionary. Ed. J. A. Simpson and E. S. C. Weiner. 2nd ed. Oxford: Clarendon Press, 1989.

Rollins, Hyder Edward, ed. *The Pack of Autolycus; or, Strange and Terrible News of Ghosts, Apparitions, Monstrous Births, Showers of Wheat, Judgments of God, and Other Prodigious and Fearful Happenings as Told in Broadside Ballads of the Years 1624-1693.* Cambridge: Harvard University Press, 1927.

Saunders, J. W. "The Stigma of Print: A Note on the Social Bases of Tudor Poetry." *Essays in Criticism* 1 (1951): 139-64.

Schochet, Gordon J. *Patriarchalism in Political Thought.* Oxford: Basil Blackwell, 1975.

Shakespeare, William. *The Complete Works of Shakespeare.* Ed. David Bevington. 4th ed. New York: Longman, 1997.

————. *The Winter's Tale.* Ed. Stephen Orgel. Oxford: Oxford University Press, 1996.

————. *The Winter's Tale.* Ed. Ernst Schanazer. New York: Penguin, 1969.

————. *The Winter's Tale: The Norton Shakespeare.* Ed. Stephen Greenblatt et al. New York: Norton, 1997. 2883-2953.

Sidney, Philip. *An Apology for Poetry. Critical Theory Since Plato.* Ed. Hazard Adams. New York: Harcourt, 1971.

Sokol, B. J. *Art and Illusion in "The Winter's Tale."* Manchester: Manchester University Press, 1994.

"The True Description of a Monsterous Chylde, borne in the Ile of Wight." London, 1564. STC 1422.

"The True Discription of two Monsterous Chyldren Borne at Herne in Kent." London, 1565. STC 6774.

Wall, Wendy. *The Imprint of Gender: Authorship and Publication in the English Renaissance.* Ithaca: Cornell University Press, 1994.

Weimann, Robert. *Authority and Representation in Early Modern Discourse.* Baltimore: Johns Hopkins University Press, 1996.

Wilson, Dudley. *Signs and Portents: Monstrous Births from the Middle Ages to the Enlightenment.* New York: Routledge, 1993.

Wilson, Harold S. " 'Nature and Art' in *Winter's Tale* IV, iv, 86ff." *Shakespeare Association Bulletin* 18 (1943): 114–20.

Wearing Greene: Autolycus, Robert Greene, and the Structure of Romance in The Winter's Tale

STEVEN R. MENTZ

A MONG SHAKESPEARE'S MANY SOURCES in *The Winter's Tale,* the prose pamphlets of Robert Greene stand out conspicuously.[1] In several overtly incompatible guises, Greene's texts fill every corner of Shakespeare's drama. The main plot adapts Greene's most popular prose romance, *Pandosto* (1588).[2] The Autolycus subplot, often considered Shakespeare's addition to *Pandosto,* draws on Greene's "cony-catching" pamphlets (1591–92).[3] The play's conclusion, the repentance of Leontes and renewal of the kingdoms, recalls still another set of Greene texts, the repentance tracts published just after his death in 1592.[4] Even the doomed son, Mamillius, has a Greene pretext; his name masculinizes the name of Mamillia, the heroine of Greene's first printed romance in 1583.[5] These multiple borrowings from three different sets of Greene texts—romantic fiction, low-life sociology, and religiously inflected autobiography—would seem to divide *The Winter's Tale* into competing subtexts. Close examination of the lesser-known Greene sources—the cony-catching material and the repentance tracts—shows that these unruly subtexts actually contribute to the structure of the romance master plot.[6] The subsources illuminate Shakespeare's relationship with Greene and the dramatist's expansive sense of the genre of romance.[7] Greene's texts are ghosts haunting *The Winter's Tale,* and their shadowy presences reveal the heterodox generic structure of Shakespearean romance.

Shakespeare's echoes of *Pandosto* and the other Greene sources have long been noted by scholars.[8] What remains unconsidered, however, is Shakespeare's systematic combination of three different plots of survival and change. This essay focuses on the subplots of cony-catching and repentance as spaces of privileged difficulty for understanding Shakespeare's romance structure. These sometimes overlooked sources reveal how intricate a generic net Shakespeare casts in this play. At issue is not just the old question of "influence," but also the question of how Shakespearean drama imagines its relation to the public literary culture Greene's prose pamphlets embody. Numerous critics have observed that the play interrogates a variety of cultural practices, from old tales and ballads to court trials, aristocratic drama, and miracle plays.[9] The overabundance of texts by Greene, one of the most popular writers in London when Shakespeare began his career, suggests that the play enacts a nostalgic return to Shakespeare's Elizabethan roots.[10]

There are numerous critical models for explaining the impact of Greene (and other popular Elizabethan writers) on Shakespeare. The once-standard model highlights the triumph of the great artist (Shakespeare) over the lesser (Greene).[11] For Shakespeare and Greene, the infamous "upstart Crow" attack has led to the suggestion that the two were rivals, or that Greene was jealous but Shakespeare ignored him. The "anxiety of influence" has never been a popular method for reading Greene's impact on Shakespeare, since few critics give Greene much credit as a "strong" source.[12] Recent criticism, however, has largely eschewed competitive judgments and argued that middlebrow writers like Greene provide insights into Elizabethan literary culture that the overdetermined Shakespeare cannot.[13] As literary scholars have become increasingly concerned with "authorship," collaboration, and relations between writers in early modern England, the imagined relationship between Shakespeare and Greene in *The Winter's Tale* takes on new importance.[14] Shakespeare's use of Greene's texts provides an example of a writer appropriating a former rival in nonantagonistic fashion.[15] For Shakespeare, all versions of Robert Greene remain true to the master ethos of romance, in which catastrophes are made right by a last-minute reversal. An eleventh-hour repentance can always clear a conscience of sin, and Providence can turn any tragic plot to comic redemption: this homily is the lesson Shakespeare's play derives from Greene's romances, his cony-catching sociology, and his autobiographies.

Robert Greene: Source and Antisource

The Winter's Tale's solution to the crisis of the first three acts involves the prototypical romance plot, the recovery of a lost daughter.[16] For Shakespeare in 1610-11, turning to the ancient genre of romance entailed a recovery of England's recent literary past. Prose fiction based more-or-less explicitly on Greek romance, especially Heliodorus's *Aethiopian History,* had flourished in the print culture of late Elizabethan England.[17] Shakespeare had already drawn on Sidney's *Arcadia* (1590), the greatest and most thoroughly Heliodoran of Elizabethan romances, in *King Lear* (1606) and *Pericles* (1608).[18] *The Winter's Tale*'s backward "slide[ing] / O'er sixteen years" (4.1.5-6) between acts 3 and 4 parallels Shakespeare's own sliding back approximately sixteen years for the play's source, to the early 1590s when Greene's influence was at its peak.[19] (Assuming an approximate date of 1610-11, sixteen years before *The Winter's Tale*'s debut would be 1594-95, either two or three years after Greene's death in 1592. Greene's texts were widely republished in the years following his scandalous death.)[20] By appropriating Greene, Shakespeare reveals his nostalgia for an earlier cultural moment, when "Robin Greene" dominated London's literary world on both page and stage.

Greene, acknowledged in his own day as the king of the pamphleteers, whose "extemporal vein in any humor, will excel our greatest art-master's deliberate thoughts" (Nashe, "Preface to *Menaphon*" 82), has been recognized by twentieth-century criticism as the star figure of Elizabethan prose fiction and the book market. David Margolies celebrates him as "the first professional writer in England" (105), and Lori Newcomb, Lawrence Manley, Richard Helgerson, and E. H. Miller, from different perspectives, all agree on his dominance over prose fiction for a decade.[21] Greene captivated the literary scene so much that after his death in 1592, authors from Barnabe Rich to Henry Chettle appropriated his name for its market value.[22] Even Greene's death, brought on by a "surfett of pickle herringe and rennish wine" (Harvey 13) in a London tavern, was notorious, and arguing about it in print helped initiate the pamphlet war between Greene's onetime protégé Thomas Nashe and Gabriel Harvey.[23]

In making a symbolic rapprochement with Greene, whose main claim to notoriety in modern criticism is the "upstart Crow" attack, Shakespeare enacts on a metaliterary level the dialectic of aggression and forgiveness he presents on stage. Greene's posthumously published letter "To those

Gentlemen his Quondam acquaintance, that spend their wits in making plaies," in *Greenes Groatsworth of Wit* (1592), savages the young Shakespeare: "there is an upstart Crow, beautified with our feathers, that with his *Tygers hart wrapt in a Players hyde,* supposes he is as well able to bombast out a blanke verse as the best of you: and beeing an absolute *Johannes fac totum,* is in his owne conceit the onely Shake-scene in a countrey" (84–85).[24] Following this attack, which became notorious as soon as it was published, Shakespeare's return to Greene around 1610–11 is a self-conscious act of reconciliation.[25] *The Winter's Tale*'s riposte to the "upstart Crow" follows the naive plot structure of romance: a happy conclusion overcomes an early attack by containing it within a more spacious world.

Shakespeare does reply in kind, however, to Greene's "Shake-scene" play on his name. The four appearances of the word "green" in *The Winter's Tale* enact a running commentary on Greene and his literary career. They form a microcosm of the attack-forgiveness relationship the play stages between the two authors. Two early uses of the word, in the Sicilian half of the play, link greenness to youth. Leontes first imagines his son Mamillius as if he "saw myself unbreech'd, / In my green velvet coats" (1.2.155–56). At this point, "green" is the color of childhood. After the false accusation of Hermione, Paulina turns this sense of "green" against Leontes when she calls his jealousy "Fancies too weak for boys, too green and idle / For girls of nine" (3.2.181–82). In Sicilia, "green" symbolizes a literary method too young and "idle" to comprehend adult reality. This "green" envy might well succumb to the temptations of literary rivalry or professional jealousy.

As the play shifts to its Bohemian half, the two remaining uses of the word connect "green"/Greene to the pastoral mode and its ability to transform. After attacking Greene, Shakespeare uncovers his value as a generic model. Prince Florizel cites "green Neptune" as one of several gods who, "humbling their deities to love," take on human form to pursue erotic desires (4.4.28, 26). This fairly conventional passage, citing Jupiter, Neptune, and Apollo disguising themselves in humble forms for love, draws on passages from Greene's two most popular romances, *Pandosto* and *Menaphon.*[26] Shakespeare's transformation of Greene's humble source texts seems apposite as well. This version of "green" is something one can wear and be changed by; it is the color of literary metamorphosis.

The final use of "green" comes from Polixenes, who calls Perdita "the prettiest low-born lass that ever / Ran on the green-sward" (4.4.156–57). The "green-sward" of Bohemia is pastoral romance-land itself, the site of the play's redemptive movement. In this place, the transformative power of "green" becomes dominant. The phrase even suggests an imperfect pun in which the "green-sward" forms itself out of Greene's words.[27] The "green-sward" provides the broad ground of the second half of the play, embracing everything from the conventional pastoral of Perdita's sheepshearing to the threatening presence of Autolycus the thief.

In Shakespeare's most overt addition to Greene's main plot, Autolycus is a cony-catching rogue and cultural merchant who mirrors the dashing and disreputable figure Greene cut in Elizabethan London.[28] Autolycus's thievery recalls the bookselling culture in which Greene thrived, which marketed unreliable texts to a gullible public. The rogue is Shakespeare's portrait of Greene, part criminal and part artist.[29] Greene's source texts had already emphasized that the cony-catching pamphlets were, at least in part, self-portraits of the artist. Most explicitly, in *The Defense of Cony-Catching* (1592), a pseudonymous text, Greene's narrator describes writing itself as a form of cony-catching.[30] Cuthburt Cony-catcher, who defends his thieving brethren by implicating Greene in greater crimes, calls Greene "a Conny-catcher in his kinde, though not at cards" (*Life and Works* 10:47). Shakespeare's cony-catcher Autolycus, too, is an ambivalent figure. Shakespeare's play treats the rogue with suspicion, but it also uses his wiles for the recovery phase of the dramatic romance. The seacoast of Bohemia and its "green-sward" cast a providential net over Autolycus, and make his mischief guide the wanderings of the main plot.

Autolycus's three appearances outline Shakespeare's meditation on his former rival. Each of Autolycus's three scenes (4.3, 4.4, 5.2) matches a phase in Greene's career. Autolycus's first scene, in which he steals the Clown's purse, is drawn from *The Second Part of Cony-Catching*.[31] It also contains a song that summarizes the romance model Shakespeare takes from *Pandosto*. Autolycus's next scene, 4.4, moves from singing to pure thievery, taken from *The Third Part of Cony-Catching*.[32] Shakespeare's rogue, however, departs from Greene in his last scene (5.2), which parallels Greene's repentance tracts. Autolycus recants his errors to the newly gentle Clown and Shepherd, but his repentance seems paper-thin, reminding the audience that the cultural disorder he represents has not been firmly banished. The pro forma conversion Shakespeare gives Autolycus suggests that Greene's analogous conversions in the repentance tracts are unnecessary and possibly insincere. Autolycus does not repent because he need not: his thievery and deceit have proven essential to the main plot. Autolycus

lies at the heart of what Shakespeare takes from Greene: he embodies a
disruptive energy that enables the romance plot to correct itself.

Autolycus the Foist: 4.3

When Autolycus first comes on stage, he is a self-described thief, "a snapper-
up of unconsidered trifles" (4.3.26). While Shakespeare does not share
Greene's fascination with cataloging variations of thieves' cant, Autolycus in 4.3 might fairly be called a "foist." A "foist" is a pickpocket who
works without a knife and looks down on clumsy "nips" who use blades.
Autolycus, like Greene's "foist," is proud of his skill: "the Foist holdeth
himselfe of the highest degree, and therefore, they tearme themselves
Gentlemen foists, and so much disdaine to be called cut-purses . . . that
the Foist refuseth euen to weare a knife about him to cut his meat withal"
(*Life and Works* 10: 103).

Shakespeare's gentleman foist enters singing. His song bridges the gap
between his criminal behavior and the romance plot he will advance. Several critics have commented that moving Greene's thief to the countryside
pulls the con man's fangs by transferring him from a city where real harm
is possible to an idealized pastoral realm.[33] While the cony-catchers of
Greene's London threaten newly arrived farmers and merchants, Autolycus
and his gulls coexist in the country. Bohemia becomes safe for naive
country folk not by converting rogues like Autolycus to virtue, but by
reconceiving the impact of their crimes on the social order. Autolycus's
thievery has no bite in *The Winter's Tale*; even though the Clown loses his
purse, the supplies he was sent to buy for the feast are not missed.

Autolycus's song begins by describing the pastoral ideal of romance:

> When daffodils begin to peer,
>   With heigh! the doxy over the dale,
> Why then comes in the sweet o' the year,
>   For the red blood reigns in the winter's pale.
>   (4.3.1–4)

This pastoral, however, echoes the play's disastrous first three acts. The
arrival of a desirable "doxy" impinges on the blooming daffodils just as
Hermione has impinged on the friendship between Leontes and Polixenes
(1.2.76–80). Autolycus's first verse metaphorically retraces the Sicilian
plot, in which "red blood" splits the friendship between the kingdoms.

As he continues, Autolycus transforms erotic desire into his immediate and practical intention to steal sheets:

> The white sheet bleaching on the hedge,
> > With hey! the sweet birds, O how they sing!
> Doth set my pugging tooth an edge;
> > For a quart of ale is a dish for a king.
>
> (4.3.4–8)

This verse reflects the play's radical shift of scene, from urban Sicilia, where "red blood" reigns, to pastoral Bohemia, where Autolycus's desire for sheets and ale assumes top billing. The lyric's easy switch from one world to the other places Autolycus at the moment of transition between the two halves of the play. He is the bivalent figure at the drama's heart: thief and ex-courtier, singer and merchant, untrustworthy yet helpful, a product of both Shakespeare and Greene.

After a brief prose interlude, Autolycus's song defines the heart of the romance ethic:

> But shall I go and mourn for that, my dear?
> > The pale moon shines by night:
> And when I wander here and there:
> > I then do go most right.
>
> (4.3.15–18)

"Wandering" is the key to success for Autolycus, as he aligns himself with the traditions of romance, in which those who cast themselves on Fortune's mercy will triumph. The second half of the play reaps the rewards of Autolycus's connection between "wandering" and going "most right," despite—or perhaps because of—its overt naïveté. Autolycus's belief in wandering carries such weight that even the "faith" of which Paulina speaks in the play's final scene finally seems just another version of it.[34] As the play shifts to its redemptive movement, Autolycus recognizes that he flourishes under the wandering sign of Fortune.

Despite the song's allegiance to romance, Autolycus's trick on the Clown is pure cony-catching. This scene acts out Shakespeare's rapprochement between two versions of Greene, pastoral romance and cony-catching trickery. The "springe" (4.3.35) Autolycus sets for the Clown comes from *The Second Part of Cony-Catching,* where it is set by a master thief who "for his skil might haue bin Doctorat in his mistery" (*Life and Works* 10: 114).

Following Greene's model, Autolycus falls down and pretends to be sick, and he picks the Clown's pocket when he helps him.[35] Autolycus spices up the game by claiming to have been robbed and beaten by a notorious "rogue" named "Autolycus" (4.3.96–97), but the staging of the trick remains faithful to Greene. For a tense moment, pastoral Bohemia—the romance world in which the play recovers—looks uncomfortably like Elizabethan London. The countryside teems with ballad-singing con men preying on simple farmers. If the audience admires the elegance of Autolycus's theft, as readers despite themselves admire Greene's con men, then it celebrates criminal dexterity.[36]

Autolycus's Fetch: 4.4

From a singing "foist," Autolycus becomes, in the sheepshearing scene, a singing bookseller and cultural merchant like Greene himself. He continues to steal, but his gambit becomes what Greene calls a "fetch," a tactic for luring conies. His songs no longer describe the redemptive plot of romance, but rather the market imperative of print: "Come buy of me, come! come buy! come buy! / Buy, lads, or else your lasses cry. / Come buy!" (4.4.230–32).[37] Shakespeare's source for this trick is Greene's *Third Part of Cony-Catching,* where Greene exposes "[t]his trade, or rather unsufferable loytring qualitie, in singing of Ballets and songs . . . which is nothing els but a sly fetch to draw many togeather, who listening to an harmlesse dittie, afterward walke home to their houses with heauie hearts" (*Life and Works* 10: 161). Autolycus outperforms Greene's rogues; he sings, sells, and picks pockets at the same time, and, unlike Greene's thieves, he does not get caught.[38]

Autolycus connects his mercantile activity to his criminal actions. In this overlap between robbery and literary circulation, he becomes a dangerous image of cultural fecundity, a source of artistic power that Shakespeare wants to use, but also to control.[39] He combines his two careers as bookseller and thief, each of which depends on securing his audience's trust. What Autolycus wants, as his ballad about the hard-hearted maid suggests, is for everyone to "exchange flesh" (4.4.281) with his or her neighbor, although in this case, the economic subtext of "exchange" sounds more threatening than the erotic subtext of "flesh." He thrives in a world of circulation, where texts and trinkets, bodies and ballads are all for sale. His "wanderings" appear to threaten the social unity of the play, but his ballads actually promote unity by encouraging the faith that his previous song introduced (4.3).

Mopsa signals her susceptibility to Autolycus's wares by saying, "I love a ballad in print, a life, for then we are sure they are true"(4.4.261–62). Here she creates, in her simplistic submission to Greene's literary medium, precisely what the fragmented kingdoms of *The Winter's Tale* need: a source of faith. Mopsa may be naive, and probably barely literate, but her faith in the link between "print" and "truth" makes wholehearted belief possible. The ballads' truth comes neither from Delphic oracle nor king's word, but simply from their printed nature, their existence as physical things that circulate from hand to hand.[40] While the particular ballads in Autolycus's "pack" have sent numerous scholars, most recently Sharon Achinstein, searching for the ballads that Shakespeare might have known, I propose that the reference be broadened to "print" as an emerging industry in London, and specifically to the printed books Shakespeare had at hand when writing this play: Greene's books. Mopsa's belief in print parallels Autolycus's commitment to "wandering." Each character hews to the naive, quixotic promise of romance: the belief that their lives will duplicate what they find in books and songs. Mopsa finds this "truth" the same place Shakespeare does, in the printed matter before her.

The swindle of Autolycus's ballads becomes a debased reflection of Shakespeare's dramatic art, which sells its audience an idealized "truth" they pay to see. The ballad seller also starts to affect the play's main plot after this point. Autolycus, whose songs have been the play's clearest expression thus far of faith that wanderings will go right, proves essential to return the play to Sicilia.[41] His clothes provide a rustic disguise for Florizel (4.4.647), and his subsequent betrayal of the Clown and Shepherd brings them, and Perdita's treasure box, aboard Florizel's ship (4.4.797–801). Autolycus's interventions make possible the prototypical romance moment of the play, the first reunion of act 5, which reveals Perdita to her father's court.[42]

The main plot, strikingly, takes no revenge for Autolycus's misdeeds. We would expect the aristocrats to expose his thefts, as the London crowd exposes Greene's ballad-singing thieves.[43] The desire to find in Autolycus's subplot the moral correction that Greene advertises in his cony-catching pamphlets monopolized the attention of Simon Forman, who recorded his reactions to seeing the play in May 1611. Forman draws from the Autolycus subplot a practical moral: "beware of trustinge feined beggars or fawninge fellouss" (Shakespeare, *Winter's Tale,* ed. Pafford, xxii). Forman's moral, however, fails to account for Autolycus's positive role in returning the play to Sicilia. If Mopsa, the Clown, Camillo, and Florizel had taken Forman's advice and shunned Autolycus, the grand reunions of act 5 might never have taken place. Despite Forman, it appears essential in this play to rely on "feined beggars and fawninge fellouss," because even if they steal your purse, they will eventually regenerate your kingdom.

Camillo and Florizel appropriate Autolycus's clothes as a disguise, but the more important of Autolycus's two interventions in the plot comes on his own initiative. In one of his numerous asides,[44] Autolycus explains why he will bring the Clown and Shepherd to Florizel and Perdita: "Though I am not naturally honest, I am so sometimes by chance" (4.4.712-13). Under the rubric of "chance," Autolycus's nose for booty and his lingering goodwill toward Florizel conspire with Camillo to get everything needed on the boat to Sicilia. By "chance," his greed and ruthlessness help the hapless aristocrats.[45] Autolycus is no more "naturally honest" than his printed ballads are "true," but the play needs, and uses, his "unnatural" honesty.[46] Shakespeare here plays a final trick on Greene: try as he may to be roguish, Greene's surrogate Autolycus cannot but advance Shakespeare's plot. The trick turns, however, since the romance master plot is Greene's also, from *Pandosto.* Shakespeare both corrects Greene and allies himself with him.

Over the course of 4.4, Autolycus's allegiance to "chance" comes to mirror his faith in "wandering." He begins the scene looking for more chances to fleece conies. Switching his peddler's garb for Florizel's robes, he celebrates his increase in wealth: "I see this is the time that the unjust man doth thrive. . . . Sure the gods do this year connive at us, and we may do any thing extempore" (4.4.673-77). The word Autolycus uses to describe his success, "extempore," repeats the key term Nashe used in celebrating Greene's "extemporal vein."[47] For Autolycus the thief, as in Nashe's image of Greene the author, extemporaneous play provides opportunities to gain personal advantage. Autolycus will not expose the elopement to Polixenes because, he says, "I hold it the more knavery to conceal it; and therein I am constant to my profession" (4.4.681-83). His "knavery" can be read as economic self-interest: he expects more rewards from Florizel. At this point he still professes to be a cony-catcher out of Greene's London, alert for profit and the main chance.

As Autolycus guides the Clown and Shepherd onto Florizel's ship, how-ever, his "chance" becomes "Fortune," the guiding force in providential romance. His reference to "the gods [who] connive at us" implies that he recognizes divine favor in his newfound success. In romance, the gods' plan, no matter how wayward or seemingly "extempore," always transforms itself into a fortunate conclusion. Autolycus still craves profit, but his profit and the play's regeneration have become intertwined, as he himself observes: "If I had a mind to be honest, I see Fortune would not suffer me: she drops booties in my mouth. I am courted now with a double occasion—gold, and a means to do the prince my master good" (4.4.832-35). Autolycus, importantly, is the only character in the play to use the word "Fortune" in a celebratory way. (Florizel, by contrast, calls Fortune "visible an enemy" [5.1.215].) The play has converted Autolycus's "unnatural" honesty, and Fortune now bribes him with the Clown and Shepherd's gold to guide the play toward the marriage of Perdita and Florizel and the redemption of the kingdoms. As usual in romance, "Fortune" rules the final movement, but in act 4 she conspires with Autolycus.

The Repentance of a Cony-Catcher: 5.2

Autolycus's last appearance in the play comes after the offstage revelation of Perdita's parentage. Standing in the position of the audience, Autolycus listens to three Gentlemen describe the grand reunion. The play may have outgrown Autolycus's tricks by this point, as the Second Gentleman implies: "such a deal of wonder is broken out within this hour, that ballad-makers cannot be able to express it" (5.2.23-25). Autolycus sings no songs in this scene, sells no ballads, picks no pockets. The main plot contains his misrule and even makes a pro forma attempt to convert him. He has already called himself as a "Prodigal Son" (4.3.93-94), and, like Greene in his repentance tracts, he flirts with becoming a penitent prodigal in his last scene.[48]

Autolycus's penitence, however, is slight at best, and he remains excluded from the triumphs of act 5. He notes in his final soliloquy that he just missed advancement for his role in bringing Perdita's past to light: "Now, had I not the dash of my former life in me, would preferment drop on my head. I brought the old man and his son aboard the prince" (5.2.113-15).[49] His reference to his "former life" suggests that he considers leaving petty roguery behind, but his disreputable past clings to him. He avoids "preferment" in a way that suggests he will return to his "former" life once given the chance.[50] He prefers keeping his good deeds quiet, as he says, "had I been the finder out of this secret, it would not have relished among my other discredits" (5.2.122–23). He remains at heart a wandering rogue. While the master plot of romance usually returns courtly exiles to their rightful places, Autolycus never reconciles with his former master Florizel.

In his final exchange with the Clown and Shepherd, Autolycus's intimacy with the audience vanishes. He speaks no asides, and this scene is the only one of his three that does not end with a soliloquy. His submission to his new "good masters" (5.2.174–75) recalls his self-description as a "poor fellow" to Camillo (4.4.631), but this time he never sheds the servile mask to reveal the trickster beneath. The Clown's parting injunction, "be a tall fellow of thy hands" (5.2.167–68), resonates with Autolycus's career as a foist, but most editors gloss the phrase with its primary meaning, "be a valiant fellow."[51] Autolycus's reply, his last words in the play, is wholly opaque: "I will prove so, sir, to my power" (5.2.169). This statement may be another ruse, a prelude to picking the Clown's pocket for a third time, but a veneer of conversion prevents the audience from knowing the truth.

Robert Greene, too, converted in his final days, and like Autolycus's, his reform seems suspiciously like a prelude to another trick. At least two of Greene's literary conversions shadow Autolycus's final scene. The first is "The Conversion of an English Courtesan," published as the second half of the *Disputation between a Hee Cony-catcher and a Shee Cony-catcher* (1592). This tale tells a streamlined version of the medieval parable of the penitent prostitute.[52] The tale's critical moment comes when the soon-to-be-reformed courtesan falls in love with the virtuous merchant who will marry her and free her from her past. In Greene's telling, their erotic temptation is mutual: "thus we sat both amorous of the other, I lasciviously and he honestly" (*Life and Works* 10: 271). Greene's ironic point is that "lascivious" love and "honest" love look exactly the same, and the courtesan can convert to "honesty" without changing very much. She, like Autolycus, is "not naturally honest," but she has no problem seeming so for profit. She will accept a handsome and well-to-do husband when he offers himself. She is less constant to her shady profession than Autolycus, as she does not decline "preferment," but reaches out with both hands to settle happily as a middle-class wife.[53] For her, a life of sin does not matter, since her personalized romance leads to happy marriage.[54]

Greene's own life, as fictionalized in his repentance pamphlets, had no such romance exit. He never followed romance's master plot by returning to his abandoned wife and son. Despite apparently giving his son the name "Fortunatus," Greene did not live by the romance values of his fiction.[55] Instead he excoriated his life of sin in his posthumous pamphlets. In *The Repentance of Robert Greene* (1592) he recants his entire literary career.[56] The root of the problem, he claims, was writing for profit: "I became an Author of Playes, and a penner of Love Pamphlets . . . Yong yet in yeares, though olde in wickedness, I began to resolve that there was nothing bad, that was profitable" (*Repentance* 20). Even to himself, Greene symbolized the profit-driven London book market. Like Autolycus, he links his cultural production to the marketplace, but on his deathbed he rejected it all.[57] The irony, as modern critics have observed, is that attacking the market was itself marketable. Greene's assaults on the evils of buying and selling helped sell his books after his death, as he may have intended all along.[58]

Autolycus's faux repentance balances the overblown rhetoric of Greene's multivolume conversion.[59] Shakespeare thereby suggests that Greene's literary repentances are unbelievable and unnecessary. Like Autolycus, Greene's texts place absolute faith in Fortune's capacity to turn evil into good, so that the recovery of lost maidens in pastoral romance, the salvation of a soul by repentance, and the enrichment of a rogue's purse by chance are all part of the same master plot.[60] Shakespeare reworks Greene to unearth his constant trust in a broad romance model. In a reply to Greene's nominal rejection of fiction, *The Winter's Tale* stakes out a position for romance as an all-encompassing genre.

If Greene and Autolycus represent the play's unruly subtexts, then Shakespeare's incorporation of them suggests a complex generic hierarchy. Shakespeare's play does not expel the demons of cony-catching tracts, "Love pamphlets," and two-penny ballads so much as it absorbs them. Dramatic romance becomes the ultimate hybrid genre, uniting disparate forms. The force that brings about the play's final unity Paulina calls "faith," Autolycus calls "wandering," and Mopsa, in her simplicity, calls "print." All three are ways of guaranteeing that things will turn out happily, according to the generic rules of romance. The expanse of *The Winter's Tale*, which overflows in time, in space, in genre, and even in length in its fourth act, defines romance as a meeting place of various cultural markets. By co-opting Autolycus rather than expelling him, and by using his trickery to advance the main plot, Shakespeare signals his desire for an artistic hierarchy that reconciles aristocratic drama with ballads and prose pamphlets.[61] By refusing to make Autolycus repent, Shakespeare avoids the need for

Greene's turn away from literary creation.[62] Reconciliation trumps rivalry in this play: Sicilia and Bohemia reconcile, Shakespeare reconciles himself with Greene's legacy, and the play reconciles three versions of Greene, making the romancer, the cony-catcher, and the penitent compatible.

Notes

I would like to express my thanks to the organizers of the 1997 Ohio Shakespeare Conference in Columbus for providing a forum for an early version of this essay. I would also like to thank Annabel Patterson, Elizabeth Teare, and the anonymous reader for *Renaissance Drama* for their valuable comments.

1. For a list and discussion of the sources of the play, see Muir 240-51. Several of the non-Greene sources editors mention, like Sabie's *The Fisherman's Tale* (1594) and *Flora's Fortunes* (1595) and Forde's *The Famous History of Parismus* (1598) are themselves powerfully indebted to Greene's work. For a survey of Greene's career and relevant bibliography, see Crupi. The most thorough study of Greene is by Pruvost.

2. For a reading of *Pandosto*'s importance and continuing popularity into the eighteenth century, see Newcomb, "Social Things."

3. There were six of these pamphlets, all published in 1591-92. In chronological order, they are *A Notable Discovery of Coosanage* (1591), *The Second Part of Cony-Catching* (1591), *The Thirde (and last) Part of Cony-Catching* (1592), *The Defense of Cony-Catching* (1592), *A Disputation between a Hee Cony-Catcher and a Shee Cony-Catcher* (1592), and *The Black Bookes Messenger* (1592).

4. The theme of repentance appears in the cony-catching pamphlets and as far back as part 2 of *Mamillia* (registered 1583; first surviving edition 1593). The central location of this theme in Greene's work, however, is the three posthumous repentance pamphlets: *Greenes Groatsworth of Wit, Greenes Vision,* and *The Repentance of Robert Greene,* all published in 1592.

5. *Mamillia* may also provide the name of Shakespeare's Florizel, although Greene's character Florion is Mamillia's friend, not her lover. See Greene, *Life and Works,* vol. 2.

6. Mowat has usefully adapted the term "infracontexts" from Claes Schaar to describe source texts that serve "as the base for the surface context" which for this play is pastoral romance. For her reading of the cony-catching pamphlets as an "infracontext" for the second half of *The Winter's Tale,* see Mowat, "Rogues, Shepherds" 59.

7. Romance, as numerous recent critics have noted, is a problematic generic description that often gets used imprecisely. For critiques of the term in relationship to Shakespeare's last plays, see Wells; Palfrey 14; and Felperin.

8. Muir describes these echoes as more frequent and direct than "from any other novel used by Shakespeare as a source" (247). While the influence of Lodge's *Rosalynd* on *As You Like It* or Barnebe Riche's "Apolonius and Silla" on *Twelfth Night* suggests that Muir's claim for uniqueness may be overstated, the number of close verbal parallels in *Pandosto* and *The Winter's Tale* is striking.

9. Enterline cites Morse on the play's interest in " 'myriad forms of human narration'—old tales, reports, ballads, oracles." See Enterline 17; Morse 283-304.

42. If the Clown and Shepherd had taken the fardel to Polixenes, and he had let them open it rather than throwing them directly in prison, the revelation of Perdita's parents might have taken place without Autolycus's intervention. It is characteristic of romance, however, for all unveilings to be put off until the last moment, so Autolycus's maneuver ensures that the recovery of the lost child will take place at the right time (near the end) and in the right place (Sicilia).

43. Autolycus does worry that his crimes will be exposed. His fears vanish when Camillo and the aristocratic plot "make an instrument" (4.4.626) of him by disguising Florizel in his clothes.

44. In the space of three scenes, Autolycus speaks five soliloquies and six asides, according to Pafford's edition. This count omits his confession of his crimes (4.4.596-620), which he thinks is a soliloquy before he sees Camillo and the others on stage. For these scenes, Autolycus is as intimate with the audience, measured in the number of his soliloquies and asides, as Prince Hamlet himself.

45. The more obvious help comes from Camillo, the loyal retainer. Without examining Camillo's honesty, it is worth noting that despite always mirroring the audience's sympathies, he betrays higher-ranking nobles three times in the play. First, he betrays Leontes when he flees Sicilia; second, he betrays Polixenes when he conspires in Florizel's elopement; and third, he betrays Florizel by following him to Sicilia with Polixenes.

46. Winkler provides a compelling reading of the positive moral status of deception in romance.

47. See page 143 for Nashe's description of Greene's style.

48. Helgerson has noted that the Prodigal Son story served as a generational metaphor for Greene and other Elizabethan prose writers (esp. 1-15, 79-104). Barker also notes that Greene's version of the Prodigal Son story differed substantially from Luke's, most obviously in that Greene's prodigals returned home newly married and thereby reformed (95).

49. Perdita's seasickness, which Autolycus mentions (5.2.117-21), also keeps the origin of the fardel quiet and thus keeps Autolycus's "honesty" out of sight.

50. If Autolycus represents Greene, or Greene's generation of writers, they were notoriously bad at getting the preferment they sought.

51. Shakespeare, *Winter's Tale,* ed. Pafford glosses the phrase as a "doughty man," and Shakespeare, *Winter's Tale,* ed. Orgel as a "brave man."

52. For consideration of the tale's medieval sources, see Macdonald, "Robert Greene's Courtesan" 210.

53. See Macdonald, "Robert Greene's Courtesan" for a radically skeptical reading of her conversion.

54. Interestingly, she refuses to act as a thief during her career as a prostitute, unlike the "shee cony-catcher" of Greene's *Disputation,* and unlike Defoe's Moll Flanders as well. See Greene, *Life and Works* 10: 269.

55. See Greene, *Groatsworth* 90-91 for a letter purportedly written by Greene to his wife on his deathbed.

56. See Barker 97 and Miller 67, 215-16.

57. Macdonald notes that he derives much of his material from Philip Stubbes's *The Anatomy of Abuse.* See "Complex Moral View" 123-24.

58. For the "devastating" cynicism of this deathbed ploy, see Barker 97.

59. This dramatization was cut short by his death, as he had promised a tale called "The Conversion of a Cony-Catcher," which was to be published with the long-awaited *Black Booke*.

60. Helgerson notes a basic affinity between "romance" and "repentance" in Greene's work (101).

61. For an alternate account of generic hierarchy that emphasizes drama's connections with elite culture, see Achinstein 326.

62. Autolycus cannot sit in on the miraculous revival of Hermione in 5.3, the triumph of aristocratic drama, but his roguish persona colors it nonetheless. From Autolycus's point of view, the miracle of the statue is a particularly clever fetch, bringing Leontes and the two courts out to Paulina's garden where they can be tricked into reinstating Hermione as queen, not to mention giving Paulina a noble husband in Camillo. It is not hard to imagine that the next ballad he sells might be entitled, "Stone Queen Lives!"

Works Cited

Achinstein, Sharon. "Audiences and Authors: Ballads and the Making of English Renaissance Literary Culture." *Journal of Medieval and Renaissance Studies* 22 (1992): 311-26.

Auberlen, Eckhard. *The Commonwealth of Wit: The Writer's Image and His Strategies of Self-Representation in Elizabethan Literature*. Tubingen: Narr, 1984.

Barker, W. W. "Rhetorical Romance: The 'Frivolous Toyes' of Robert Greene." *Unfolded Tales: Essays on Renaissance Romance*. Ed. George M. Logan and Gordon Teskey. Ithaca: Cornell University Press, 1989.

Cavell, Stanley. *Disowning Knowledge in Six Plays of Shakespeare*. Cambridge: Cambridge University Press, 1987.

Chettle, Henry. *Kind-hearts Dreame. Early English Poetry V.* London: Percy Soc., 1842.

Crupi, Charles W. *Robert Greene*. Boston: Twayne, 1986.

Dionne, Craig. "Playing the 'Cony': Anonymity and Underworld Literature." *Genre* 30 (1997): 29-49.

Enterline, Lynn. " 'You speak a language that I understand not': The Rhetoric of Animation in *The Winter's Tale." Shakespeare Quarterly* 48 (1997): 17-44.

Felperin, Howard. "Romance and Romanticism: Some Reflections on *The Tempest* and *Heart of Darkness,* Or, When is Romance No Longer Romance?" *Shakespeare's Romances Reconsidered*. Ed. Carol McGinnis Kay and Henry E. Jacobs. Lincoln: University of Nebraska Press, 1978. 60-76.

Forcione, Alban K. *Cervantes, Aristotle, and the 'Persiles.'* Princeton: Princeton University Press, 1970.

Greene, Robert. *Greenes Groatsworth of Wit, Bought with a Million of Repentance*. Ed. D. Allen Carroll. Binghamton: Medieval and Renaissance Texts and Studies, 1994.

―――. *The Life and Complete Works in Prose and Verse of Robert Greene,* M.A. Ed. Alexander Grosart. 12 vols. London: Huth Library, 1881-83.

―――. *Pandosto: The Triumph of Time. An Anthology of Elizabethan Prose Fiction*. Ed. Paul Salzman. Oxford: Oxford University Press, 1987.

―――. *The Repentance of Robert Greene*. Ed. G. B. Harrison. London: Bodley Head, 1923.

Halasz, Alexandra. *The Marketplace of Print: Pamphlets and the Public Sphere in Early Modern England.* Cambridge: Cambridge University Press, 1997.

Hamilton, A. C. "Elizabethan Prose Fiction and Some Trends in Recent Criticism." *Renaissance Quarterly* 37 (1984): 21-33.

Harvey, Gabriel. *Foure Letters and Certeine Sonnets, Especially Touching Robert Greene and Other Parties by Him Abused.* Ed. G. B. Harrison. London: Bodley Head, 1922.

Helgerson, Richard. *The Elizabethan Prodigals.* Berkeley: University of California Press, 1976.

Hunt, Maurice. "Elizabethan 'Modernism,' Jacobean 'Postmodernism': Schematizing Stir in the Drama of Shakespeare and His Contemporaries." *Papers on Language and Literature* 31 (1995): 115-44.

Knight, G. Wilson. " 'Great Creating Nature': An Essay on *The Winter's Tale.*" *Shakespeare: Modern Essays in Criticism.* Ed. Leonard F. Dean. Oxford: Oxford University Press, 1967. 423-55.

Kurland, Stuart M. "Political Realism in *The Winter's Tale.*" *Studies in English Literature* 31 (1991): 365-86.

Lawlor, John. "*Pandosto* and the Nature of Dramatic Romance." *Philological Quarterly* 41 (1962): 96-113.

Macdonald, Virginia L. "The Complex Moral View of Robert Greene's *A Disputation.*" *Shakespeare-Jahrbuch* 119 (1983): 122-36.

———. "Robert Greene's Courtesan: A Renaissance Perception of a Medieval Tale." *Zeitschrift für Anglistik und Amerikanistik* 32 (1984): 210-19.

———. "Robert Greene's Innovative Contributions to Prose Fiction in *A Notable Discovery.*" *Shakespeare-Jahrbuch* 117 (1981): 127-37.

Margolies, David. *Novel and Society in Elizabethan England.* London: Croom Helm, 1985.

Manley, Lawrence. *Literature and Culture in Early Modern London.* Cambridge: Cambridge University Press, 1995.

Masten, Jeffrey. *Textual Intercourse: Collaboration, Authorship, and Sexualities in Renaissance Drama.* Cambridge: Cambridge University Press, 1997.

McMillin, Scott. *The Elizabethan Theatre and "The Book of Sir Thomas More."* Ithaca: Cornell University Press, 1987.

McPeek, James A. S. *The Black Book of Knaves and Unthrifts in Shakespeare and Other Renaissance Authors.* Storrs: University of Connecticut Press, 1969.

Miller, Edwin Haviland. *The Professional Writer in Elizabethan England.* Cambridge: Harvard University Press, 1959.

Morse, William R. "Metacriticism and Materiality: The Case of Shakespeare's *The Winter's Tale.*" *English Literary History* 58 (1991): 283-304.

Mowat, Barbara. "Rogues, Shepherds, and the Counterfeit Distressed: Texts and Infracontexts of *The Winter's Tale* 4.3." *Shakespeare Studies* 22 (1994): 58-76.

———. "The Theater and Literary Culture." *A New History of Early English Drama.* Ed. John Cox and David Scott Kastan. New York: Columbia University Press, 1997. 213-30.

Muir, Kenneth. *Shakespeare's Sources I: Comedies and Tragedies.* London: Methuen, 1957.

Nashe, Thomas. "Preface to Greene's *Menaphon.*" *Menaphon.* Ed. Brenda Cantar. Ottawa: Dovehouse, 1996.

————. *Strange Newes. The Complete Works of Thomas Nashe.* 5 vols. Ed. R. B. McKerrow. London: Sidgwick and Jackson, 1911.

Newcomb, Lori Humphrey. "The Romance of Service: The Simple History of *Pandosto*'s Servant Readers." *Framing Elizabethan Fictions: Contemporary Approaches to Early Modern Narrative Prose.* Ed. Constance C. Relihan. Kent: Kent State University Press, 1996. 117–39.

————. "'Social Things': The Production of Popular Culture in the Reception of Robert Greene's *Pandosto.*" *English Literary History* 61 (1994): 753–81.

Palfrey, Simon. *Late Shakespeare: A New World of Words.* Oxford: Clarendon, 1997.

Pruvost, René. *Robert Greene et ses romans (1558-1592): Contributions à l'historie de la Renaissance en Angleterre.* Paris: Sociétié d'Edition "Les Belles Lettres," 1938.

R. B. *Greenes Funerals.* 1594. Ed. R. B. McKerrow. London: Sidgwick and Jackson, 1911.

Shakespeare, William. *The Winter's Tale.* Ed. Stephen Orgel. Oxford: Clarendon Press, 1996.

————. *The Winter's Tale.* Arden Shakespeare. Ed. J. H. P. Pafford. London: Routledge, 1963.

Watt, Tessa. *Cheap Print and Popular Piety, 1550-1640.* Cambridge: Cambridge University Press, 1992.

Wells, Stanley. "Shakespeare and Romance." *Later Shakespeare.* Ed. John Russell Brown and Bernard Harris. London: Edward Arnold, 1966. 49–80.

Winkler, John J. "The Mendacity of Kalasiris and the Narrative Structure of Heliodoros' *Aithiopika.*" *Yale Classical Studies* 27 (1982): 93–158.

Wolff, Samuel. *The Greek Romances in Elizabethan Prose Fiction.* New York: Columbia University Press, 1912.

William Shakespeare's
Sir John Oldcastle

JAMES J. MARINO

I N 1619, WILLIAM JAGGARD reprinted *The First Part of Sir John Oldcastle* with a falsified date, 1600, and added a new byline: William Shakespeare. Had this been intended as fraud, it would have been remarkably unconvincing, since Jaggard also kept the phrase "Acted by the Lord Admiral His Servants" on the title page, which clearly identifies the play as belonging not to Shakespeare and his company but to their chief rivals during the late Elizabethan era. Moreover, Jaggard's reasons for falsifying the date would deter him from adding Shakespeare's name unless he considered the addition valid; his deception was not aimed at the reading public but at Shakespeare's acting partners, whom no false attribution would be likely to fool. But since Jaggard knew his copy text had come from the Admiral's Men, he must have known that the words he printed had not been written by Shakespeare.[1] The authorship Jaggard asserted for Shakespeare was not a claim about the composition of a specific text, but Jaggard's recognition of "Shakespeare's" claims upon a property in which *Oldcastle*'s 1619 publisher also had rights. The imagined property was not confined to a single text, nor were early modern printers bound to later notions about what Margreta de Grazia and Peter Stallybrass have called "the self-identity of the work," the idealized singularity of the verbal artifact (255). Early modern players and stationers had competing, and often incompatible, notions of what constituted an intellectual property and what claims might be made upon it. A property, or a play, might under some circumstances be construed not as one text but a group of texts, or as a distinctive element within a text. Jaggard's *Oldcastle*, and the plays with which it was bound, show the actors' and printers' rival models of property in contest.

The stationers habitually identified multiple plays on the same topic (most notably history plays) as a single play. Congruities of title and plot, or shared characters, sufficed to constitute a unified property as far as print rights were concerned. The actual wording of the texts was largely irrelevant; one play might have two or more texts, sharing little common language, or none. The multiple texts might be attributed to a single writer, even if he had composed only one of them. The writer's authority was not imagined as preceding or originating the work, which is to say that the writer was not imagined as generative "author" at all. Any principle of "authorship" was applied retroactively, as a sign of shared, coherent identity between divergent texts. The writer's name, added to title pages, affirmed the unity of an intellectual property (or, in at least one case, served to split a property in two). Such retroactive ascriptions allowed a writer who had adapted an older play to be identified as the author of the source from which he'd borrowed.

Actors, on the other hand, deployed writers' names to deny, rather than affirm, any identity between similar texts. The playing companies had a vested interest in construing their revisions of older dramas as new plays, radically distinct from any textual predecessor. Strenuous competition and the demands of an insatiable theatrical market required the players to constantly revise older scripts: to keep up their supply of presentable material, to match and overgo the successes of rival companies, and to keep their repertory from growing old-fashioned in an age of rapid theatrical innovation. It was crucial for the actors that their rewritten scripts be acknowledged as new, independent plays, upon which the owners of earlier versions could make no claim. The theater placed a premium on the new, and acting companies often competed to displace other troupes' successful plays with improved versions and occupy the cultural space the competitor's plays had once held. When plays went on the print market, the players would sometimes attach a writer's name to individuate the script they currently owned, forestalling or dissolving any rival claims on their property. This tactic was especially helpful when the name, like William Shakespeare, stood as a trope for the interests of the playing company as a whole. The attribution of *Oldcastle* to Shakespeare rises from stationers' attempts to anticipate, and counter, the players' revision-based claims on dramatic properties.

The 1619 edition of *Oldcastle* is one of the so-called Pavier quartos, ten Shakespeare plays which were printed, as A. W. Pollard first established, to be bound and sold as a single volume (Pollard viii–ix; Greg, *Bibliography* 3: 1107–9). Since the scholars who discovered these editions' bibliographical quirks were committed to a narrative of literary "piracy" (and treated these quartos as an example), they emphasized the involvement of Thomas Pavier, who held six of the relevant copyrights, rather than the embarrassing participation of Jaggard, who printed all ten plays but also helped produce the new bibliography's holy of textual holies, the first folio, in 1623.[2]

Seven of the ten "Pavier" (or Jaggard) quartos bear false dates, to circumvent a May 1619 edict by the Lord Chamberlain which banned any further printings of the King's Men's plays without the company's permission (de Grazia 30; Kastan 84–85; Kirschbaum 198–99, 298–300). The prohibition was not limited to previously unpublished scripts, which would have sufficiently protected the players' acting repertory from any rivals. Republication of the King's Men's plays, some of which had been in print for more than twenty years, was also forbidden, preventing the stationers who held those copyrights from making any further profit without license from the actors. In effect, the players had used their ongoing performance rights to their plays and their favor with the Chamberlain (William Herbert, to whom they would dedicate the first folio) to regain control over print rights they had alienated long before.

The edict forced Jaggard and his colleagues to exercise their rights through deception, disguising most of the 1619 quartos as copies left over from earlier editions.[3] *Pericles, The Yorkshire Tragedy,* and the play we now call *The Merry Wives of Windsor* are dated 1619, indicating that they had been printed before the Lord Chamberlain's ban. *Oldcastle* kept the date from its first quarto in 1600, and its theatrical owners were still called the Admiral's Servants although that company had changed its name several times.[4] But there would be no reason to backdate *Oldcastle* if the printers did not believe the King's Men had some claim on it; there was no edict against publishing another company's plays. Neither did the 1619 printers put Shakespeare's name on any other plays without some reasonable basis for the attribution: all the rest had been ascribed to Shakespeare already or were associated with him strongly enough to be claimed as his in the later folio. And "piracy" of play scripts, in A. W. Pollard's imagination of the term, was hardly the booming criminal enterprise he supposed. (Peter Blayney has dismantled Pollard's narrative most thoroughly and convincingly in his essay on "The Publication of Playbooks" in *A New History of Early English Drama*.) The profits of piracy would have been particularly underwhelming to substantial and respected stationers like Jaggard, or his friend Pavier, who was promoted to high guild office in 1619 and therefore, as Gerald D. Johnson argues, had far more to lose than gain by any fraud (Johnson 21-22, 35, 36). The evidence suggests that Jaggard (and Pavier, to the extent of his involvement) did consider *1 Sir John Oldcastle* Shakespeare's in 1619, even if it had not been in 1600.

What now seem the oddities of Jaggard's collection, its bibliographic deceptions and apparently miscellaneous contents, are traces of the labor that would produce the first folio, a volume which displaces the 1619 quartos and obscures their role in the formation of the Shakespeare canon. The false dates are signs of the King's Men's struggle to control the texts which later became the Shakespeare canon; controlling the rights was a necessary prerequisite to the codification of that canon in 1623. Until that work was done, using Shakespeare's authority as a ruling idea to provide "unification and integration" for a set of "heterogeneous plays," as Margreta de Grazia has written, "the Shakespearean corpus had not yet been defined" (30-31, 44).[5] The collection of 1619 has been acknowledged as one attempt to define that nascent canon, an attempt contingent upon circumstance and the control of rights but not much more contingent on those factors than the production of the folio would be (de Grazia and Stallybrass 261-62).

Typically, the ten plays from 1619 are imagined as seven canonical plays (eight, including *Pericles*), authorized in every sense of that word by their inclusion in the first folio, and three (or two) apocryphal plays, excluded from that work and its textual authority. But only hindsight makes this division visible. It is at least as valid, and a far better representation of the printers' circumstances, to classify the plays as six works previously ascribed to Shakespeare and four newly attributed to him. But the six attributed to Shakespeare before 1619 are not exactly the same as those attributed to him in the folio.

Four Jaggard plays are approved as Shakespeare's by both previous and posterior authority: *A Midsummer Night's Dream, The Merchant of Venice, King Lear,* and the play known since the folio as *The Merry Wives of Windsor* but previously titled (significantly for the case of *Sir John Oldcastle*) *Sir John Falstaff and the Merry Wives of Windsor.* Two plays previously published as Shakespeare's, *Pericles* and *The Yorkshire Tragedy,* were to be excluded from the folio. The four newly attributed plays are *Oldcastle, Henry V,* and the second and third parts of *Henry VI,* the last two combined under the title *The Whole Contention of Lancaster and York. Sir John Oldcastle* is clearly the odd play out here, never cited as Shakespeare's before or again, but its condition is far closer to the histories' than to the apocryphal plays'. By including *Pericles* and *A Yorkshire Tragedy,* Jaggard merely follows the example of others, but printing *Oldcastle* and the other histories requires him to assert Shakespeare's authorship and contribute to the public sense of his emergent canon. But he excludes the previously anonymous *Titus Andronicus,* to which his friend Pavier had at least a partial claim, perhaps because he did not recognize the play as Shakespeare's.[6] The assignment of the three *Henry* plays and of *Oldcastle* to Shakespeare, the "correct" and "incorrect" attribution, must be considered part of one process.

If *Oldcastle* is the singular error in the collection, the one mistake made without precedent, the question must be: What connection to Shakespeare's work did Jaggard and his confederates perceive? The obvious link is with Falstaff, who had once been called "Oldcastle" himself. To understand how the stationers of 1619 thought of that connection, one must consider Oldcastle and Falstaff's relationship on the stage and the importance of disputed titles and blurred identities to the Jaggard collection as a whole.

Considering the play's content, it may be difficult to believe any reader would mistake *Oldcastle* for one of Shakespeare's Falstaff plays. Its Sir John, "the Good Lord Cobham" as proto-Protestant martyr, is a stark contrast to Shakespeare's licentious clown, and the texts insist on the distinction explicitly. (Brooks, *Playhouse* 75) *Oldcastle*'s prologue doesn't want its saint mistaken for the fat rogue at the Globe: "It is no pampered glutton we present, / Nor agèd counsellor to youthful sins" (6–7).[7] Meanwhile, the epilogue of *2 Henry IV* is just as afraid of its fat rogue being taken for the Rose's saint: "Oldcastle died a martyr, and this is not the man" (31–32).[8] Yet conflation of the characters persisted.

Eight performances of a play identified as *Oldcastle* or *Sir John Oldcastle* appear in the records: three by the Admiral's Men, two by Worcester's, and three by the Chamberlain's or King's (Kawachi 111, 113, 122, 207, 232). Unless the Chamberlain's-cum-King's Servants acquired the Admiral's

Men's text or, as Roslyn Knutson believes, commissioned their own Old-castle play (which might amply justify confusion in 1619), at least two witnesses, decades apart, identified a Falstaff play as *Oldcastle* (Knutson, *Shakespeare's Company* 95–96).

The first reference to *Oldcastle* is in October 1599, when Henslowe pays Anthony Munday, Michael Drayton, Robert Wilson, and Richard Hath-way for the script and, unusually, adds a ten-shilling bonus after the first performance (Henslowe 125–26; Gurr 245). The Admiral's Men repeated their successful new history in November 1599 and March 1600, at their soon-to-be-abandoned Rose theater, which had in 1599 acquired a new, uncomfortably close neighbor, the Chamberlain's Men's Globe (Kawachi 111, 113; Gurr 116, 294; Knutson, *Shakespeare's Company* 79).

The prevailing view of *Oldcastle,* persuasively championed by Andrew Gurr, sees it as an attempt to renew the Chamberlain's Servants' embarrass-ment over *1 Henry IV,* whose depiction of Sir John Oldcastle, Lord Cobham, had so offended the incumbent Lord Cobham that the character had to be renamed Falstaff (Gurr 76, 245, 287). The close proximity between the Rose and the Globe serves, in this view, to maximize the Chamberlain's Men's discomfort (Gurr 245, 320). And certainly, *Oldcastle* was in some powerful sense a Rose play, peculiarly connected to its theater. There is no record of the Admiral's Men performing the play elsewhere. If it remained in their repertory after they had built the Fortune in the northern suburbs, which reestablished their original distance from their rivals, all performances went unrecorded; the Admiral's Men may never have acted it again. The play, and the Rose, were eventually given to Worcester's Men, who acted *Oldcastle* twice near the start of their tenancy, in August and September 1602 (Kawachi 122; Gurr 245, 320). Indeed, Henslowe opens his accounts with the new company by listing a payment to Dekker for additions to *Oldcastle;* readying that particular play was apparently the first order of business for occupants of the Rose (Henslowe 213–16). But like the play's previous owners, Worcester's Men seem to have allowed it to lapse from their repertory and cannot be shown to have performed it after abandoning the Rose for other quarters in 1603.

The Chamberlain's Men, however, are described in a letter by Rowland White as playing "Sir John Old Castle"[9] on March 6, 1600, at the Blackfriars address of their patron George Carey, the Lord Chamberlain, just when the new, rival history play is supposed to have been embarrassing them most (Kawachi 113; Knutson, *Company* 95; Brooks, *Playhouse* 76). Of course, an even better time to embarrass the Chamberlain's Men would have been during William Brooke, Lord Cobham's brief tenure as Lord Chamberlain, from 1596 to 1597. But Henslowe did not commission *Oldcastle* until autumn 1599, when Brooke had been dead for more than two years (Kinney 4, 31). *Oldcastle* was written well after the furor over Sir John's name but fairly soon after the Globe was built, and the Chamberlain's Men seem perfectly comfortable with their Blackfriars "Oldcastle" within six months of the Rose play's debut.

If the play performed for Carey had been lifted from their competitors' repertory, and such transgressions were rare, Shakespeare's company could not have picked a better occasion; the Lord Chamberlain's pleasure would outweigh any niggling complaints from rival players, and the Chamberlain's servants would have demonstrated their proper reverence for the Lollard martyr. If, on the other hand, the Chamberlain's Men put on one of their Falstaff plays, which White identified as "Oldcastle," some auditors must have continued to identify Falstaff with his original prototype.[10]

This double identification long outlived the original controversy over *1 Henry IV.* David Scott Kastan cites various writers from the Caroline period and the Commonwealth who, in his phrase, "saw through Shakespeare's fiction" to Falstaff's initial identity as Oldcastle (93–96). Moreover, Sir Henry Herbert, Master of the Revels, who would have been an infant when *1 Henry IV* debuted, records the King's Men's performing "Old Castle" at court twice, in 1631 and 1638 (Kawachi 207, 232; Herbert 76; Bentley, *Jacobean* 1:28). If Herbert saw *The Merry Wives of Windsor* or a *Henry IV* play, Falstaff and Oldcastle were still sharing their identities two decades after the Jaggard *Oldcastle.*

That identification has led to a rich critical debate over the last fifteen years, beginning with Gary Taylor's "Fortunes of Oldcastle" and still far from resolved; the best recent contribution is Kastan's essay in his *Shakespeare after Theory.* The relationship between the characters was more complicated than simple equivalence, where one could be reduced into merely an alias for the other; one might "see through" Falstaff, and remember his original identity, without losing sight of his new. Indeed, as Kastan notes, there are far more references to Falstaff in the early modern period "than to any other Shakespearean character" (105). Clearly, the fat knight had appeals beyond his historical or religious identity, and the widely circulating discourse about him allowed him to be understood, as least sometimes, as distinct from his original. Falstaff never precisely ceased to be Oldcastle, but neither was he strictly confined to that identity.

Nor should his reception be understood in the terms of any single text. Most of the debate Taylor has generated has been grounded in one intertext or another. Taylor, "restoring" the character's name to Oldcastle for the complete *Oxford Shakespeare,* appeals to the uncensored urtext of *1 Henry IV,* before external conditions forced the name change; David Bevington, having retained the Falstaff name in Oxford's stand-alone *1 Henry IV,* writes of the continuity between the fictional creature of *1 Henry IV* and those in *2 Henry IV* and *Merry Wives of Windsor.* Kristen Poole illuminates Oldcastle/Falstaff's place in a tradition of satire upon Puritans, particularly in the Martin Marprelate tracts. Foxe's *Acts and Monuments* and John Bale's *Brief Chronicle* of Oldcastle's examination and execution loom as intertexts, as does *The Famous Victories of Henry V,* which sets the precedent for the later depiction of Oldcastle and (unless it is itself Shakespeare's) complicates any argument about Shakespeare's purposes in using the martyr's name. (I would not argue that Shakespeare retained Oldcastle's name unreflectively, but the difference between endorsing a precedent and setting one should not be ignored.)

Falstaff/Oldcastle is fundamentally intertextual: derived from a character in an earlier play and a still earlier set of stage traditions, engaged in what Bakhtin calls a "hidden polemic" with the literature of Puritan hagiography, carrying his multiple names and multiple histories with him through a series of heterogeneous texts and inconsistent narratives. And the question of "Falstaff's" relationship to "Oldcastle" should not be limited to a single play. Although the character should not be fetishized as a consistent or "real" individual, part of Oldcastle/Falstaff's theatrical power is the persistence of his recognized identity from play to play, an identity which presents itself as extratextual to some degree because it is confined to no single script, nor indeed to any single chronology or genre. The imaginary character and his imaginary personality, like the imagined personality of the writer-as-author, serve as a unifying principle for disparate performances in a miscellany of texts, some written by William Shakespeare and some by others; the continuing associations between those performances enrich the figure on the stage. Oldstaff, or Falsecastle, is a series of allusions to himself. If viewers associated the Falstaff in *1 Henry IV* with Sir John Oldcastle, it would be difficult not to bring that association to *2 Henry IV* or to *Sir John Falstaff and the Merry Wives of Windsor.* Nor would the boundaries between one text and another, so important to literary critics, strike the early modern playgoer as more real or significant than the persistence of their theatrical memory.

The durable entanglement of Oldcastle and Falstaff suggests a reason for Henslowe's commission of *Sir John Oldcastle,* and for the peculiar advantages of playing it at the Rose. If *Oldcastle* was designed only as polemic, or theater criticism, the Admiral's Men might have polemicized freely from either side of the Thames. They chose not to. Instead, they used *Oldcastle* in ways likely to exploit Falstaff's popularity. The closeness of the new Globe and old Rose, nearer together than any permanent London theaters had been before, was apparently an advantage to *Oldcastle*'s owners.[11] Part of the play's value lay in its proximity to the Chamberlain's Men and the Globe, making it more valuable to the Rose's tenants than to anyone else. The Rose *Oldcastle* was intended for Falstaff's audience, the playgoers who were now frequenting Southwark and the neighborhood of the Globe. Oldcastle, returned to his original name, was offered as an alternative Falstaff, or indeed as a new development in the evolution of a character who had been treading the stage, in one form or another, before Shakespeare had gotten hold of him. By reforming Oldcastle, in every sense of that verb, transfiguring him from low comedy to pious historical tragedy, the Admiral's Men simultaneously appealed to the popular taste for Protestant patriotism and assumed the greater cultural weight afforded tragedy. The collaboration of the stage populist Munday and the courtly nationalist Drayton suggests the company's aesthetic goals, and their sense of how the playgoers' tastes would develop. The goal was not simply to critique Falstaff, but to supersede him and create the Falstaff of the future.[12] Success would not have ended conflation between the Sir Johns, of course; revision could not and was not meant to induce cultural amnesia in the audience. But one stage knight, having defeated his rival on the grounds of theatrical sophistication, would occupy the other's theatrical space and be enriched by the audience's memories of his predecessor. The eventual victor was called Falstaff.

It was customary for the Admiral's and Chamberlain's Men to mirror one another's repertory, imitating their competitors' successes (Gurr 76, 287; Knutson, *Shakespeare's Company* 48-50). A popular city comedy or revenge tragedy would spawn more of its genre in other playhouses; a successful history play, whose subject matter was public domain, could acquire a very close double indeed. While the actors would not generally pirate or play another company's actual scripts, they would imitate, and strive to displace, their competitors' successes (Knutson, "Repertory" 469–70). A sophisticated rewriting of a rival's property might render the older play obsolete and draw away its audience to a new, superior version. At the same time, a company's own repertory had to be kept updated so it could not be superannuated by competitors. Henslowe famously hired Jonson to write a "Richard Crookback," obviously meant to match or overmatch Shakespeare's *Richard III*, but he also paid Jonson for additions to *The Spanish Tragedy* so it could hold its ground against newer revenge tragedies (Henslowe 182, 203; Knutson, "Repertory" 470; Riggs 87–91). Other poets were routinely hired to update Admiral's Men's plays, and the varied editions of several Chamberlain's Men's plays testify to the changes they routinely underwent over years of repertory performance (Bentley, *Profession* 237–40, 245–52, 262–63).

In this context, revision becomes a key strategy for controlling theatrical properties. Many of the Chamberlain's Men's plays which changed most drastically had originally been written for another company and were acquired after the original troupe dissolved. *The Famous Victories of Henry V, The Troublesome Reign of King John,* and *The True Tragedy of King Richard III,* plays which have been variously construed as independent "source plays" or as the worst of bad quartos, were originally published as properties of the Queen's Men, while the "bad" quarto of *3 Henry VI* and *A Taming of a Shrew* belonged to Pembroke's Men (Greg, *Bibliography* 1: 178–80, 203–5, 211, 222–25, 243–44). Both companies had collapsed by 1594, when the Lord Chamberlain's Men were formed.[13] Two plays without attribution to any company, *King Leir* and the "bad" *2 Henry VI,* were also printed or registered in 1594, too early to have been written for the new group (Greg, *Bibliography* 1: 222–25, 337–38). Perhaps the Chamberlain's Men thoroughly rewrote scripts which individual members had brought from their former troupes, or perhaps they annexed lapsed properties. In either case, the rewriting solidified the company's claim to the piece. Revision seems to have been the best part of possession, a way of distinguishing the script a group currently possessed from an earlier version whose rightful ownership was open to contest.

The actors' revision-centered notion of literary property was not universally embraced by printers and booksellers, however, as Jaggard's 1619 quarto of *Henry V* demonstrates. Thomas Pavier had acquired the rights to *Henry V* from Thomas Creed, who had come by them on the basis of his rights to *The Famous Victories of Henry V,* a Queen's Men's play whose plot and characters parallel Shakespeare's *Henry IV* and *Henry V* plays but whose text is verbally distinct from Shakespeare's (Greg, *Bibliography* 1: 243–44). *The Famous Victories,* most recently edited by Peter Corbin and Douglas Sedge, features such familiar set pieces as the Dauphin's gift of tennis balls, the French King and Dauphin's disparate evaluations of the English, Henry's byplay with a French herald before Agincourt, and Henry's final courtship of Princess Catherine. Moreover, it features a decidedly Falstaffian Sir John Oldcastle, a jocular "Jocky" who plots highway robberies with Prince Henry, feuds with the Lord Chief Justice, and finds himself exiled by the new king on much the same terms Falstaff will suffer.

The Stationers' Company seems to have considered *The Famous Victories* not merely analogous to *Henry V* but identical (Blayney, "Publication" 399). Creed's 1594 registration of *The Famous Victories* and his 1598 quarto apparently sufficed as copyright for the Chamberlain's Servants' *Henry V* as well, which Creed printed for the first time in 1600, with an attribution to its current theatrical proprietors (Greg, *Bibliography* 1: 243–44, 268–70). On August 14, 1600, "the history of Henry the Vth with the battle of Agincourt," which might legitimately describe either the Queen's Men's or Chamberlain's Men's production, was "set over to the said Thomas Pavier" among several other "things formerly printed" (Greg, *Bibliography* 1: 16). Although the 1600 *Henry V* was printed for Thomas Millington and John Busby, it was Creed's rights which were "set over" to Pavier, and neither Millington nor Busby asserted further rights to the text.[14] It was the Chamberlain's Men's version which Pavier had printed by Creed in 1602 and again by Jaggard in 1619. Pavier never published a copy of *The Famous Victories,* and Creed printed neither play after 1602.

W. W. Greg speculates that the transfer in the Stationer's Register refers to *The Famous Victories,* which Pavier used to gain control of the Shakespeare text instead, an action Greg considered "shady" (Greg, *Bibliography* 1: 16; Greg, *Folio* 64). If so, Pavier must have been a skillful confidence man indeed, since he got Creed, the defrauded owner, to print the text for him. What seems more likely is that Creed and Pavier conceived both texts as a single intellectual property, and that the Stationers' Register does not indicate which play was transferred in 1600 because the Stationers did not distinguish between the Queen's and Chamberlain's versions.

The Famous Victories reappears in 1617, after Creed's death, when Bernard Alsop, the junior partner who inherited his business, printed a quarto of the play, with some copies to be sold by Timothy Barlow (Greg, *Bibliography* 1: 243-44). Alsop's edition might suggest that he considered *Henry V* and *The Famous Victories* as separate properties, one of which had been sold by Creed and the other bequeathed to him, except that he attributes *The Famous Victories* to "The King's Majesty's Servants." Clearly, Alsop identifies his text with the play in the King's Men's repertory. Although *The Famous Victories* had once belonged to another troupe, if the King's Men had the current performance rights to *Henry V,* the earlier versions must belong to them as well.

Alsop was not alone in his reasoning. Several printers would retroactively ascribe Queen's or Pembroke's play to Shakespeare and his company, many years after the first edition. *The Taming of a Shrew* only gained a King's Servants ascription in 1631, after the first folio had established its provenance (Greg, *Bibliography* 1: 203-5). *The Troublesome Reign of King John* (like *The Famous Victories* an analogous play which shares much of its plot, but little of its language, with Shakespeare's text) receives a credit "by W. Sh." in 1611, and "By W. Shakespeare" in 1622, when work on the folio had already begun (Greg, *Bibliography* 1: 178-80).[15]

These late ascriptions were not ineffectual; the publishers of the first folio had to acknowledge their validity. When, on November 8, 1623, Isaac Jaggard and Edward Blount registered "so many of the said Copies" of Shakespeare's plays "as are not formerly entered to other men," their list omitted both *The Taming of the Shrew* and *King John* (Greg, *Bibliography* 1: 33), although nothing resembling the texts Jaggard and Blount used for those plays had previously been published. As Peter Blayney and others have shown, Jaggard and Blount had to accept *A Shrew* and *The Troublesome Reign* as identical with the Shakespeare plays and secure the copy holders' permission to include Shakespeare's texts in the folio (Blayney, *Folio* 2; Kastan 82). They also had to register *1 Henry VI* as the "third part" of *Henry VI,* because the plays which the folio calls *2* and *3 Henry VI* had been published earlier as *1* and *2 Henry VI*; registering their new first part as the "third" kept their title from intruding on existing rights. The Stationers did not necessarily consider a literary property as a "text" in our understanding of the word, as a specific, unique literary artifact. At least one viewpoint saw a "play" as a title, plot, and set of characters, and construed any revised texts as part of the original work. And a character who had achieved extratextual recognition, like Falstaff or Oldcastle, could itself become the principle which bound various properties together, in some sense becoming the "author" of a whole cluster of plays: a fictive personality that organizes texts into a visible bibliographic category.

The Stationers' position on intellectual property is not only logically consistent but also quite reasonable. If a printer or bookseller paid a playwright or some actors for the rights to a play, and some years later another group of players (or perhaps, more provokingly, the same players) began to hawk about a "new" play on the same subject, with substantially the same title, it would be natural for the publisher to suspect chicanery. A claim that the play had been put into new words (in effect, paraphrased, no matter how gloriously superior that paraphrase might be) and had thus become a new property, could not have been overwhelmingly persuasive. The new version's glorious superiority could only make matters worse. In Blayney's words, the Stationer's Company guaranteed a copy registrant "not only the exclusive right to reprint the text, but also the right to a fair chance to recover his costs" and intervened to block publications which would compete too closely for the same readers (Blayney, "Publication" 399). Certainly, a new *Henry V* or *King John* would compete directly with earlier editions and bring direct economic harm to the original publisher (particularly in a business which required long-term investments in inventory, because a single printing might not sell out for years). And a vastly improved *Henry V* or *King John* would provide more powerful competition, making the earlier version worthless. Indeed, the players specifically intended their revised scripts to compete with and displace older texts. Their business methods were, by necessity, antithetical to the Stationers'.

The publishers who ascribed *The Famous Victories* or *The Troublesome Reign* to Shakespeare did not necessarily believe Shakespeare had penned the precise assortment of words that went onto their pages, nor would they need to believe so, as their interest was not in the precisely assorted words. Rather, the phrase "by William Shakespeare" signals a property to which he, and his company, might assert some claim; the words "William Shakespeare" themselves can be taken as a figure for the interest of the King's Men (de Grazia and Stallybrass 275–76). That interest might not have arisen until long after the original text had been written and set in print; the issue was how the claim might affect control of the property. To place Shakespeare's name on a text was to assert identity between the play one owned and the play the King's Servants currently performed. Asserting that identity protected the stationer's interest in the work and forestalled attempts to displace one's text with a newer, more "authentic" version.

Claims of authorship could be deployed for the opposite purpose as well. Before *King John* or *Oldcastle* gained their ascriptions to Shakespeare, Nathaniel Butter registered and published a new version of the old chronicle play *King Leir,* which had been registered in 1594 and printed in 1605 (Greg, *Bibliography* 1: 11, 20, 337–38). Butter's name for his text, both in the Register and on the title page, was *Mr. William Shakespeare His True Chronicle History of the Life and Death of King Lear . . .* (Greg, *Bibliography* 1: 24, 398–401), the one occasion in Shakespeare's life when his name went above the title. In fact, Shakespeare's name is an integral part of this title; Butter and his occasional partner John Busby were specifically registering Shakespeare's version of the play, as distinct from the older text published by Simon Stafford and John Wright three years before Butter and Busby's entry. Stallybrass argues that Shakespeare's name is not placed above *Lear*'s title to herald the "arrival of the 'author' in his most heroic form" but to prevent *Lear* from being "mistaken for . . . *Leir,*" and Kastan considers the authorial name a tool to "individualize and protect Butter's property," a "mark of distinction" to "differentiate" it from the early play (Stallybrass 597; Kastan 37, 81; Brooks, *Playhouse* 70). In fact, Shakespeare's name differentiates *Lear* from *Leir* in the most literal way, not merely avoiding confusion between two existing titles but creating the perception of difference where none had been.

Butter's title page goes on to mention the Gloucester plot and the royal favor the play has received: "*with the unfortunate life of Edgar, son and heir to the Earl of Gloucester, and his sullen and assumed humor of Tom of Bedlam. As it was played before the King's Majesty at Whitehall upon St. Stephen's night in Christmas Holidays. By His Majesty's Servants playing usually at the Globe on the Bankside.*" All of this is to some extent advertising for the book buyer, but it also functions as a property claim, specifically listing the elements which set this text apart from its predecessor. The addition of the Gloucester material, adapted from a story in Book 2 of the *Arcadia,* is the most obvious difference between the two plots, and the royal pleasure is a valuable imprimatur. (What could be dishonest, if the King approves it? And if *Lear* were simply an old play, would the Master of Revels have scheduled it first in the Court's Christmas season?) *Lear* is being identified as the version performed by the King's

Men, the version given at Court, the version with Edgar, and, first of all, the version written by Shakespeare. The claim begins with the author, and a separate copyright was granted, although the economic competition could hardly have been more direct.

Here is the author as creator: Shakespeare's name creates two plays as individual properties where there had been only one. The author's name, his authority, becomes the distinctive element that differentiates the text from its predecessor and provides the new work an independent existence. Just as Heminges and Condell use Shakespeare's name "synecdochally," in de Grazia's formulation, as a "bibliographical rubric" to make the "heterogeneous printed and scripted textual pieces" collected in the folio "coalesce," so Butter uses the author's name as a synecdoche for a whole generation of development in dramatic technique (de Grazia 39). The difference between *Leir* and *Lear* is the 1590s and the artistic growth that English theater saw in those years. The change, however rapid, was collective, and in many ways incremental, the work of dozens of actors and poets in the London playhouses, but Butter reduces that activity to the achievement of an individual personality, the author, whose labor transforms an old play into something new and different. *Lear* will no longer be identified with its previous self, but with its new "author," and so Butter uses the principle of authorship to dissolve previous claims on his property. His stratagem must have taught the other stationers how tenuous their rights to "Shakespeare's" works really were and given a strong incentive for adding Shakespeare's byline to new editions. If the existing print rights to a play could be abrogated by adding an author's name to a new imprint, the current owners had to make that addition themselves, before an interloper did. Attributions were not added to plays like *The Famous Victories* and *The Troublesome Reign* with an intent to defraud buyers; rather, they were meant to block an anticipated fraud against the legitimate owners.

Most of the 1619 quartos had vexed ownerships or murky provenances, or both. *Henry V* and the *Henry VI* plays have been discussed. *Pericles*'s print rights had changed hands several times, but the terms of the transactions are lost. Blount had registered the play in 1608 but not printed it, and after Pavier's death in 1626, the successors to his copyrights seem to have believed they owned *Pericles* (Greg, *Bibliography* 1: 34–35). In the meantime, two 1609 quartos were printed by Henry Gosson, Pavier's partner in a ballad-publishing combine, while Simon Stafford, who had known Pavier since their days in the Drapers' Company, printed another

quarto in 1611. How the play first left Blount's control isn't certain, but
when he turned his hand to the first folio, *Pericles*'s attribution, like *The
Yorkshire Tragedy*'s, would be denied by Heminges and Condell (Greg,
Bibliography 1: 419-22, 3: 1107-9; Johnson, 14, 24).

The original publishers of *The Merchant of Venice* and *A Midsummer
Night's Dream* were dead and the rights unclear. Lawrence Heyes claimed
his father's lapsed rights to *The Merchant of Venice* in July 1619, officially
registering the claim on July 8, which has been construed as a response to
the 1619 quartos (Greg, *Bibliography* 1: 31, 278-81). Jaggard's quarto
does not name the senior Heyes but rather James Roberts, who had
first registered the work and whose business Jaggard had bought around
1608 (Greg, *Bibliography* 3: 1107-9; McKerrow et al, *Dictionary* 229).
Jaggard may have believed that the rights had reverted from Heyes to
Roberts and thereafter transferred to him; in any case, Lawrence Heyes's
entry underscores *Merchant*'s insecure title in early 1619. The apparent
extinction of the legitimate rights made these plays especially vulnerable to
appropriation; but the King's Men, intent on voiding the extant print rights
to their plays, were the most likely to appropriate it, and a new impression
was the best defense against their revisions of copyright history.[16]

Mr. William Shakespeare His True Chronicle History of King Lear may
have been printed with Nathaniel Butter's permission, as Greg speculates,
especially if he felt the King's Men might try to supersede his text, as he
had superseded *King Leir* (Greg, *Bibliography* 3: 1107-9). But his title
to the "authorial" *Lear* did not necessarily inspire universal respect, and
the 1619 quarto may be a kind of retaliatory trespass, reappropriating the
literary property Butter had appropriated from the owners of *Leir,* John
Wright and Simon Stafford, the most recent publisher of *Pericles* (Greg,
Bibliography 1: 337, 420).

Neither would Arthur Johnson's rights to *Sir John Falstaff* inevitably
command recognition from the owner of *Sir John Oldcastle*. Radical differences of genre and tone notwithstanding, the ongoing identification between the title characters would undermine any certain boundary between
the two plays as literary properties. One of the titles might even be used to
gain possession of the other. The best available protection for a stationer
was to assert control of both texts, and as many other texts featuring
the lead character as possible, so that his claim on Oldcastle/Falstaff was
beyond dispute. *Sir John Oldcastle* was a Shakespeare play in this sense,
a play that Shakespeare's partners might appropriate through a textual

double. His name on the title page asserts the identity of the publisher's and author's property, so that the differentiating power of the authorial name cannot create a second property from the first.

The King's Men's response to the 1619 quartos, and the property claims they embodied, is inscribed in the first folio. Of Jaggard's ten quartos, only the two dead men's texts, *Midsummer Night's Dream* and *Merchant of Venice,* enter the folio largely unchanged. Heminges and Condell discarded three of the other plays and provided new texts for the remaining five. Even the quartos of *Lear* and *Henry V,* which had supplanted earlier texts, were exchanged for revised versions. *Sir John Falstaff and the Merry Wives of Windsor* not only gained a new text but lost the first half of its title, becoming *The Merry Wives of Windsor* thereafter (or at least until Verdi decided *Falstaff* made the better title after all). Although *Falstaff* might seem the more logical name, the folio's truncated title bears no dangerous resemblances to the title of *Sir John Oldcastle.* At the same time Shakespeare's name, no longer necessary, is dropped from the title of *Lear.* Shakespeare's authorizing name was now attached to the whole volume and could be removed from individual plays.

At first glance, it seems paradoxical that booksellers, who dealt in the permanent medium of the printed text, championed a fluid, inclusive concept of literary property, in which a single work might have many versions, while actors like Heminges and Condell, adapting their scripts to suit opportunity and need, would promote the notion of a fixed and singular literary object, of "the perfect and full originals" that would later be advertised in the first Beaumont and Fletcher folio (Bentley, *Profession* 241). The actors' and stationers' positions were dictated by practical economics more than deep philosophical principle; some individuals, like Butter, might embrace the actors' model for intellectual property (differentiating *Lear* from *Leir*) rather than the stationers', if it happened to give him a commercial advantage. As a group, the printers and booksellers needed to preserve their expensive, slow-selling wares from any rapid change and to discourage radical revisions (although small-scale additions and corrections, which enhanced the value of a second edition without affecting title, were naturally welcome). The actors, whose art was confined to the moment of performance and whose business demanded swift adaptation, naturally valued their newest texts and sought recompense for the cost and labor of revision. The King's Men's story of "stolen and surreptitious copies" and their related account of Shakespeare's compositional process dehistoricize the texts in the hope of current gain, disowning all previous incarnations and disinheriting previous owners (*Norton Facsimile* A3r). Heminges and Condell were revisionists committed to denying revision.

In the folio's address "To the great Variety of Readers," Heminges and Condell offer the elusive ideal of a definitive Shakespeare text, with copies "perfect of their limbs, and . . . absolute in their numbers, as he conceived them," and a yearning for that promised Grail has haunted textual scholars since (*Norton Facsimile* A3r).

But Heminges and Condell's promise is not about the text at all. One of their motives is frankly commercial, and they make no attempt to hide it (Brooks, *Playhouse* 11). The first paragraph of their preface to the general reader exhorts customers to read the work "but buy it first," since payment "commends a Book best, says the Stationer" (*Norton Facsimile* A3r). Heminges and Condell may ascribe their economic motives to a proverbial, straw-man "Stationer," but the message is their own: "whatever you do, buy" (A3r). Naturally, the charge of "stolen and surreptitious copies" suits their business agenda by discrediting any rival editions of the plays. But Heminges and Condell's idealized notion of the text is also an expression of their trade.

Margreta de Grazia has explored how the folio's prefatory materials use the imagery of the natural body and familial succession to construct authorship (40–42). But Heminges and Condell's account of Shakespeare the author also depicts writing in largely theatrical terms. Shakespeare,

as he was a happy imitator of Nature, was a most gentle expresser of it. His mind and hand went together: And what he thought, he uttered with that easiness, that we have scarce received from him a blot in his papers. (*Norton Facsimile* A3r)

Shakespeare's talent as a poet or "expresser" of nature is linked to his gift as a "happy imitator" on the stage. His effortless "easiness," the synchronized purpose of his mind and hand, suggest not the labors of composition but rather a *performance of composition,* a present-tense speech act with the theatrical illusion of spontaneity. Most interestingly, Heminges and Condell imagine Shakespeare's words not as what he penned but as what he *uttered,* as words spoken aloud at the moment of conception and also, in the prevalent seventeenth-century meaning of "uttered," as things offered for sale upon the market (*OED*).

Heminges and Condell's account should not be taken for literal truth; the extent of Shakespeare's borrowings from other sources and the divergent versions of his texts disprove it. But the actor's trade demands that he conceal the work preparatory to performance, that his actions in front of the spectators seem unpremeditated and effortless. The idealized Shakespeare text which Heminges and Condell imagine is a copy without compositional history, eclipsing past indecisions and labors in an eternal, superbly consummated present. It is the text on stage: not the legendary playhouse copy, or a faithful record of any performance, but a performance of its own, a self-representation that denies its own prior history. Those who have taken Heminges and Condell at their word, hoping for some unmediated record of the authorial intent, have made a serious miscalculation. The writer, William Shakespeare, is not to be found in the folio pages. The figure critics have embraced is an actor.

Notes

1. The most recent and comprehensive account of *Oldcastle*'s publication can be found in Douglas A. Brooks's "Sir John Oldcastle and the Construction of Shakespeare's Authorship," since revised as a chapter in his *From Playhouse to Printing House,* which illuminates the parallel developments of Oldcastle and Shakespeare's iconographies. Brooks is deeply engaged with questions of material culture and of the dialectical relationships between rival texts, but less concerned with the exact nature and consequences of the 1619 attribution, or with the inconsistencies in traditional accounts of that attribution, which have been my chief interests here. Brooks's argument allows for, but by no means depends upon, the narrative that I contest, and my conclusions would tend to strengthen his basic claims about authorship while recognizing the complications and significance that previous explanations for Jaggard's quartos deny.

2. Jaggard's name does not appear on title pages, some of which bear the names of stationers who were dead, but beneath each title is a unique ornament from Jaggard's shop, cataloged by Ronald B. McKerrow as device 283, which establishes that the work was done in Jaggard's printing house (*Devices* 110).

3. W. W. Greg made the first case for the 1619 quartos' fraudulent dates, converting Pollard to his cause, and William Neidig provided the conclusive proof. Pollard recounts these events in his *Shakespeare's Fight with the Pirates,* viii–xiii. See also Greg's "On Certain False Dates in Shakespeare Quartos" and Neidig's essays, "The Shakespeare Quartos of 1619," and "False Dates on Shakspere Quartos."

4. The 1619 title page is reproduced in *Life of Sir John Oldcastle,* xxi.

5. The constitution of the folio has been examined recently by Jeffrey Masten, who also considers the Jonson and Beaumont and Fletcher folios, in his *Textual Intercourse;* Peter Blayney in his *First Folio of Shakespeare;* and David Scott Kastan in *Shakespeare after Theory.* Arthur Marotti explores the parallel topic of Shakespeare's lyric canon, including Jaggard's *Passionate Pilgrim* anthology and his successor John Benson's *Poems Written by William Shakespeare,* in "Shakespeare's Sonnets as Literary Property."

6. Alternately, *Titus* might not have been printed in 1619 because its owner's rights needed less defense; the 1619 plays all had troubled provenances of one kind or another, but the history of *Titus*'s ownership had already been established beyond doubt. The title page of 1594's first quarto lists it as the property of Derby's, Pembroke's, and Sussex's Servants, presumably in succession; all successive quartos, from 1600 on, add the Chamberlain's Servants to the list (Greg, *Bibliography* 1: 116–17). Under those circumstances, the King's Men could not possibly dissociate the *Titus* acted by earlier companies (and sold to the stationers) from the play in their own repertory.

7. All citations from *Sir John Oldcastle* are taken from *Oldcastle Controversy*.

8. Citations from the works of Shakespeare are drawn from *Riverside Shakespeare*.

9. Here, as elsewhere throughout the essay, I have standardized early modern spellings wherever practical to do so.

10. The King's Men are also recorded giving a play called "Sir John Falstaff" at court twice, in 1612–13 and in 1625, and performing a piece John Greene referred to as "Falstaff" at the Blackfriars in 1635 (Gurr 389; Bentley, *Jacobean* 1: 128; Herbert 52).

11. Some part-time theatrical venues, such as inns, could be fairly close, but by the late 1590s professional companies were no longer using such places and had probably never used them as their sole professional base.

12. Oldcastle and Falstaff had parallel careers in print as well as onstage. *Oldcastle* was registered and published hot on the heels of the Chamberlain's Men's *Henry V,* which had connections to the Oldcastle and Falstaff material; *2 Henry IV* followed immediately after that (Greg, *Bibliography* 1: 268–72). This seems to be a case where, as Blayney argues, the players used publication as advertising ("Publication" 386); here, the publicity for each company's property spurred the other troupe to advertise its counteroffering.

13. A later incarnation of Pembroke's company had the same patron as the earlier group, but not the same personnel or plays (Gurr 106–9, 272–73).

14. Blayney presents a somewhat different explanation of these events, including the "staying" of the later *Henry V* ("Publication" 399). My main difference from Blayney lies in our views of Millington and Busby's role; that they published the 1600 quarto, with Creed as printer-for-hire, might indicate that they gained control over a separate property, but there were other instances where the printer, rather than the "publishers," was the registered owner of a copy. More important, Millington and Busby's subsequent lack of control over the text suggests that the unified *Henry V* title lay with Creed.

15. For the chronology of the folio's production, see Peter Blayney's *First Folio* and also *The Norton Facsimile,* for which he wrote the introduction.

16. Technically, the rights to such "derelict" titles, in Greg's phrase, would revert to the Stationers' Company at large, but without an interested party to press his claims, such titles would likely be left undefended (Greg, *Folio* 67).

Works Cited

Bakhtin, M. M. (Mikhail Mikhailovich). *The Dialogic Imagination: Four Essays.* Trans. Caryl Emerson and Michael Holquist. Ed. Holquist. Austin: University of Texas Press, 1981.

Bale, John. *Brefe chronycle concernynge the examinacyon and death of the martyr Syr J. Oldecastell.* Antwerp: A. Goinus, 1544. STC 1276.

Bentley, Gerald Eades. *The Jacobean and Caroline Stage.* 7 vols. Oxford: Clarendon, 1941-68.

————. *The Profession of Dramatist in Shakespeare's Time.* Princeton: Princeton University Press, 1971.

Bevington, David. "Determining the Indeterminate: The Oxford Shakespeare." *Shakespeare Quarterly* 38.4 (Winter 1987): 501-19.

Blayney, Peter W. M. "Introduction." *The Norton Facsimile: The First Folio of Shakespeare.* 2nd ed. Ed. Charlton Hinman. New York: Norton, 1996.

————. "The Publication of Playbooks." *A New History of Early English Drama.* Ed. John D. Cox and David Scott Kastan. New York: Columbia University Press, 1997. 383-422.

————. *The First Folio of Shakespeare.* Washington, DC: Folger Library Publications, 1991.

Brooks, Douglas A. "Sir John Oldcastle and the Construction of Shakespeare's Authorship." *SEL: Studies in English Literature, 1500-1900.* 38.2 (Spring 1998): 333-61.

————. *From Playhouse to Printing House: Drama and Authorship in Early Modern England.* Cambridge: Cambridge University Press, 2000.

de Grazia, Margreta. *Shakespeare Verbatim: The Reproduction of Authenticity and the 1790 Apparatus.* Oxford: Clarendon, 1991.

de Grazia, Margreta and Stallybrass, Peter. "The Materiality of Shakespeare's Text." *Shakespeare Quarterly* 44.3 (Fall 1993): 255-83.

Greg, W. W. *A Bibliography of the English Printed Drama to the Restoration.* 4 vols. London: Printed for the Bibliographical Society at the University Press, Oxford, 1939-59.

————. *The Shakespeare First Folio.* Oxford: Clarendon, 1955.

————. "On Certain False Dates in Shakespeare Quartos," *The Library,* 2nd series. 9 (1908): 113-31.

Gurr, Andrew. *The Shakespearian Playing Companies.* Oxford: Clarendon, 1996.

Henslowe, Philip. *Henslowe's Diary.* Ed. R. A. Foakes and R. T. Rickert. Cambridge: Cambridge University Press, 1961.

Herbert, Henry. *The Dramatic Records of Sir Henry Herbert, Master of the Revels 1623-1673.* Ed. Joseph Quincy Adams. New Haven: Yale University Press, 1917.

Johnson, Gerald D. "Thomas Pavier, Publisher, 1600-1625." *The Library,* 6th series, 14:1 (March 1992): 12-50.

Kastan, David Scott. *Shakespeare After Theory.* New York: Routledge, 1999.

Kawachi, Yoshiko. *Calendar of English Renaissance Drama 1558-1642.* New York: Garland, 1986.

Kinney, Arthur F. *Titled Elizabethans: A Directory of Elizabethan State and Church Officers and Knights, with Peers of England, Scotland, and Ireland, 1558-1603.* Hamden, CT: Archon Books, 1973.

Kirschbaum, Leo. *Shakespeare and the Stationers.* Columbus: Ohio State University Press, 1955.

Knutson, Roslyn. "The Repertory." *A New History of Early English Drama.* Ed. John D. Cox and David Scott Kastan. New York: Columbia University Press, 1997. 461-80.

————. *The Repertory of Shakespeare's Company, 1594-1613.* Fayetteville: University of Arkansas Press, 1991.

The Life of Sir John Oldcastle, 1600. Malone Society Reprint. Ed. Percy Simpson. London: Printed for the Malone Society by Charles Whittingham & Co. at the Chiswick Press, 1908.

Loewenstein, Joseph. "The Script in the Marketplace." *Representations* 12 (Fall 1985): 101–14.

Marotti, Arthur. "Shakespeare's Sonnets as Literary Property." *Soliciting Interpretation: Literary Theory and Seventeenth-Century English Poetry*. Ed. Elizabeth D. Harvey and Katharine Eisaman Maus. Chicago: University of Chicago Press, 1990.

Masten, Jeffrey. *Textual Intercourse: Collaboration, Authorship, and Sexualities in Renaissance Drama*. Cambridge: Cambridge University Press, 1997.

McKerrow, Ronald Brunlees. *Printer's and Publisher's Devices in England & Scotland 1485–1640*. London: Printed for the Bibliographical Society at the Chiswick Press, 1913.

McKerrow, Ronald Brunlees, et al. *A Dictionary of Printers and Booksellers in England, Scotland, and Ireland. And of Foreign Printers of English Books 1557–1640*. London: Printed for the Bibliographical Society by Blades, East, & Blades, 1910.

Neidig, William. "False Dates on Shakespeare Quartos." *Century Magazine* October 1910: 912–19.

———. "The Shakespeare Quartos of 1619." *Modern Philology* October 1910: 145–64.

The Norton Facsimile: The First Folio of Shakespeare. 2nd ed. Ed. Charlton Hinman. New York: Norton, 1996.

The Oldcastle Controversy: Sir John Oldcastle, Part 1, and The Famous Victories of Henry V. Ed. Peter Corbin and Douglas Sedge. Manchester: Manchester University Press, 1991.

The Oxford English Dictionary. 2nd ed. Prepared by J. A. Simpson and E. S. C. Weiner. Oxford: Clarendon, 1989.

Pollard, A. W. *Shakespeare's Fight with the Pirates and the Problems of the Transmission of His Text*. 2nd ed. Cambridge: Cambridge University Press, 1920.

Poole, Kristen. "Saints Alive! Falstaff, Martin Marprelate, and the Staging of Puritanism." *Shakespeare Quarterly* 46.1 (Fall 1995): 47–75.

The Riverside Shakespeare. Ed. G. Blakemore Evans et al. Boston: Houghton Mifflin, 1974.

Riggs, David. *Ben Jonson: A Life*. Cambridge, MA: Harvard University Press, 1989.

Stallybrass, Peter. "Shakespeare, the Individual, and the Text." *Cultural Studies*. Ed. Lawrence Grossberg, Cary Nelson, and Paula Treichler. New York: Routledge, 1992. 593–610.

Taylor, Gary. "The Fortunes of Oldcastle." *Shakespeare Survey* 38 (1985): 85–100.

The Veil of Manuscript

LEAH S. MARCUS

A s RANDALL MCLEOD and others have been suggesting of late, we are in the throes of a crisis in editing.[1] The strategies editors have traditionally used to disambiguate textual evidence do not sit well with the present generation of poststructuralist critics, who like to have their editions served up medium rare, thank you, with cruxes and variants left unresolved and clearly visible as evidence of the early reception and dissemination of the text in question, and of its embeddedness in broader cultural practices. But how, and to what extent, do we allow our appetite for textual undecidability to influence our transcription and interpretation of manuscript materials? The present study will use experiences derived from my recent immersion in a single manuscript text in order to question some of the interpretive practices we still depend on in working with early modern manuscript materials. Polysemy is often easier in theory than in practice.

Shakespeareans in particular, deprived of even a single precious holograph of a poem or play, invest the lost evidence with almost apocalyptic status as authorial witness. Toward the end of his life, the distinguished scholar-editor Fredson Bowers was haunted by what he termed the "veil" of print that lay between himself and Shakespeare's manuscripts. In a chapter revealingly entitled "The Search for Authority: The Investigation of Shakespeare's Printed Texts," he surveys various forms of printing-house "despoliation" inflicted upon Shakespeare's and other playhouse manuscripts and advocates the study of habits of individual compositors as a way of coming closer to those lost materials: "Ultimately we shall know more about the characteristics of these compositors so that something may be attempted in the way of lifting a corner of the veil of print that hides the underlying copy."[2] At other points in the essay he finds different terms for the process of progressive revelation he envisions: "the peeling off of as much of the veneer of print as we can manage" (37), or the gaining of insight into materials "preserved in the disguise of print" (38). Bowers did not, of course, suppose that all manuscript copy had the same degree of "Authority": he distinguished carefully among authorial manuscripts, revisions, playhouse adaptations, official "books" of the play, and scriveners' copies and weighed them differentially in terms of what each could contribute to the reconstruction of a Shakespearean text. Nevertheless, in his thinking, there was a significant dichotomy between the putative clarity and "Authority" of manuscript evidence and the obfuscating "despoliation" of print. If only Shakespeareans could penetrate beyond that unliftable veil—now we see through a glass darkly, but then face-to-face.

The assumption of Bowers—and indeed of most editors of Shakespeare—is that if only we possessed some or all of the manuscript evidence, whether fair copy or foul papers, we would be brought considerably closer to the plays as the author intended them, or at least as he prepared and perhaps revised them repeatedly for performance. It is, of course, possible that we do possess a single, precious fragment of Shakespeare's own play script: Hand D of British Library MS Harley 7368, folios 8 and 9, the "Ill May Day" addition to *Sir Thomas More,* dated circa 1601. I do not want to focus here on presenting evidence against that attribution, though I am one of the scholars who considers the matter far from settled.[3] In their preface to the first folio of *Shakespeare* (1623), Heminge and Condell assert that Shakespeare never blotted a line—nearly every line of Hand D contains a blot. But the hand, by the standards of the period, is wonderfully legible— the "foul papers" of most playtexts from the period are quite a bit harder to read—and our inclination to attribute Hand D to Shakespeare may well stem in part from that legibility. If Hand D is indeed Shakespeare, then we can feel some confidence that our possession of his play scripts for *Romeo and Juliet* or *Hamlet* or *King Lear* might indeed enlighten us as to what he actually wrote.

Some scholars have used the evidence of Hand D to justify emendations, as in John Dover Wilson's alteration of "blew-ey'd" in the description of Sycorax in *The Tempest* to "blear-ey'd" on the grounds that in the hand of the *Thomas More* passage, final *r* and *w* are easily confused, and that Shakespeare in any case would not have created a blue-eyed witch.[4] But whatever we may think of that particular textual intervention, there are other textual difficulties that Hand D doesn't help us with at all. In Hand D, words are clearly demarcated from each other, unlike the hand behind *King Lear*'s "A dog so bade in office," emended in modern editions to "A dog's obeyed in office." Nor is Hand D much help with the frequent problems in Shakespeare's early printed texts relating to word endings— not only the lack of subject-verb agreement, which was endemic to the period, but also singulars where we would be much happier with plurals and plurals where we would be much happier with singulars: "Oh, ye are men of stones, [or stone?] / Had I your tongues and eyes . . ." Both the first quarto and the folio texts of this famous line from *King Lear* read "stones." Did Shakespeare write "stone" or "stones"? In Hand D, final *s* is clearly legible, and plurals are easily distinguished from singulars.

Of course, we have no guarantee that early modern printing-house copy texts were Shakespeare's own manuscripts. We are relatively certain, for example, that some of the plays were printed from copies made by the professional scrivener Ralph Crane, and it is highly likely that many more were printed from playhouse copies of one kind or another. But whatever the nature of the manuscript copy behind the printed editions, the assumption of Shakespearean editors seems to be that manuscript copy will carry far greater authority than the "despoiled" early printed versions. It would be wonderful to have such copy, of course, or even non-Shakespearean manuscript copy used for printed editions of his plays. But it is highly likely that for every interpretive difficulty the manuscript evidence solved, another would be created. Indeed, as I shall demonstrate, there is an uncanny resemblance between the scholarly method that studies the habits of any given compositor as a way of determining as closely as possible his departures from the manuscript he was using to set his copy and the scholarly method that studies the habits of manuscript scribes as a way of determining as closely as possible the wording of a manuscript text. In the former case, editorial tradition has tended to demonize the hapless compositor, while in the latter, modern textual scholars in effect become the compositors—they control important elements of the process by which the handwritten words on a manuscript page will be translated into print. But in neither case is the elusive manuscript "original" as lucidly "present" and revealing as Bowers's dichotomy between print and manuscript would suggest. Behind the veil of print there lies yet another veil—and sometimes multiple veils—of manuscript.

As Trevor Howard-Hill and Grace Ioppolo have noted, we have a superb example of the vagaries of manuscript evidence in Thomas Middleton's *A Game at Chess,* for which we possess several manuscripts, some of them in the author's own hand.[5] But this relative abundance of manuscripts cannot be arranged as an orderly stemma from late, corrupted copies back to early, authoritative authorial originals. Quite the reverse: Middleton seems to have felt no compunction about "mutilating" his own play in copying it out for friends and patrons. One copy he made displays startling differences from the other—he was either incapable of or uninterested in making copies that were faithful to some "authoritative" version of the play but instead saw each session of copying as an opportunity for reshaping. From everything we know about the fertile brain of Shakespeare, he was equally likely to compose afresh in the act of copying. If we did possess multiple authorial manuscripts of, say, *Hamlet,* the textual situation of the play would likely be even more impossibly unsettled and complex than it is at the present time. Here, however, I would like to concentrate not on the variability among different manuscript copies, a phenomenon which by now has become familiar to scholars, but on ways in which an individual manuscript can differ from itself and thereby complicate our efforts to interpret it. Even if we only had one manuscript of one of Shakespeare's plays, we still might have considerable difficulty establishing its text— unless, of course, it was written in a hand as legible as Hand D in the manuscript of *Sir Thomas More.*

I will illustrate this contention by discussing a manuscript that has no known connection to Shakespeare beyond the fact that it was, like Hand D, in all likelihood produced in 1601 and probably transcribed from dictation, as some of the playhouse manuscripts may well have been. This manuscript comes out of research for a recent project, *Elizabeth I: Collected Works.* The particular manuscript I will be discussing is the only full version we have found of Queen Elizabeth's final speech before Parliament on December 19, 1601, a little less than three weeks after she had delivered her more famous "Golden Speech." The manuscript is British Library MS Cotton Titus C.VI, fols. 410r–411v, from a bound volume entitled "Original Letters and Papers of Henry Howard, Earl of Northampton," who was Lord Privy Seal in 1601 and was doubtless present at the queen's delivery of the speech. The manuscript, however, is not in Northampton's own hand, or so my historian friends assure me. Very likely he dictated his recollection of the speech to a secretary shortly after its delivery by the queen.

Elizabeth's speeches are like Shakespeare's plays in that they had their fullest existence not as written texts but as performance, and in that, with the exception of one or two speeches written by the queen for delivery by court officials, we lack her written "originals" just as we lack Shakespeare's "originals." Indeed, in the case of Elizabeth's speeches, written originals may never have existed. She tended not to compose her remarks in writing in advance of their delivery, but rather to speak from memory, as rhetorical manuals frequently advised, and to amplify and embroider upon her planned topoi with a good deal of freedom in order to suit them as closely as possible to the immediate circumstances of their delivery.[6] The Earl of Northampton's copy of Elizabeth's last speech before Parliament does not show the typical signs of having been copied from a previous manuscript but instead has an unusual pattern of revision. Often the scribe strikes through one word or phrase and substitutes another, as though he were composing rather than copying. The scribe at one point scores through a whole paragraph for deletion and then reproduces it almost in the same wording, with only very minor changes. The manuscript seems to record the results of dictation, perhaps by the earl himself to a secretary, and very likely from memory or from hasty notes of the queen's speech made at the time of its delivery. The earl (or whoever was doing the dictation) remembered a phrase or passage, then decided he had got it wrong and requested its deletion or correction. In the case of the deleted paragraph, he then made another stab at remembering the speech that turned out to differ very little from his first attempt.

Like most other versions we have of Elizabeth's speeches, the Northampton text is therefore a "memorial reconstruction," as were perhaps rather more of the manuscripts behind printed editions of Shakespeare than most of his editors would comfortably admit.[7] Since the Northampton copy is the fullest version of the speech we have, there is no parallel independent authority by which to judge its accuracy to Elizabeth's spoken original, although a much briefer summary of the same speech exists in a contemporary diary by Sir Roger Wilbraham, another member of Parliament, and confirms its major points.[8] On the basis of evidence offered by other, similar transcripts that can actually be corroborated by reference to other source materials, we can be fairly confident that Northampton's version was relatively "authoritative" in Bowers's sense of the term—close to Elizabeth's spoken "original" and perhaps closer to her performance than our edited version in *Elizabeth I: Collected Works* will be to an accurate rendering of Northampton's manuscript. In this case, and it is by no means atypical of documents from the period, huge difficulties in interpretation inhere in the manuscript itself. My coeditor Janel Mueller and I both sweated blood over this manuscript and are painfully aware that much interpretive energy has gone into our transcription of it. And yet, for all our effort, it is unlikely that we have produced a version that corresponds word for word with what the scribe wrote. This particular manuscript is an unusually opaque "veil."

As will become evident from the excerpts offered in this essay, the Northampton manuscript is written in a fairly uniform mixed hand, part secretary and part italic, which is what we would expect from the beginning of the seventeenth century, but with a rather "modern" overall look of italic in that its general tendency is to slant the letters uniformly all one direction rather than looping back on most of the ascenders, as was still the tendency in secretary hands of the period. In some words, this hand is quite legible, but the scribe has a rather maddening tendency—which becomes more marked as he tired in the course of the transcription—to run words together and to swallow up word endings. This hand, so far as we know, has nothing to do with Shakespeare, but it serves well to illustrate the kind of interpretive cruxes we might well encounter if we still had the manuscripts that lay behind the printed texts. We would be spared the need to make conjectural readings on the basis of hypothesized printing-house errors and the known habits of compositors, but we would still be dealing in conjecture and would encounter scribal idiosyncrasies just as elusive and complicated as the compositorial "lapses" Bowers associated with the printing house.

The speech's most noteworthy crux will serve as an introductory illustration of problems in interpreting this manuscript. In the speech, Elizabeth surveys key foreign policy issues of her reign in order to demonstrate—yet once more, as she had only weeks before in her "Golden Speech"—her unfailing care and solicitude for her "dear" subjects. At one point early in the speech, she discusses her "care" for "proceeding justly and uprightly to conserve my people's love" and offers an arresting simile: "I look ever as it were upon a plain table wherein is written neither partiality nor prejudice."[9] Here is an excerpt from the beginning of the speech; the phrase in question is on line 17:

The queen's rather lovely (and early) evocation of the idea of tabula rasa is utterly lost in the most recent and authoritative edition of the speech, T. E. Hartley's collection of *Proceedings in the Parliaments of Elizabeth I,* which translates the phrase "I look ever" as "I took ever." A glance at the excerpt will demonstrate how easily the "error," assuming that it is one, was made: "look" ⟨look⟩ in line 17 has a strong upstroke that looks like a crossing on a *t.* In such a case of scribal ambiguity, standard procedure is to compare other instances of the same letter, and other initial *l*'s in the same hand show the same characteristic upstroke. See, for example, "looking" ⟨looking⟩ in line 7—and there are many other examples in the text. The transcription using "took" was made by the eminent historian Patrick Collinson: we are not talking here about an ignorant error but about a genuine difficulty in interpretation. In our edition we preferred "look" for the solid paleographic reasons just explained but also for felicity in interpretation: "look ever as it were upon a plain table" is immediately comprehensible and aesthetically pleasing, while "took ever as it were upon a plain table" requires great interpretive ingenuity to untangle since the sentence offers no object for the verb "took." We chose, in other words, the interpretive option that was most economical in determining meaning—a form of thrift that might give pause to any reader for whom polysemy is more interesting than clarity.[10]

A more difficult case in this hand is final *d* versus final *e*. In discussing the revolt in the Netherlands, for example, Elizabeth refers to the subjects' opposition to Spanish rule, which she claims to have tried to keep from festering any deeper than it already was: "I advertised the king of Spain at sundry times and by sundry messengers of this intent, advising him to be wary lest his grieved subjects, being brought to despair, did not closely put the state into the protection of some other prince that might turn this advantage to his prejudice . . ." (fol. 411r):

A glance at "aduertised," "kinge," "Spaine," "warie," and "greiud" in this single sentence alone will demonstrate how much final *d* and final *e* resemble each other in this hand. Both loop back, though in some cases (such as "kinge"), final *e* has a higher loop than final *d*. In other cases, however, the two letters are indistinguishable, and the transcriber must fall back upon the dangerous prop of context in order to discern one from the other. Since Elizabeth is talking about her past policy decisions, it "makes sense" to read "aduertised" in the past tense rather than the present tense as "aduertise," and if we interpret the word in the present tense, there is an unnecessary downstroke before the final *e*. But by making the word past tense, we preclude the (admittedly faint) possibility that Elizabeth is still "advertising" and admonishing the King of Spain in the present. To what extent might the manuscript's undecidability between readings suggest a veiled threat against Spain that was also present in the queen's delivery of the speech?

Moreover, in the word "warie" a little later in the same sentence, if the word's final *e* is interpreted instead as a *d*, "warie" can easily be read as "warnd" (warned), except that there would then be only one hump on the *n* that precedes the final *d*. However, this hand frequently swallows up parts of letterforms, which is a major reason for its difficulty. If "warie" is read as "warnd," the meaning of the queen's admonition is further altered in the direction of continuing belligerence against Spain: "warie" allows more scope for King Philip's powers of judgment, while "warnd" shifts more agency to Elizabeth and arguably intimates that she collaborated in the rebellion against his rule of the Netherlands. Indeed, in 1586, Elizabeth had been offered, and had declined, the position of Supreme Governor of the Netherlands, a sequence of events she refers to elsewhere in the speech. At the time of its delivery before Parliament in 1601, England was still at war with Spain: Habsburg troops had invaded Ireland, and a much more massive Spanish invasion was feared in England. Basing ourselves on scribal evidence, we can be confident that we made the right choice in our reading of the passage: the word is "warie," not "warnd." Nevertheless, by choosing the wording we did—on strong paleographic grounds, but also on the basis of our preexisting knowledge of the history of the period—we arguably removed some of the passage's ambiguous aura of menace against Spain, an aura kept alive by the undecidability between "warie" and "warnd."

Most intransigent of all in this maddening and interesting hand is the matter of final *e* versus final *es* or final *s*. Some cases are almost impossible to judge. Here is a passage occurring immediately before the second passage displayed in this chapter, indeed as an earlier part of the same sentence:

In the sentence that begins with the final two words of the first line, Elizabeth avers, attesting to her shock at the Netherlands' attempt to overthrow Spanish rule in the time of Charles V, "And though they [the Netherlands] sought to clear this scandal by vouching books and records of an oath taken to the States by Charles the emperor, for maintenance of their liberties with this condition: that it should be for them to revolt from obedience whensoever he should any way infringe or impugn their liberties (a very strange oath, I confess, but such a one as they produced. . . ." (fol. 411r). In the sixth line of this excerpt is the word [handwriting] to be read as "libertie" with a final reverse-style secretary *e*, or is the word instead "libertes" with *es?* The "liberties" [handwriting] two lines above is much clearer, and on the basis of its final sigma-style *s* we read the lower word as "libertes." The difference in meaning is significant, for "libertie" is a more general concept, while "libertes," as specific rights, are more restricted.

Many other passages show the same type of ambiguity between final *e* and *s* or *es*. The next example to be considered comes from an early portion of the speech in which the queen speaks generally (and eloquently) of her love for her subjects: "Beside your dutiful supplies for defense of the public—which, as the philosophers affirm of rivers coming from the ocean, return to the ocean again—I have diminished my own revenue that I might add to your security, and been content to be a taper of true virgin wax, to waste myself and spend my life that I might give light and comfort to those that live under me" (fol. 410r). The quotation begins with the fourth word in the first line:

The word "Beside" [handwriting] at the beginning of this excerpt rings somewhat false to modern ears—shouldn't it be "Besides"? A question to be asked, indeed. There is a clear *s* on "philosophers" [handwriting] on the line below "Beside," but what of "Beside" itself? Should it read "Beside" or "Besids"? "Philosophers" ends in a sigma-style *s* familiar from the passage about "liberties," and it is barely possible that the indeterminate squiggle at the end of "Beside" can be interpreted as a similar sigma-style *s*. But at the time that we prepared our transcription of the passage, we were scrupulously bending over backward not to impose our sense of syntactic correctness on the texts. We would very much have liked the reading to be "Besids," but we could not see any way to interpret the final letter as *s*. The difference in meaning is not vast between the two possibilities: "Besids" suggests "in addition"—the queen adds her own

revenues on top of her subjects' "supplies for defense of the public."
"Beside" instead suggests a parallel action—she would be arguing that
she lay her own revenues beside, or along side of, her subjects' for the
defense of the public. One reading suggests hierarchy, while the other tilts
the meaning a bit toward commonality. Whether fortuitously or not, the
undecidability between "Beside" and "Besids" in this passage registers an
ambiguity that Elizabeth used fruitfully in speeches throughout her reign:
while asserting her authority, she managed to convince large numbers of
her auditors of her deep fellow feeling for their hopes and desires. We will
never know certainly which reading is closer to what the scribe thought
he wrote. If we had expanded our sample to include all the possible *s* and
es terminals in the manuscript, however, we might have decided the case
differently.

Let us look at the problem of terminal *e* and *es* (or *is*) in a broader
paleographic perspective. The problem exists in its acutest form in this
manuscript in our attempts to distinguish "the" from "this." The difference
between the two words is clear enough when the scribe uses the sigma-
style *s* at the end of "this": I offer two instances in the first column of the
following chart:

This	?	The

The first "this" is from line 4 of the manuscript as reproduced
earlier in this chapter. Elizabeth begins the speech, "Before your going
down at the end of the Parliament, I thought good to deliver unto you
certain notes for your observation that serve aptly for the present time,
to be imparted afterward where you shall come abroad, to *this* end:
that you by me, and other by you, may understand to what prince, and
how affected to the good of this estate, you have declared yourself so
loving subjects. . . ." In the case of the emphasized "this," paleographic
evidence and our aesthetic preference correlate nicely. Either "the" or

"this" would be possible readings, but "this" is more emphatic. The same
is true for the second entry 𝗛𝗟 ⌣ in the first column on the chart, a
"this" that occurs toward the bottom of the third page of the Northampton
manuscript (fol. 411r):

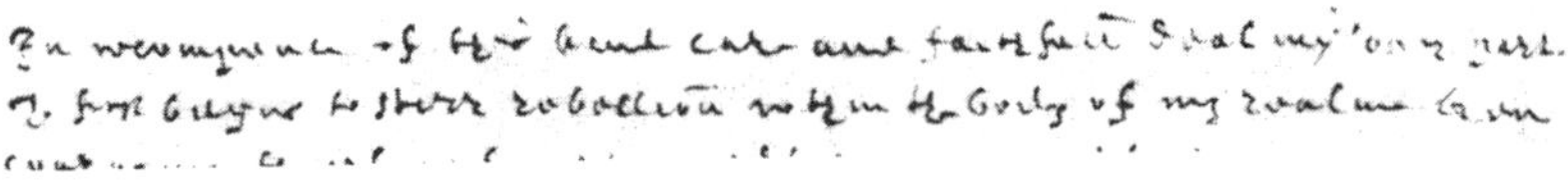

[handwritten manuscript line]

In this passage, discussing the perfidy of King Philip, Elizabeth says, "In
recompense of *this* kind care and faithful dealing on my part, he first
begins to stir rebellion within the body of my realm. . . ." And there are
other similarly clear cases of "this" in the manuscript—too many to require
enumeration here.

As anyone versed in the reading of early modern hands is well aware,
however, few writers of the period were content to repeat a single letterform with utter consistency; rather, they varied their usage with a freedom
that often seems almost random. If we assume that this writer prefers to use
the sigma-style *s* at the end of "this," we can safely assume that the examples
in the second column of the chart are all "the" rather than "this." The first
"The" *[handwritten]* in the third column is unequivocal, if somewhat blotted:
it appears as the first word in a sentence, "*The* strange devices, practices and stratagems," *[handwritten]* on the
first page of the manuscript. The "the" *[handwritten]* immediately below it in
the third column of my chart seems equally unequivocal, occurring before "world" on the third page of the manuscript in the phrase "in the
manner of the world": *[handwritten]*. But before
"manner" in the same phrase there occurs a "the" *[handwritten]* that is less clear,
and this is the third "the" down in the third column of the chart. In
this word, the *e* is rather extended, moving, perhaps in the direction of
the *is* ending in the second example under the first column. Did Elizabeth say "this manner of the world" or "the manner of the world"? Most
likely the latter—we are still safely within the realm of "the" as opposed
to "this."

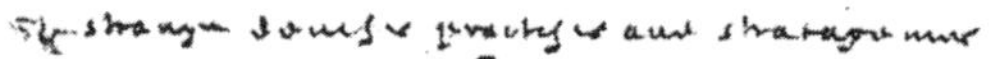

But what of the next example *[handwritten]*, which I have placed alone in the
second column to indicate its uncertain status? It occurs two lines down
in the manuscript from "the manner of the world," which we have just
discussed. Here is a fuller version of the passage in which it appears:

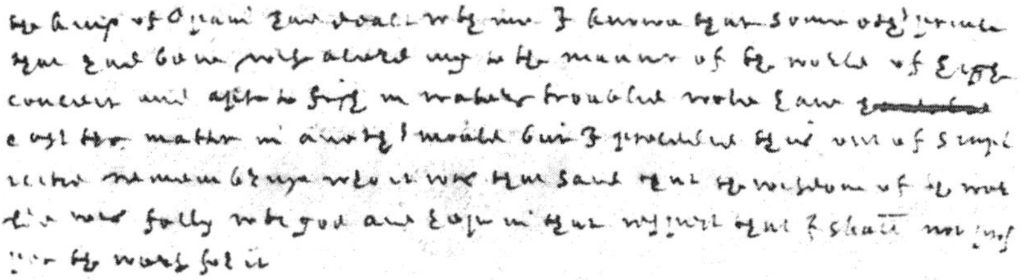

[handwritten manuscript lines]

Continuing her discussion of her rectitude in dealing with Philip II, Elizabeth states, beginning in the middle of the first line, "I know that some other prince that had been wise according to the manner of the world, of high conceit and apt to fish in waters troubled, would have cast *this* matter in another mold, but I proceeded thus out of simplicity, remembering who it was that said that the wisdom of the world was folly unto God, and hope in that respect that I shall not suffer the worse for it." Did Elizabeth say "this matter" or "the matter"? If we inspect the final word on the chart, it seems equidistant in terms of its letterforms between "the" and "this." It has only three discernible letters, which might incline us to place it in the "the" column. But in this final ambiguous case, we opted for "this," on grounds that the slight jog in the final stroke signaled the beginning of an *s* in the manner of the sigma-style *s* at the end of the two examples of "this" in the first column of the chart. Luckily, the meaning of the passage was not strongly affected either way, although by opting for "this matter" rather than "the matter" we arguably lost an interesting stylistic pointing in the passage between "the manner" and "the matter."

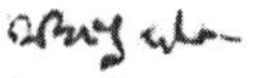

Although our interpretation of this final, highly ambiguous case did not make a huge difference to the meaning of the passage in question, it did have huge implications for the rest of our transcription. On the basis of our reading of a twitch in the final stroke of a word in this hand as signaling an *s*, we altered a number of other singulars in our transcription of the manuscript to plurals. But we may not have changed enough of them. What about the problem of deciding between "Beside" and "Besids" in our reading of *[handwritten word]* as discussed earlier, from the first page of the manuscript in the phrase "Beside your dutiful supplies for defense of the public"? We kept the word as "Beside," but based on the cases of "this" in which a small jog in the final stroke seems to signify an *s*, we probably should have preferred "Besids" because the final stroke of the word shows a similar jog (which is not as clearly visible in the scanned image as might be wished). Similarly, in the fourth line from the beginning of the speech there is an "other" *[handwritten]* in the phrase "that you by me and other by you" *[handwritten]* that probably should have been transcribed (more felicitously for modern ears) as "others." We took the scribe's final stroke to be an *e,* resembling final *e* as it occurs several other places in the manuscript. But by analogy with several instances of "this" we have already discussed, the final letter in the word may well be yet another idiosyncratic sigma-style *s.* The hand of the Northampton manuscript is extreme in the uncertainty of its word endings. The frequent confusions between "the" and "this" are largely peculiar to this scribe, but the difficulty in distinguishing singulars from plurals is also common in other hands of the period. By deciding unequivocally between singulars and plurals in our transcription of the manuscript, we surely flattened out a trait—closely associated with the texts of Elizabeth, but certainly not limited to them—that may have important cultural implications. Could this indifference be related, for example, to a broader sense of collectivity in which the singular had not yet acquired the solidity of individuation that it would acquire during the seventeenth century? The question is worth pursuing at greater length than can be attempted here.

The uncertainty of final letters in the hand of this 1601 Northampton manuscript highlights the degree to which our choices in transcribing are plastic and interpretive rather than simply a mechanical application of paleographic principles. Just as the associates and followers of Fredson Bowers who are interested in distinguishing one compositor from another in the printing house single out specific features of a text and base their differentiation of compositors A and B on the occurrence of those features, so in editing Elizabeth's writings in manuscript we sometimes were compelled to single out specific elements of a letterform as part of an effort to determine whether a word is, say, "the" or "this," "Beside" or "Besids." And as in the case of the study of compositorial practices, our attempt at objective analysis and the establishment of valid criteria for distinguishing one letterform from another gave way eventually to a more intuitive process of determination based on criteria that are far from objective. Moreover, in working with manuscript materials, we were brought to recognize elusive but suggestive possible connections between scribal practice and broader habits of mind that were obliterated by our normal habits of transcription.

In compositorial analysis, the number of typesetters involved in bringing Shakespeare into print keeps going up as the evidence is scrutinized more closely and inconsistencies in the analytic scheme are recognized. According to Bowers's overview of the process in "A Search for Authority," the first analysts identified two compositors at work on the first folio, compositors A and B. Charlton Hinman looked much more closely at the folio text and added compositors C, D, and E. John O'Connor added Compositor F, and, more recently, Gary Taylor has proposed H, I, and J.[11] This Cat-in-the-Hat multiplication of persons is very much like the multiplication of criteria that is required if one is to attempt a "scientific" study of letterforms in the Northampton copy of Queen Elizabeth's final speech before Parliament, or any other really difficult manuscript. Eventually, in both cases, the enterprise topples from the weight of its own burgeoning complexity. Manuscript work does not simplify the determination of textual meaning; rather, it suffers from a similar propensity for reductio ad absurdum that seems to intensify along with the investigator's meticulousness.

In reading manuscript materials, we are guided partly by context, which, as we know well, is no safe guide at all since it encourages us to find the likeliest, most "normal" reading, when the writer may have intended something more extraordinary and "abnormal." There have been many examples of this in the course of our editing of the writings of Elizabeth, only a few of which come from this manuscript discussed here. In the Northampton manuscript, a word we initially identified as "some" eventually turned out to be "sundrie." Elsewhere in Elizabeth's writings, "hiddenest" sometimes turned out to be "hideousest" and "cautious" turned out to be "cautelous." Or so we have judged. Then again, as illustrated more than once during my discussion here, scholars may well defend themselves too strongly against the tendency to normalize, in which case we may resist textual elements that appear suspiciously modern. Even more than reading early modern print, reading manuscript leaves much material open for interpretation. Some of that material may finally prove indecipherable according to a uniform set of rules and may be more fruitfully approached as symptomatic of yet unrecognized cultural differences or alien habits of mind.

As a group, we Shakespeareans have tended to disparage Shakespeare's compositors for their strange idiosyncrasies and blind spots. But they did a pretty fair job, given the manuscripts they had to work from. If the Northampton manuscript can boast of no known connection with Shakespeare, it at least illustrates idiosyncrasies like those of manuscripts that may have lain behind printing-house copy for some of the plays. It, like the first folio but unlike Hand D from *Sir Thomas More,* shows a strong propensity to run words together and/or create artificial spaces within them. As we have seen in some detail, it also tends to make singulars and plurals difficult to distinguish from each other. We need to consider the possibility that our faith in the identification of Hand D with Shakespeare is based on a wish-fulfillment fantasy that his manuscripts, if we had them, would indeed offer clarity rather than a new array of interpretive challenges. There is no reason to suppose that Shakespeare's texts would have presented markedly fewer complexities for those laboring in the printing house than did the texts of Elizabeth. Behind the veil of print there lies the veil of manuscript. The editing of Shakespeare would hardly be made more straightforward—and would be transformed in ways that we cannot presently imagine—if we were to encounter one of those much desired manuscripts face-to-face.

Notes

1. See, among many other recent studies, Randall M Leod [McLeod], ed., *Crisis in Editing: Texts of the English Renaissance* (New York: AMS Press, 1994).

2. Fredson Bowers, "A Search for Authority: The Investigation of Shakespeare's Printed Texts," *Print and Culture in the Renaissance: Essays on the Advent of Printing in Europe,* ed. Gerald P. Tyson and Sylvia S. Wagonheim (Newark: University of Delaware P; London: Associated University Press, 1986) 17–44; quotation is from 32.

3. See in particular Trevor Howard-Hill, ed., *Shakespeare and Sir Thomas More: Essays on the Play and Its Shakespearean Interest* (Cambridge: Cambridge University Press, 1989); and the review of this volume by Paul Werstine in *Essays in Theatre* 9 (1990): 91–94.

4. See the textual notes by Wilson in Sir Arthur Quiller-Couch and John Dover Wilson, eds., *The Tempest* (Cambridge: Cambridge University Press; New York: Macmillan, 1921) 93; and the discussion of the crux in Leah S. Marcus, *Unediting the Renaissance: Shakespeare, Marlowe, Milton* (London: Routledge, 1996) 1–25.

5. See Trevor Howard-Hill, "The Author as Scribe or Reviser? Middleton's Intentions in *A Game at Chess,*" *TEXT* 3 (1987): 305–18; Grace Ioppolo, *Revising Shakespeare* (Cambridge: Harvard University Press, 1991) 70–76; and Stephen Orgel, "Acting Scripts, Performing Texts," *Crisis in Editing: Texts of the English Renaissance,* ed. Randall M Leod [McLeod] (New York: AMS Press, 1994). 251–91.

6. For a more detailed discussion of Elizabeth's speech-writing practices, see the introduction and notes to Leah S. Marcus, Janel Mueller, and Mary Beth Rose, eds., *Elizabeth I: Collected Works* (Chicago: University of Chicago Press, 2000), and Leah S. Marcus, "From Oral Delivery to Print in the Speeches of Elizabeth I," *Print, Manuscript, Performance: The Changing Relations of the Media in Early Modern England,* ed. Arthur F. Marotti and Michael D. Bristol (Columbus: Ohio State University Press, 2000) 33–48.

7. As I have argued elsewhere, Shakespeare himself may have been a "memorial constructor." See Marcus, *Unediting the Renaissance,* chap. 5, 132–76.

8. For full texts of both versions of the speech, see Marcus. Mueller, and Rose, *Elizabeth I* 346-54.

9. Here and throughout, excerpts from the speech are cited from the modernized text in Marcus, Mueller, and Rose, *Elizabeth I.* However, discussions of the orthography or interpretation of individual words cite them in original spelling. For a justification of our difficult decision to modernize the texts within the main volume of the edition, see its introduction and also Leah S. Marcus, "Confessions of a Reformed Uneditor (II)," *PMLA* 115 (Oct. 2000): 1072-77. A second volume of the edition, which will include original-spelling versions of all materials in Elizabeth's hand as well as foreign language originals, is forthcoming from the University of Chicago Press.

10. T. E. Hartley, *Proceedings in the Parliaments of Elizabeth I* (Leicester: Leicester University Press, 1981-95); Patrick Collinson, personal communication, NEH Summer Seminar, Claremont, California, July 1995.

11. My summary is derived from Bowers 22-37; see also D. F. McKenzie, "Printers of the Mind: Some Notes on Bibliographical Theories and Printing-House Practices," *Studies in Bibliography* 22 (1969): 1-75.

King Lear *(1608) and the Typography of Literary Ambition*

DOUGLAS A. BROOKS

Introduction

Most readers of *Renaissance Drama* know that since 1623 there have been two substantively different texts of *King Lear:* the 1608 quarto printed by Nicholas Okes for Nathaniel Butter (Q *Lear*) and the text included in the first folio of Shakespeare (F *Lear*). The posthumous publication of the 1623 folio, of course, constituted a major event both in the formation of Shakespeare's authorial canon and in the history of early modern English printed drama. The 1608 text of *Lear,* on the other hand, as many readers may also know, was disparaged for much of the twentieth century as a "bad" quarto: that is, an ineptly printed, perhaps pirated or memorially reconstructed text, which—in the opinion of a number of prominent Shakespearean textual scholars—represented a gross distortion of the play Shakespeare must have originally written. What may be less well known is that the 1608 text of the play is the only extant printed quarto to prominently feature Shakespeare's name at the top of the title page. At the very least, the rather stark disparity between the singular authorial status of the 1608 *Lear* quarto and its subsequent inauthorial status in twentieth-century textual scholarship deserves attention. Indeed, I believe that a careful examination of the specific cultural, material, and historical circumstances in which Q *Lear* was produced sheds much needed light not only on the physical coming into being of one of Shakespeare's most important works but also more generally on the production, circulation, and reception of printed drama written for the early modern London stage.

From the perspective of Shakespearean textual scholarship, a reconsideration of the 1608 quarto text of *King Lear* can bring new evidence to recent scholarly debates over the authorial status of Q *Lear.* And while these debates have often enough focused on somewhat arcane bibliographic matters of little interest to many students and scholars of early modern English drama, I hope to show how the analysis of a literary work as a material book can provide the grounds for generating larger historical and hermeneutical insights. Accordingly, from the wider perspective of early modern drama studies, I want to suggest that an examination of Q *Lear* that seeks to recover the text's material origins within the early modern London book trade can help to elucidate emergent notions of dramatic authorship and literary ambition in the period. Such notions have received considerable attention in a number of important scholarly studies of early modern literary production written in the past two decades.[1] Jeffrey Masten, for example, has astutely observed that "first, dramatic authorship emerges from the publishing house and only indirectly from the theatre and, second, that authorship in its emergence is as much about marketing as about true attribution."[2] The 1608 quarto text of *Lear* represents a striking piece of evidence in support of Masten's claims.

Moreover, my analysis of Q *Lear* suggests that the oft-noted role played by Ben Jonson in the eventual transformation of acting scripts written for the playhouse into literary texts and, concomitantly, in the transformation of jobbing playwrights into literary authors is in need of reevaluation. Concurring with G. E. Bentley's assertion that "probably no other publication before the Restoration did so much to raise the contemporary estimate of the generally belittled form of plays,"[3] most scholars have readily acknowledged the impact that the 1616 Jonson folio had on the authorship of early modern drama and, more important for many critics, on Shakespeare's literary reputation as it was posthumously constructed by the 1623 folio. Alternatively, my analysis of the 1608 *Lear* quarto suggests that Jonson's influence on the marketing of Shakespeare's plays—via the printers and printing-house practices that linked the two playwrights—to readers was already being felt nearly two decades before Jonson was called upon to write a commendatory verse for the planned collection of his late rival's plays. In this specific context, this chapter strives to shift the ground of recent debates over dramatic texts away from authorial intention in the direction of what I would call printers' intentions. If, as Masten is suggesting, we need to seek the dramatic author not in the London playhouses, but in the bookstalls of Paul's Cross Churchyard, then certainly the activities of printers/publishers who produced and marketed dramatic texts deserve our attention. Finally, I want to suggest that an examination of Q *Lear* has implications for thinking about early modern drama theatrically, because, like *Lear,* a number of plays by Shakespeare and his contemporaries have come down to us in unstable, variant textual form. In a recent essay, for example, that examines some modern productions of *King Lear,* Benedict Nightingale reminds his reader that "[i]t goes without saying there is no such thing as a 'complete' production of *Lear.* The biases of the director, the design he chooses, the peculiarities of the actors he casts, and the kind of rapport they achieve with each other, the theater in which they are performing, the nature of the audience to whom they are performing, and intangibles ranging from the atmosphere of the evening to the cultural context in which the event is occurring—together, they will obviously slant and therefore in some sense limit the play."[4] Though Nightingale is careful to mention a range of tangibles and "intangibles" that can shape a production of *Lear* (or any play, for that matter), one particularly tangible—indeed material—consideration is rather conspicuous in its absence from his list. Surely, in the specific case of *Lear,* the choice of the 1608 text or the 1623 text will have a significant impact on a given theatrical production of the play. Furthermore, in the recent work of textual scholars, the theater in turn has been marshaled to the task of validating one text of *Lear* over another. Coming to the defense of Michael J. Warren and Gary Taylor's once controversial argument that the folio text represents a later version of the play revised by Shakespeare,[5] Stanley Wells, for example, observes, "It would probably be over-optimistic to expect professional directors to give us either the quarto or folio text uncut, but it would be perfectly easy for a director to base his production on one or the other text, not admitting any degree of conflation. And it would be especially valuable to have such a production based on the folio as a way of testing, in the only way that is ultimately valid, the belief that the revisions are theatrically justified."[6] Such a production was indeed realized in the 1990 RSC production directed by Nicholas Hytner, in whom, as Robert Clare notes, "Wells found his man."[7]

The 1608 quarto text of *Lear* has generated a more contentious critical reception than perhaps any other extant early modern playtext. Initially disparaged by textual scholars because of its hypothesized distance from century. When A. W. Pollard inaugurated the era of "bad" quartos in his 1909 book *Shakespeare Folios and Quartos,* the 1608 quarto of *King Lear* was not included in that exclusive group of unfortunate plays "which have 'bad' texts, differing widely and for the worse from those of the First Folio" and whose entry in the Stationers' Register was either missing or "of an unusual nature."[11] Of course, since a quarto's status was primarily judged according to how closely it resembled its folio alter ego, all of the extant quartos were always already bad ontologically,[12] though some like Q *Lear* were less bad enough to be considered good. In a chapter devoted to "A Bibliography of the Quarto Editions of Shakespeare's Plays Published Previously to 1623," Pollard provides the following analysis, under the heading "Source of Text," for the *Lear* quarto:

> An unusually illegible playhouse copy. While the edition was being printed the proofs of several sheets seem to have been read with the manuscript, and numerous corrections introduced. The copies of these sheets which had been printed without corrections were not, however, destroyed, but mixed promiscuously with corrected copies, so that there are different combinations of corrected and uncorrected sheets in the different extant copies of this edition.[13]

The hypothetically unusual illegibility of the playhouse copy would subsequently become the grounds for a number of scholars to argue that the text was set from Shakespeare's "foul papers,"[14] but what interests me most about this passage is the prominence of the printing house. Pollard's narrative, in which proofs of several sheets get read and numerous corrections get introduced, is a tale of good intentions subsequently negated at the gathering stage. Here, in the space of his bibliographical description allocated to speculating on the source of a given quarto text, Pollard actually has very little to say about the source of the 1608 *Lear* quarto and a great deal to say about the printing house that produced it. In his next chapter, devoted to discussing "The Good and the Bad Quartos," Pollard has even more to say about the printing of Q *Lear*.

Noting that Q *Lear* was the first play of Shakespeare's to be published in the reign of James I, Pollard then provides the following description of its coming into being before decisively ruling on its status as a "good" quarto:

> The text is one of the best known instances of the correction of a book while it was on the press, so that there is an uncorrected and a corrected edition of several of the sheets, which were bound up, however, at haphazard, so that scarce any two copies agree. Save for the mistakes in the uncorrected sheets the text is satisfactory, and

was used as a basis for the folio of 1623, in which, however, nearly three hundred of its lines disappear and over a hundred others are added. . . . There is no division into acts and scenes, and the stage directions are brief and very slightly descriptive. Thus everything about the book is normal and regular—entry, text, subsequent use by Folio editors . . . .[15]

Here, Pollard's earlier privileging of the quarto's production over its source seems to be justified by the text's exemplary status as a book that was corrected "while it was on the press," and the good/bad binary that grounds his analysis of Shakespeare's texts throughout again seems to structure his specific appraisal of Q *Lear*'s engendering in the printing house. He describes two distinct phases of printing-house activity: the "good" phase of the text's printing and the "bad" phase of its gathering—the latter characterized as "promiscuous" in the first account and "haphazard" in the second. Even the issue of memory, which will come to play such a powerful role in subsequent critical determinations of a given quarto's status, makes an appearance here when Pollard finally moves backward from printer to the copy he printed from. Seeking to validate the *Lear* transcript that survived the perilous journey from playhouse to printing house, Pollard asserts that "the suspicions which the name of John Busby may have aroused are groundless. He was obviously the provider of the copy, as his name disappears from the imprint, but no doubt if he could not pirate a book he was ready to pay for it, if need be, and no one seems to have cherished *long memories* in these matters" (my italics).[16]

In the space of some twenty pages, then, the story of how a printer's good intentions—to produce a correct text of *Lear*—are undermined by the economic realities of early modern printing, especially the high cost of paper, is told twice. Pollard's privileging of Q *Lear* for its press corrections is substantiated by Peter W. M. Blayney's more recent analysis which indicates that nearly half of the text's twenty-one formes were corrected at press, and that at least four formes were corrected before presswork began.[17] Remarkably, neither authorship nor the theater—except for the brief identification of Q's source as "playhouse copy"—are given any consideration. To fully appreciate the singularity of this narrative in Pollard's thinking about Shakespeare's texts, however, it must be viewed in the context of what he has to say about the "Source of Text" for the other pre-1623 quartos he examines. Here are his speculations about the sources of their first editions:

1. *Titus Andronicus*—Source of Text

2. *Richard II*—Source of Text

3. *Richard III*—Source of Text: "A copy of the play slightly cut down and altered for stage representation"[18]

4. *Romeo and Juliet*—Source of Text

5. *Henry IV*— Source of Text

6. *Love's Labour's Lost*—Source of Text

7. *The Merchant of Venice*—Source of Text

8. *Henry V*—Source of Text: "A grossly imperfect version of the play as abridged for the stage."[19]

9. *Much Ado About Nothing*—Source of Text: "In Act IV, Sc. ii, the names of the actors, Kemp and Cowley, are substituted for Dogberry and Verges, proving that the text was set up from a prompt copy or a transcript of one."[20]

10. *Henry IV, Part 2*—Source of Text: "That the text is taken from an acting version, made for use in the playhouse, is proved (a) by its omission of 171 lines found in the folio; (b) by the use of the name of the actor "Sincklo" for the part assigned to the "Officer" in the folio in Act V, sc. iv; (c) by signs of the text being in an unedited state as compared with that of the folio, e.g., in its retention in I, I, 161, of the part of Sir John Umfreville merged in the folio in that of Bardolph."[21]

11. *A Midsummer Night's Dream*—Source of Text

12. *The Merry Wives of Windsor*—Probable Source of Text: " 'The true origin of the quarto I believe to be as follows: The play was first shortened for stage representation: to the performance the literary hack, employed by the stationer to obtain a copy, resorted with his note-book. Perhaps he managed to take down some portions of the dialogue pretty accurately in short-hand, or obtained them by the assistance of some of the people connected with the theatre; but for the larger portion of the play it seems evident that he must have relied on his notes and memory only, and have clothed with his own words the bare ideas which he had stolen.' "[22]

13. *Hamlet*—Source of Text

14. *Troilus and Cressida*—Source of Text

15. *Pericles*—Evidence as to Source of Text: "Full of mistakes, which can

only be explained by the copy having been taken down by shorthand writers at the theatre."[23]

16. *Othello*—Source of Text

What even a cursory glance at this list makes clear is that Pollard actually has very little to say about the source of the other quartos. Indeed, of the seventeen quarto first editions for which he offers a bibliographical description, he is unwilling to speculate at all about the sources of ten of them. Of the remaining seven quartos, one (*Much Ado*) is derived from a prompt copy, another (*Pericles*) is—to adapt Thomas Heywood's infamous phrase—"by Stenography dr[a]w[n]," and the other four (*Richard III, Henry V, 2 Henry IV,* and *Merry Wives*) are said to be based either on transcripts abridged for the stage or "taken from an acting version, made for use in the playhouse." Thus, in a sense, the theatrical legitimacy of this last group of texts was established at the very moment the critical binary of good/bad quartos was introduced. For my purposes at this point, however, what seems most significant about Pollard's effort to describe bibliographically the extant first-edition quartos is the fact that only the 1608 *Lear* quarto generates a twice-told narrative about what happened to the transcript in the printing house.

The vicissitudes of Q *Lear*'s scholarly fate after Pollard's 1909 study are too numerous—and perhaps too frequently narrativized[24]—to merit anything more than a brief review here, but in the specific context of his preoccupation with the text's production, one point needs to be made. Within the conspicuously grammatological trajectory of the critical tradition that followed Pollard, *graphos* gave way to *logos* as the singularity of the 1608 quarto's printing was gradually placed under erasure. Arguably, this all-too-predictable repression was initiated by Leo Kirschbaum in 1938 when he included Q *Lear* as one of twenty texts he identified as bad quartos.[25] That *Lear*'s significance as an exemplar of a press-corrected book had been eclipsed upon its induction into the bad quarto club was confirmed a year later in W. W. Greg's Clark Lectures at Trinity College, Cambridge. Observing that "not all the 'good' quartos have, according to the latest theory, quite so respectable an origin as Pollard allowed them," Greg promptly offers an example of a text that has recently been humbled: "This applies particularly to *King Lear.* Unless I am mistaken, and what would be more surprising Sir Edmund Chambers is equally and independently so, the text of the quarto of 1608, though on a very different level of accuracy from those of the recognized 'bad' quartos, is like these a report based on actual performance, and therefore presumably piratical and surreptitious."[26] The source of Q *Lear* is no longer "[a]n unusually illegible playhouse copy" extensively corrected as it was printed, but rather a memorially reconstructed report of the play as it was actually performed. Thus, Q *Lear*'s "bad"ness is now contingent upon its theatrical origins, and the text's "good"ness, formerly contingent upon its translation from stage to page, has been powerfully repressed by "the latest theory."

Greg's prominence in the scholarship on early modern dramatic texts would pretty much guarantee that Pollard's recognition of Q *Lear*'s significance as an artifact of the printing house would stay repressed, though the *graphos,* like the ghost of Hamlet's father, has occasionally returned with a vengeance—for example, in Blayney's monumental study of the 1608 quarto.[27] Even the two-text controversy, first sparked by Michael J. Warren's contention that "Q1 and F1 are not corrupted versions of a single Shakespearean original but two separate authoritative versions of the play,"[28] later ratified in *The Division of the Kingdoms* and subsequently canonized in both the Oxford and Norton editions of Shakespeare's plays, was primarily an attempt to overturn Greg's thinking about Q *Lear.*[29] Consequently, the "good" intentions of Q *Lear*'s printer in Pollard's analysis of its source have been further displaced by the "bad" authorial intuitions of a playwright who would subsequently attempt to improve *King Lear* by revising it after seeing it staged.[30]

Although the twentieth century was a time of tremendous change, the 1608 quarto of *Lear* has been a site of some stability and constancy. Initially singled out as an exemplar of a press-corrected book and classified as "normal and regular" in the context of other Shakespearean quartos, Q *Lear*'s fortunes quickly fell, and it has spent the remainder of the century lacking either unmediated access to its author's pen or unmediated access to its author's mature pen. In the next section of this chapter, I want to sketch out briefly and tentatively a context in which Q *Lear* can be restored to its formerly singular printed state of grace in Pollard's account. To accomplish this admittedly nostalgic project, the goal of which is to provide a foundation for rethinking Q *Lear*'s literary and theatrical legitimacy, I will attempt to relocate the text within a specific phase of early modern dramatic publication which, I believe, influenced the material production of the 1608 quarto. While this approach may seem as paradoxical as the modern scholarly trajectory I critiqued at the outset, I hope to demonstrate that its virtue lies in its focus on a set of practices that was gaining currency at precisely the moment Q *Lear* was in the printing house.

Bad Theater/Good Text/Good Printer

I want to begin some four years after Q *Lear* was published and work back to it. My principal piece of evidence consists of the following lines from a note "To the Reader" included in the 1612 quarto edition of John Webster's play, *The White Devil:*

For my owne part I have ever truly cherisht my good opinion of other mens worthy Labours, especially of that full and haightned stile of Maister *Chapman*. The labor'd and vnderstanding workes of Maister *Johnson:* The no lesse worthy composures of the both worthily excellent Maister *Beamont* and Maister *Fletcher:* And lastly (without wrong last to be named) the right happy and copious industry of M. *Shake-speare*, M. *Dekker,* and M. *Heywood,* wishing what I write may be read by their light.[31]

I have examined this passage in great detail elsewhere,[32] but here I want to focus on its value for determining the context in which Q *Lear* was published. Although Webster cautions his reader against equating the order in which he mentions these seven dramatists with some qualitative judgment of their merits as writers, I believe that in fact he has arranged his list of "cherisht" colleagues in the playwriting profession according to a hierarchy which, although indiscernible from the perspective of current critical practices, nevertheless holds a significant insight into the publication of dramatic texts in early seventeenth-century England. Specifically, I want to argue that Webster's assessment of the milieu in which he works is guided by an insider's knowledge of the relationship between playhouse and printing house. Chapman is praised for his "full and height'ned style," while Jonson is credited for producing "labour'd and understanding works." Four years later, Jonson would make good on the compliment by controversially publishing his folio collection of plays, masques, and epigrams under the title of *Workes*—a fairly involved printing project which, according to C. H. Herford, Percy Simpson, and Evelyn Simpson, may have been in the planning stages when Webster's play went to the press.[33] Beaumont and Fletcher are recognized for their "no less worthy composures." Lastly, Webster groups Dekker, Shakespeare, and Heywood together, praising them for their "right happy and copious industry."

In a recent essay that examines the initial performance and publication history of *The Knight of the Burning Pestle,* staged in 1607 and printed six years later, Zachary Lesser has argued that the play's publisher, Walter Burre, believed that "he could exploit a new and important cultural division in the theatrical market."[34] Hoping to generate a market for printed drama consisting of well-educated readers who may not have frequented the theater, Burre used the only tool available to him, the printing press. Among the specific features which characterize this nascent effort are the prominence of author attributions and Latin epigraphs on title pages and the use of what Greg identified as "continuous printing"—a method of setting type in which verse lines broken between two speakers are set on one line.[35] The practice of continuous printing, which began in the universities and with translations from classical drama, certainly had a distinctly elitist heritage. For this reason, Lesser argues that

the technique came to seem "literary" and classical, serving to distance the play from its theatrical origins and from the "vulgar" plays which win the favor of audiences in the theater. Of the first twenty plays printed continuously, dating from c. 1530 to 1604, all but four are either university drama, literary translations, or closet drama.[36]

Arguably, the presence of author attributions, Latin epigraphs, and continuous printing conferred a certain literary status upon a given dramatic text, and it is likely that seventeenth-century publishers such as Burre trusted that a specific readership's familiarity with such features would enable it to readily distinguish their plays from less literary fare. If we apply this insight to Webster's assessment of his esteemed playwriting colleagues, we will see that the order in which he mentions them is particularly meaningful.

The 1612 quarto edition of *The White Devil,* printed by Q *Lear*'s printer, Nicholas Okes, is in fact continuously printed. For Webster the printed text of *The White Devil*—replete with singular authorial attribution ("Written by Iohn Webster"), Latin epigraph ("Non inferiora secutus"), and continuous printing—typographically constitutes his literary debut. Moreover, the self-consciously literary status of the play is reiterated thematically in the prefatory note "To the Reader," which not only appeals to an educated readership through its reliance on six lines of Latin but also rather explicitly attempts to designate its target readership by referring to the performed play's inept audience:

I have noted, most of the people that come to that Play-house, resemble those ignorant asses (who visiting Stationers shoppes their vse is not to inquire for good bookes, but new bookes) I present it to the generall view with this confidence.[37]

The audience, Webster asserts, was comprised of "ignorant asses" who prefer new plays to good plays. An earlier but similar lament about play-goers' preferences had been articulated more graphically in the preface to another printed dramatic text that appeared in the same year Q *Lear* was published. In a note entitled "To the Reader," included in the 1608 quarto text of *The Familie of Love,* a writer complains,

Plaies in this Citie are like wenches new falne to the trade, onelie desired of your neatest gallants, whiles the'are fresh: when they grow stale they must be vented by Termers and Cuntrie chapmen.[38]

The subtle wordplay on "Cuntrie chapmen," a chapbook being one of the most common items sold in London's bookstalls, succinctly brings together sexual and textual intercourse, a convergence that is already at work in the larger analogy structuring the passage. As such, the writer has wandered into a rather conventional early modern gendered discourse of publication employed in the prefaces of any number of books printed in the period.[39] What is new, however, in the preface to Webster's typographically literary debut as an individualized author is that he relies on the example of ignorant book buyers to discredit the theater. Conflating the playhouse and the printing house in order to promote his play to a new marketplace, Webster has already sought out a printer who has learned to rely on a set of typographic conventions to create and foster a market of readers who not only may buy a play like *The White Devil* but also may accord it the kind of respect and appreciation its writer thinks it deserves. Thus, in the case of one printed dramatic text, something like literature has been typographically born out of an individual playwright's effort to distance his play from the audience who saw it performed in the theater.[40] As such, Webster's final move in his note "To the Reader," listing the names of seven writers whose "worthy Labours" he admires, must be seen as a fantasy of belonging to an elite club of playwrights.

George Chapman's literary reputation was already secure by the time *The White Devil* was printed. He had studied at both Oxford and Cambridge and had done more than any of his contemporaries to make Homer available to English readers. Thus, he alone gets praised for his "haightned stile."

Indeed, Chapman's translations of Homer may have earned him a privileged position in Webster's prefatory effort at authorial self-construction, for, as Barbara A. Mowat observes, "[t]he several editions of Homer published between 1581 and 1616 illustrate the gradual construction of a great Author in England's early modern period."[41] Having contributed a significant final chapter to this lengthy, collaboratively produced narrative, Chapman was in a particularly excellent position to benefit from it. Beyond his significant literary credentials, Chapman had also produced a body of plays which, compared to Webster's output at this stage in his career, was considerable. Between 1598 and 1612, nine plays were published under his name, and one collaboratively written play—*Eastward Hoe* (1605)—was attributed to Chapman, Ben Jonson, and John Marston. One of these plays, *The Gentleman Usher,* was published in the self-consciously literary style of *The White Devil* two years before Q *Lear* and six years before Webster's play. Another of Chapman's dramatic texts to be printed continuously— *The Revenge of Bussy d'Ambois* (1613)—appeared a year after Webster placed him at the top of his list of playwrights who had earned his "good opinion." Arguably, the recognition accorded Chapman in the preface to *The White Devil* gave his publisher some ideas about how his next play should be printed and marketed.

Alternatively, Jonson was known primarily at this stage in his career as a playwright who wrote plays for the theater and masques and entertainments for James I's court. Jonson, of course, had done more in the period prior to the publication of Webster's play to bolster the literary reputation of and create a new reading market for printed drama than any of the six other playwrights Webster mentions. Jonson's belief—so fully articulated in the preface "To the Readers" of the 1605 quarto of *Sejanus, his Fall*— that the publication process could deliver some modicum of legitimacy to the profession of playwriting must have deeply influenced Webster's thinking about the literary status of his authorial debut—especially in terms of how he viewed the relation between the playhouse and the printing house.

In the dedication included in the first quarto edition of *Catiline, his Conspiracy* (1611), Jonson had critiqued popular audiences in terms that would be appropriated a year or so later by Webster, complaining of the "so thicke, and darke, an ignorance, as now almost couers the Age" (A2r).[42] Moreover, Jonson offered different readers' addresses to the play's two very different kinds of readers: one is aimed at the "reader in ordinarie" who will "commend out of affection, selfe tickling, an easinesse, or imitation"; the other addresses the "Reader extraordinary" (A3r) who not only knows a great piece of literature when he or she reads it but also perhaps has the money to buy it. A year later, in the address to the reader of *The Alchemist* (1612), Jonson takes aim at playwrights who "are esteem'd the more learned, and sufficient for this, by the Multitude," and blames this unfortunate fate on "the disease of the unskilfull, to thinke rude things greater then polish'd: or scatter'd more numerous than compos'd" (A3r–A3v).[43]

Given the intensity of Jonson's desire to distance himself from "the loathed stage," it should come as no surprise that he takes greater advantage of the publication process to mark his plays typographically as literary than any of the other playwrights Webster mentions. Of the five Jonson plays that were published between 1605 and 1612—*Sejanus, his Fall* (1605); *Volpone* (1607); *The Case is Altered* (1609); *Catiline, his Conspiracy* (1611); and *The Alchemist* (1612)—all of them make use of continuous printing (see figure 1). (When these plays were reset for the *Workes,* William Stansby also opted for continuous printing.) Thus, it seems clear that Jonson had already begun to take advantage of the printing house to further his literary ambitions as much as a decade before he began to work with Stansby on the printing of the 1616 folio.

Only two authors into Webster's list, the nature of its hierarchy should already be apparent. Chapman, the university man with an established literary reputation comes first; Jonson, the professional playwright who has aggressively used publication to create for himself an extratheatrical literary reputation, comes second. Oddly however, Webster concludes by praising three playwrights who have each been professionally involved in the theater for nearly two decades. Indeed, given the context in which they appear, it seems likely that Webster put them together because their strong associations with playing companies marked them as popular playwrights who had lower literary ambitions than the other writers who precede them in his list. In other words, those playwrights who aspire to the "heighth of stile" go at the top, while those who appeal to the groundlings go at the bottom.

Unlike Jonson, for example, who presciently saw in the printing press the possibility of distancing himself and his career as an author from "the loathed stage," Shakespeare was involved in the publication of only two works, *Venus and Adonis* and *The Rape of Lucrece*. As Bentley observes

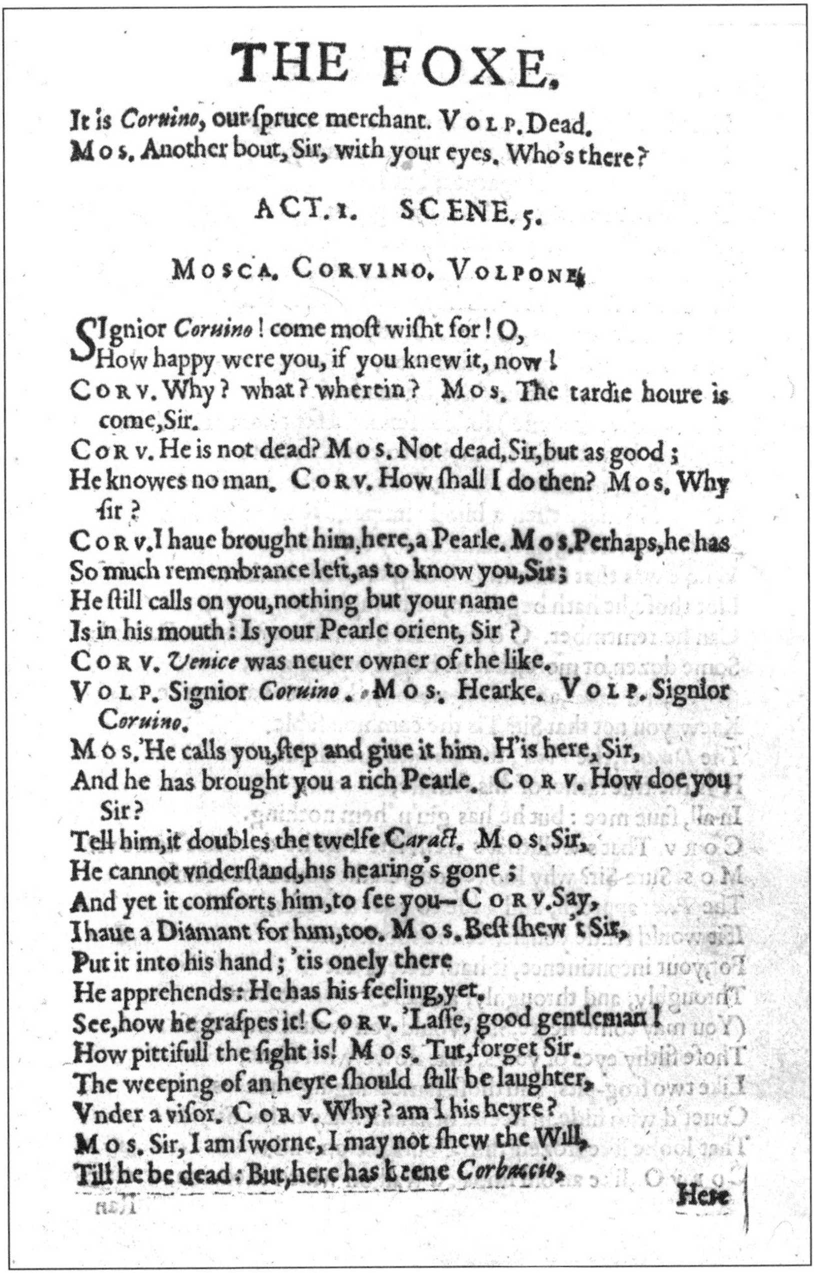

THE FOXE.

It is *Coruino*, our spruce merchant. V o l p. Dead.
M o s. Another bout, Sir, with your eyes. Who's there?

ACT. 1.   SCENE. 5.

M o s c a. C o r v i n o. V o l p o n e.

SIgnior *Coruino*! come moſt wiſht for! O,
How happy were you, if you knew it, now !
C o r v. Why? what? wherein? M o s. The tardie houre is
come, Sir.
C o r v. He is not dead? M o s. Not dead, Sir, but as good ;
He knowes no man. C o r v. How ſhall I do then? M o s. Why
ſir ?
C o r v. I haue brought him, here, a Pearle. M o s. Perhaps, he has
So much remembrance left, as to know you, Sir ;
He ſtill calls on you, nothing but your name
Is in his mouth : Is your Pearle orient, Sir ?
C o r v. *Venice* was neuer owner of the like.
V o l p. Signior *Coruino*. M o s. Hearke. V o l p. Signior
Coruino.
M o s. He calls you, ſtep and giue it him. H'is here, Sir,
And he has brought you a rich Pearle. C o r v. How doe you
Sir ?
Tell him, it doubles the twelfe *Caract*. M o s. Sir,
He cannot vnderſtand, his hearing's gone ;
And yet it comforts him, to ſee you— C o r v. Say,
I haue a Diamant for him, too. M o s. Beſt ſhew 't Sir,
Put it into his hand ; 'tis onely there
He apprehends : He has his feeling, yet.
See, how he graſpes it! C o r v. 'Laſſe, good gentleman !
How pittifull the ſight is! M o s. Tut, forget Sir.
The weeping of an heyre ſhould ſtill be laughter,
Vnder a viſor. C o r v. Why? am I his heyre?
M o s. Sir, I am ſworne, I may not ſhew the Will,
Till he be dead : But, here has beene *Corbaccio*,

Here

FIGURE 1.   A page from *Volpone*, 1607 (by permission of the Huntington Library).

with reference to these two poems, "[Shakespeare] not only provided dedications but gave his readers excellent texts, far cleaner than those displayed in any of his play quartos."[44] Alternatively, Shakespeare seems to have been singularly indifferent about whether and how the plays he wrote made it into print, an indifference that has troubled critics from Samuel Johnson to the present. As Richard Dutton succinctly characterizes the playwright's selective involvement with publication, "Shakespeare was not shy of print, it seems, only of printing plays (and sonnets)."[45]

Struggling to rationalize his lack of interest in publication, critics have sometimes called attention to Shakespeare's unparalleled professional involvement with the same company; and it seems likely that the playwright's status as a sharer discouraged him from engaging in the kind of authorial self-promotion for which Jonson has often been celebrated. In fact, after comparing available evidence of contractual agreements between theaters and playwrights in the period, Dutton concludes that Shakespeare "was bound by constraints of corporate bonding virtually unparalleled in the period," adding that "[s]ince these constraints commonly seem to have put an embargo on the printing of corporately owned playbooks for both shareholders and 'ordinary poets,' Shakespeare must have felt massively restricted."[46] Whereas Jonson was keenly aware that the "Stage" and the "Booke" afforded him distinct opportunities for authorship and relied on the publication process to excise his early collaborative works from his authorial canon, Shakespeare may have been content to or compelled to sidestep an emergent author function for the sake of the collaborative well-being of the company.

Shakespeare's lack of interest in publication has been a bit embarrassing, given his singular position in the West, and commentators have frequently apologized for it or attributed it to paranoia about piracy. There is, however, one important exception in the prefolio printing history of Shakespeare's plays which, although it cannot be traced back to the author's agency, nevertheless places him for a moment in the self-consciously literary company of Webster and Jonson. Moreover, this exceptional case, remarkably enough, is precisely the one that gets accorded a special place in Pollard's account because of its exemplarity as a press-corrected book. In other words, although seventeen extant quarto first editions of Shakespeare's plays found their way into print with the help of nearly as many different publishers,[47] only one of them, the 1608 quarto text of *King Lear* published by Nathaniel Butter and printed by Okes, seems to target the same kind of select, literary readership to which Jonson and Webster sought to market themselves.

The *Lear* quarto was the first play that Okes, who became a master printer in 1607, had ever worked on,[48] and it is therefore rather likely that Butter and Okes looked around for a model to imitate. Given the fact that Q *Lear* is the only quarto to prominently feature Shakespeare's name at the top of the title page (see figure 2), Jonson's earlier texts may well have been a model. When, for example, Jonson's play *Volpone* was published a year before Q *Lear,* the author's name, set in larger type than any other word on the title page, seemed to be the primary reason for buying and reading the text that follow (see figure 3). But putting the playwright's name at the top of the title page was a strategy of authorial self-presentation already used by Jonson's printers for the 1604 quarto of *B. Jon: his part of King James his Royall and Magnificent Entertainement* (see figure 4). Furthermore, because Q *Lear* is the first extant Shakespeare play to be published after the Chamberlain's Men had become the King's Men, an allusion to an earlier publication that chronicled James I's entry into London may have subtly registered the author's recent promotion as playwright to the king's company. Indeed, the link between Shakespeare's company and James is emphasized in the center of the title page by the italicized phrase, "*As it was played before the Kings Maiestie at Whitehall upon* / S. Stephans *night in Christmas Hollidayes.*" Thus, the title page asserts that it fronts the printed transcript of a unique and special court performance, a performance that gets further individualized retroactively by the subsequent and final piece of information offered about the King's Men: "By his Maiesties seruants playing vsually at the Gloabe / on the Bancke-side." In other words, the title page suggests that this is not the play as it would have been performed at the playhouse, but rather as it was performed before the king. Moreover, the anomalous typographic overdetermination of the quarto's authorship differentiates Shakespeare's "True Chronicle historie of the life and death of King LEAR and his three Daughters" from a non-Shakespearean "True Chronicle History of King LEIR and his three daughters" published in 1603. Indeed, the author's name is printed a second time in the same large type as a head-title on the first page of playtext, and once again a genitive relation between author and play is emphasized: "M. William Shak-speare / *H I S* / Historie, of King Lear." In short, Shakespeare's name functions on the title page of Q *Lear* less to identify the playwright than to identify the playbook: the "Shak-speare" of the title page here, as David Scott Kastan

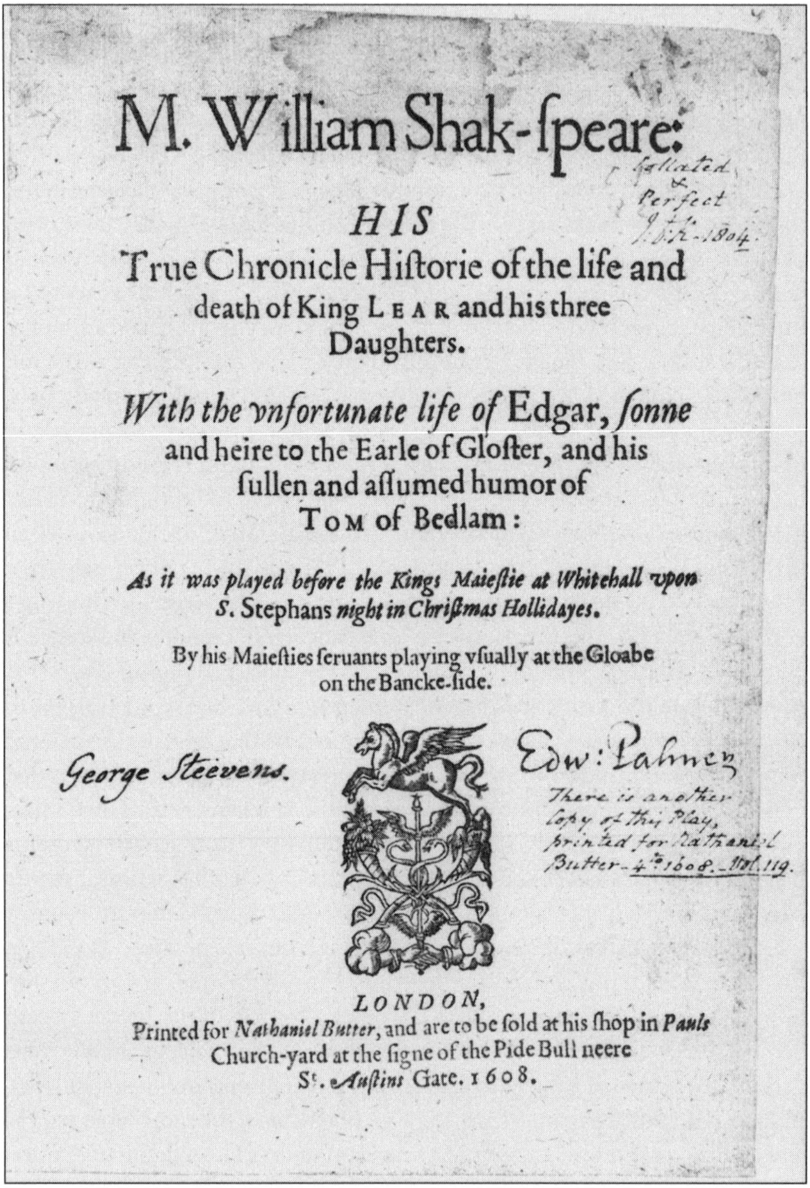

M. William Shak-ſpeare:

HIS

True Chronicle Hiſtorie of the life and
death of King L E A R and his three
Daughters.

With the vnfortunate life of Edgar, *ſonne*
and heire to the Earle of Gloſter, and his
ſullen and aſſumed humor of
T O M of Bedlam:

As it was played before the Kings Maieſtie at Whitehall vpon
S. Stephans night in Chriſtmas Hollidayes.

By his Maieſties ſeruants playing vſually at the Gloabe
on the Bancke-ſide.

George Steevens.

Edw: Palmer
There is another
Copy of this Play,
printed for Nathaniel
Butter—4º 1608.—Nol. 119.

Collated
&
Perfect
J.R.—1804.

LONDON,

Printed for *Nathaniel Butter*, and are to be ſold at his ſhop in *Pauls*
Church-yard at the ſigne of the Pide Bull neere
S^t. *Auſtins* Gate. 1 6 0 8.

FIGURE 2. Title page from *King Lear,* 1608 (by permission of the Huntington
Library).

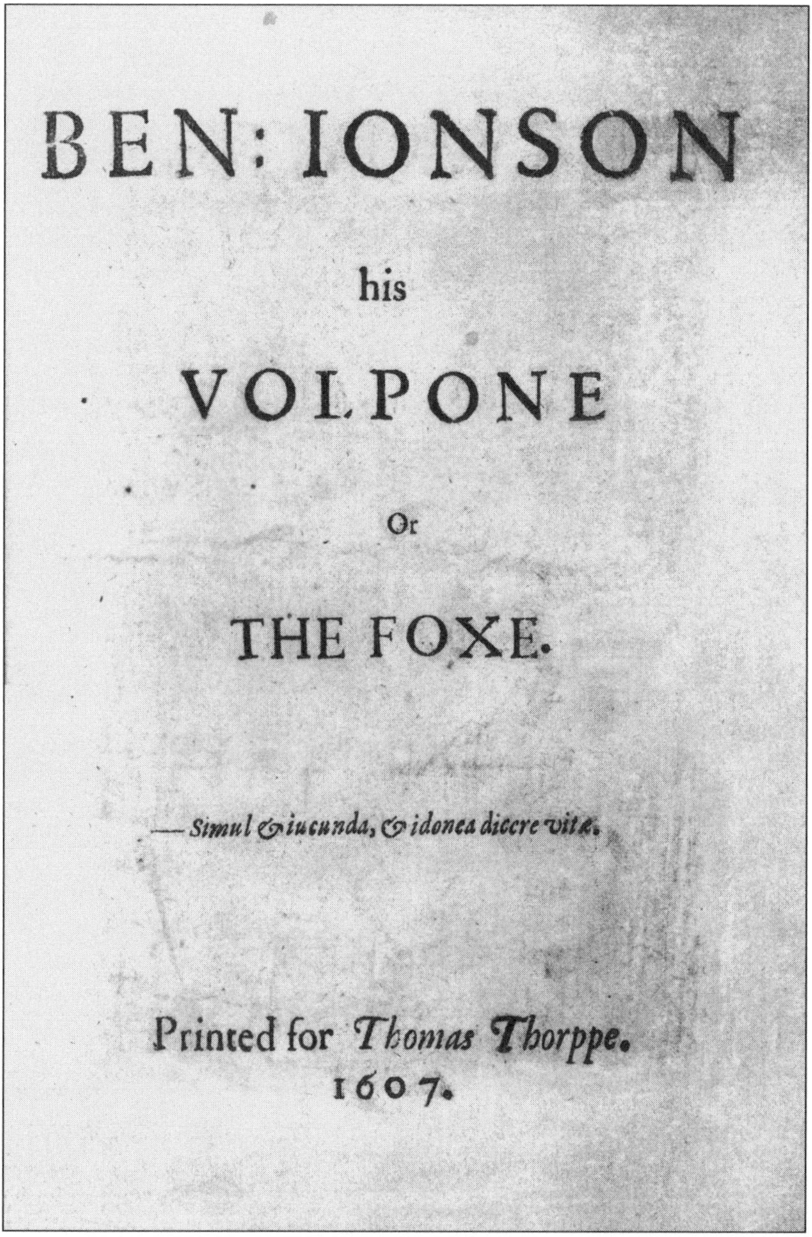

BEN: IONSON

his

VOLPONE

Or

THE FOXE.

—— *Simul & iucunda, & idonea dicere vitæ.*

Printed for *Thomas Thorppe.*
1607.

FIGURE 3. Title page from *Volpone*, 1607 (by permission of the Huntington Library).

B. JON:

HIS PART OF

King James his Royall and Magnifi-
cent *Entertainement through his*
Honorable Cittie of London,
Thurſeday the 15. of
March. 1603.

So much as was preſented in the firſt and laſt of
their Triumphall Arch's.

With his ſpeach made to the laſt Preſentation, in the
Strand, erected by the inhabitants of the Dutchy,
and *Weſtminſter.*

Alſo, a briefe *Panegyre* of his Maieſties firſt and well
auſpicated entrance to his high Court of Parliament,
on Monday, the 19. of the ſame
Moneth.

With other Additions.

Mart.   *Quando magis dignos licuit ſpectare triumphos.*

Printed at London by V.S. for
Edward Blount, 1604.

FIGURE 4.   Title page from *B. Jon: his part of King James his Royall and
Magnificent Entertainement,* 1604 (by permission of the Huntington Library).

observes, is "the publisher's Shakespeare, a simulacrum who will help sell books"[49]—a kind of Foucauldian author function invented to individualize and protect the publisher's property and investment. And it is tempting to speculate that a year after Q *Lear* was published, Jonson and Okes slyly alluded to the Jonsonian nature of Okes and Butter's previous project on the title page of *The Case is Altered.* Like the title page of the 1608 text, this newly published play was marketed to readers as an author's possession: "Ben Jonson / His Case is Altered."

The singularity of Q *Lear*'s title page cannot, perhaps, be overemphasized. In the specific context of Shakespeare's career in print, it is without precedent. The title pages of the following quartos were printed without any indication of Shakespeare's authorship: *Titus Andronicus, The First Part of the Contention betwixt the two famous Houses of York and Lancaster, The True Tragedy of Richard Duke of York, Romeo and Juliet* (Q1 and Q2), *Richard III, I Henry IV,* and *Henry V.* Thus, nearly half of the plays that appeared in print before the 1623 folio laid no claims to Shakespeare's paternity. Those quartos that did acknowledge Shakespeare's authorship merely placed his name in relatively small type beneath seemingly more important information. Only the title page of Q *Lear* seeks to market the play it fronts on the merits of its author's name. In the larger context of printed drama written for the London stage, Q *Lear*'s title page also stands out. With the exception of those Jonson plays discussed earlier, no other contemporary play offered a comparably spectacular attribution on its title page. Indeed, the significant typographic link between these two authors' playtexts strongly suggests that Jonson's strategies of publication and authorial self-promotion, both of which might be seen as symptoms of what Joseph Loewenstein aptly terms "the bibliographic ego,"[50] constitute a kind of palimpsestic shadow beneath the materialization of *King Lear*'s debut in print. Even the inclusion of an author's name on the title pages of published plays was not yet a given, though during the decade in which Q *Lear* appeared, author attribution rose to its highest level since the opening of the first public playhouse in 1576. For the year 1608, we know the titles of some seventeen plays that have been attributed to an author or authors. We know the titles of nine other plays performed and/or published in the same year that remain unattributed.

It is not always wise to judge a book by its cover, and in the case of Q *Lear* the text that follows the title page does not live up to that page's typographically literary promise. Unlike the majority of Jonson play quartos published in the first decade of the seventeenth century, Okes did not typographically mark Q *Lear* for a select readership by printing the text continuously.[51] Nevertheless, some of the continuities between Okes's inexperienced approach and the practices of Jonson's printers I have touched on suggest that Okes and/or Butter not only gave some thought to how plays by Shakespeare's contemporaries were being translated from stage to page, but that they ultimately settled on the Jonsonian model. Much has been written about the first folio's debts to Jonson's *Workes,* but the printing-house practices that link Q *Lear* to contemporary Jonson quartos suggest that a Jonsonian procedure for embalming and monumentalizing Shakespeare's corpus had already been tested some fifteen years earlier.

At least once in Shakespeare's pre–first folio publication history a printing house took it upon itself to distance one of his plays from the "smoky breath of the multitude," an audience which—if the title page of Q *Lear* is to be believed—perhaps had not breathed on the play in the first place. Remarkably, the next extant Shakespeare quarto to be published, *The Historie of Troylus and Cresseida* (1609), is the first extant Shakespeare quarto to include an address to the reader—a paratextual strategy that Jonson had already deployed in published quarto texts of his plays for the sake of relocating them from the theater to the archive. Written by Henry Walley, the address constitutes an attempt to disassociate the play from uneducated theater audiences like the ones Webster and Jonson deplore. Walley assures the "Eternall reader," an eternity secured through publication, that "you have heere a new play, neuer stal'd with the Stage, neuer clapper-clawd with the palmes of the vulger, and yet passing full of the palme comicall."[52] After comparing Shakespeare's dramas with "the best Commedy in *Terence* or *Plautus*" and prophesying that "when [Shakespeare] is gone, and Commedies out of sale, you will scramble for them, and set vp a new English Inquisition,"[53] Walley returns to the subject of the play's theatrical innocence:

Take this for a warning, and at the perrill of your pleasures losse, and Iudgements, refuse not, nor like the lesse, for not being sullied with the smoky breath of the multitude; but thanke fortune for the scape it hath made amongst you.[54]

Whereas other publishers/playwrights encourage prospective readers to distinguish between the book and the theater, Walley tries to convince readers to buy a play that he claims was never staged. The only other reader address to preface a Shakespeare quarto is a note from "The Stationer to the Reader" that was written by Thomas Walkley and included in the 1622 edition of *Othello* printed for him by Nicholas Okes. In the thirteen years that separate the two addresses, theater audiences have all but disappeared as a defining oppositional context for promoting the publication process. Instead, one year before the appearance of the first folio, the authorial ghost of Shakespeare has already emerged as a Jonsonian author figure with his "name" and his "worke" at the center of Walkley's commodification strategy: "To commend it, I will not, for that which is good I hope every man will commend, without intreaty: and I am the bolder, because the Authors name is sufficient to vent his worke" (A2r).[55]

Conclusion

Until the printer's copy for Q *Lear* and the folio text of the play are located, we can only continue to speculate as to the authorial status of both editions. Indeed, in the absence of such evidence, we will never be completely sure that the 1623 text of *Lear* represents a later, more mature, authorially revised version of the play. Major productions of *Lear* by the Royal Shakespeare Company and the National Theater during the past three decades have regularly included eleven substantive Q *Lear* passages omitted from F,[56] a pattern of inclusion that would seem to support Q's theatrical validity. In this sense, the version of *Lear* that many recent critics believe did not benefit from Shakespeare's postperformance revisions has proven itself quite worthy of the stage. Thus, in the particular case of Q *Lear,* the current critical wisdom that folio versions of plays, as opposed to extant quarto editions of the same plays, are closer to hypothetical performance texts as Shakespeare and his playing company intended them, may not hold true in all cases. A group of actors/directors I worked with a few years back on a production of the play by the Columbia University MFA program in drama were astonished when I informed them that the "mock trial" does not appear in the supposedly later, authorially revised F version; and, in fact, that scene was one of the more stunning elements in their production. Influenced—and perhaps *impressed*—by the extent of Q *Lear*'s press corrections, Pollard decided that the 1608 text of the play was a "good" quarto and even accorded it a singular status in his bibliographical description of the extant prefolio canon. I hope this brief analysis of the text and the context in which it was printed suggests that not only did Okes do what he could to produce a "good" quarto—stopping the press at least eight times to make corrections—but also that he and/or Butter gave some thought to how dramatic texts by some of Shakespeare's contemporaries were being printed and, in the end, chose as their model texts by one of the few playwrights in the period who openly endorsed and encouraged the transmission of drama from playhouse to printing house. Whether Q *Lear* is successfully retransmitted from the page back to the stage will always depend, ultimately, on the kinds of extratextual factors Nightingale mentions in the passage I quoted earlier. Nevertheless, I believe there is one thing about Q *Lear* that we can be reasonably sure of: few, if any, prospective book buyers in Paul's Cross Churchyard thought they were being sold a "bad" quarto.

Notes

An early version of this chapter was submitted as an essay to the seminar on "Performing 'Bad' Quartos" at the 1998 annual meeting of the Shakespeare Association of America in Cleveland, Ohio. I want to thank the leaders of that seminar, Skip Shand and Dale Churchward, for letting me sign on to their seminar very late in the game and for providing me with three single-spaced typed pages of comments on my paper. I also want to thank my colleague Jim Harner for reading a draft of the essay and making a number of helpful suggestions. Two anonymous readers for *Renaissance Drama* helped me to see the forest beyond the trees, and I am very grateful to Paul Werstine for his continuous encouragement of my work.

1. These studies include Stephen Greenblatt, *Renaissance Self-Fashioning: From More to Shakespeare* (Chicago: University of Chicago Press, 1980); Greenblatt, *Shakespearean Negotiations: The Circulation of Social Energy in Renaissance England* (Berkeley: University of California Press, 1988); Richard Helgerson, *Self-Crowned Laureates: Spenser, Jonson, Milton, and the Literary System* (Berkeley: University of California Press, 1983); Richard Wilson, *Will Power: Essays on Shakespearean Authority* (Detroit: Wayne State University Press, 1993); Jonathan Crewe, *Trials of Authorship: Anterior Forms and Poetic Reconstruction from Wyatt to Shakespeare* (Berkeley: University of California Press, 1990); Kevin Dunn, *Pretexts of Authority: The Rhetoric of Authorship in the Renaissance Preface* (Stanford: Stanford University Press, 1994); Leah Marcus, *Puzzling Shakespeare: Local Reading and its Discontents* (Berkeley: University of California Press, 1988); Gary Taylor, *Reinventing Shakespeare: A Cultural History from the Restoration to the Present* (New York: Oxford University Press, 1989); Michael Dobson, *The Making of the National Poet: Shakespeare, Adaption and Authorship, 1660-1769* (Oxford: Clarendon, 1992); Margreta de Grazia, *Shakespeare Verbatim: The Reproduction of Authenticity and the 1790 Apparatus* (Oxford: Clarendon, 1991); Jean L. Marsden, *The Re-Imagined Text: Shakespeare, Adaptation, and Eighteenth-Century Literary Theory* (Lexington: University Press of Kentucky, 1995); Kevin Pask, *The Emergence of the English Author: Scripting the Life of the Poet in Early Modern England* (Cambridge: Cambridge University Press, 1996); Jeffrey Masten, *Textual Intercourse: Col-*

laboration, Authorship, and Sexualities in Renaissance Drama (Cambridge: Cambridge University Press, 1997).

2. Jeffrey Masten, "Playwriting: Authorship and Collaboration," *A New History of Early English Drama,* ed. John D. Cox and David Scott Kastan (New York: Columbia University Press, 1997) 357-82; quotation at 371.

3. G. E. Bentley, *The Profession of Dramatist in Shakespeare's Time, 1590-1642* (Princeton: Princeton University Press, 1971) 55-56.

4. Benedict Nightingale, "Some Recent Productions," *Lear from Study to Stage: Essays in Criticism,* ed. James Ogden and Arthur H. Scouten (Crambury, NJ: Associated University Press, 1997) 226-46; quotation at 229.

5. The article that first generated the controversy over F *Lear*'s status as an authorially revised version of the 1608 quarto was Michael J. Warren, "Quarto and Folio *King Lear* and the Interpretation of Albany and Edgar," *Shakespeare, Pattern of Excelling Nature,* ed. David Bevington and Jay L. Halio (Newark: University of Delaware Press, 1978) 95-107. See also Steven Urkowitz, *Shakespeare's Revision of "King Lear"* (Princeton: Princeton University Press, 1980); and, of course, the essays in Gary Taylor and Michael J. Warren, *The Division of the Kingdoms: Shakespeare's Two Versions of King Lear* (Oxford: Oxford University Press, 1983).

6. Stanley Wells, "The Once and Future *King Lear,*" *The Division of the Kingdoms: Shakespeare's Two Versions of King Lear,* ed. Gary Taylor and Michael J. Warren (Oxford: Oxford University Press, 1983) 1-22; quotation at 19.

7. Robert Clare, " 'Who is it that can tell me who I am?': The Theory of Authorial Revision between the Quarto and Folio Texts of *King Lear,*" *Library* 17 (1995): 34-59; quotation at 47.

8. Laurie E. Maguire, *Shakespearean Suspect Texts: The "Bad" Quartos and their Contexts* (Cambridge: Cambridge University Press, 1996) 73-74. See also Paul Werstine, "A Century of 'Bad' Shakespeare Quartos," *Shakespeare Quarterly* 50 (1999): 310-33.

9. T. H. Howard-Hill, "The Two-Text Controversy," *Lear from Study to Stage: Essays in Criticism,* ed. James Ogden and Arthur H. Scouten (Crambury, NJ: Associated University Press, 1997) 31-41.

10. For useful recent studies of such collaborative interventions, see Masten, "Playwriting" and *Textual Intercourse.*

11. A. W. Pollard, *Shakespeare Folios and Quartos* (New York: Cooper Square, 1970) 65. Indeed, as Werstine notes, it was in fact W. W. Greg's subsequent work on *Merry Wives of Windsor* that inspired followers of the new bibliography "to extend the memorial-reconstruction hypothesis to other early printings of Shakespeare's plays . . . even the 1608 *King Lear*" ("Century" 310).

12. The exception, of course, is *Pericles,* which was not included in the first folio.

13. Pollard 53.

14. For a useful discussion of these arguments, see Paul Werstine, "Narratives About Printed Shakespeare Texts: 'Foul Papers' and 'Bad' Quartos," *Shakespeare Quarterly* 41 (1990): 65-86.

15. Pollard 76.

16. Pollard 76.

17. Peter W. M. Blayney, *The Texts of King Lear and Their Origins,* vol. 1, *Nicholas Okes and the First Quarto* (Cambridge: Cambridge University Press, 1982) 150.

18. Pollard 22.

19. Pollard 38.

20. Pollard 44.

21. Pollard 44.

22. P. A. Daniel, quoted in Pollard 50.

23. Pollard 62.

24. For an excellent recent account, see Maguire 85–89.

25. Leo Kirschbaum, "A Census of Bad Quartos," *RES* 14 (1938): 20–43.

26. W. W. Greg, *The Editorial Problem in Shakespeare,* 3rd ed. (Oxford: Clarendon, 1954) 12–13. Previously, Greg had entertained the possibility that Q *Lear* was a reported text in two earlier articles: "The Function of Bibliography in Literary Criticism Illustrated in a Study of the Text of 'King Lear,'" *Neophilogus* 17 (1933): 241–62; and "King Lear—Mislineation and Stenography," *Library,* 4.17 (1936–37): 172–83.

27. Blayney.

28. Michael J. Warren, *The Complete "King Lear"* (Berkeley: University of California Press, 1989) xxix.

29. See Werstine, "Narratives" 82–83.

30. This position is particularly evident in Gary Taylor, "Monopolies, Show Trials, Disaster, and Invasion: *King Lear* and Censorship," *The Division of the Kingdoms,* ed. Taylor and Michael J. Warren (Oxford: Oxford University Press, 1983) 75–120, esp. 89–101.

31. Quoted in W. W. Greg, *A Bibliography of the English Printed Drama to the Restoration,* 4 vols. (London: Bibliographical Society, 1939–57) 3: 1213.

32. See Douglas A. Brooks, *From Playhouse to Printing House: Drama and Authorship in Early Modern England* (Cambridge: Cambridge University Press, 2000) 44–65.

33. C. H. Herford, Percy Simpson, and Evelyn Simpson, *Ben Jonson,* 11 vols. (Oxford: Clarendon, 1952) 9:14.

34. Zachary Lesser, "Walter Burre's *Knight of the Burning Pestle,*" *ELR* 29.1 (1999) 22–43; quotation at 23.

35. Greg, *Bibliography* 1: xviii.

36. Lesser 30.

37. Greg, *Bibliography* 3: 1213.

38. Greg, *Bibliography* 3: 1206–07.

39. For a useful analysis of this "discourse of violation" in the context of published early modern drama, see Wendy Wall, *The Imprint of Gender: Authorship and Publication in the English Renaissance* (Ithaca: Cornell University Press, 1993) 182–84.

40. For a useful discussion of related issues, see Barbara A. Mowat, "The Theater and Literary Culture," *New History of Early English Drama,* ed. John D. Cox and David Scott Kastan (New York: Columbia University Press, 1977) 213–30.

41. Barbara A. Mowat, "Constructing the Author," *Elizabethan Theater: Essays in Honor of S. Schoenbaum,* ed. R. B. Parker and S. P. Zitner (Newark: University of Delaware Press, 1996) 93–110; quotation at 97.

42. Ben Jonson, *Catiline, his Conspiracy* (London, 1611), found in Early English Books 1475-1640 757:04.

43. Ben Jonson, *The Alchemist* (London, 1612), found in Early English Books 1475-1640 757:01.

44. Bentley 280.

45. Richard Dutton, "The Birth of the Author," *Elizabethan Theater: Essays in Honor of S. Schoenbaum,* ed. R. B. Parker and S. P. Zitner (Newark: University of Delaware Press, 1996) 71-92; quotation at 71.

46. Dutton 78.

47. I am excluding *The First Part of the Contention betwixt the two famous Houses of York and Lancaster* and *The True Tragedy of Richard Duke of York* from consideration here because Pollard did not include them in his description. They do not, however, have any of the features that I intend to discuss in my analysis of Q *Lear*.

48. Blayney 10.

49. David Scott Kastan, "Shakespeare after Theory," *Textus* 9 (1996): 357-74; quotation at 369.

50. Joseph Loewenstein, "The Script in the Marketplace," *Representations* 12 (1985): 101-114; quotation at 101.

51. Indeed, there is more mislineation in Q *Lear* than in any other Shakespeare quarto.

52. Greg, *Bibliography* 3: 1208-09.

53. Greg, *Bibliography* 3: 1209.

54. Greg, *Bibliography* 3: 1209.

55. Greg, *Bibliography* 3: 1218.

56. See Clare 46, table 1.

Shakespeare and the Millennial Market: The Commercial Bard

KATHLEEN E. McLUSKIE

A T THE WORLD SHAKESPEARE CONGRESS in Los Angeles in 1998, a break-fast meeting was hosted by the editorial team of Routledge for the editors of the Arden Shakespeare. At that meeting, the Routledge team announced that the Arden Shakespeare was being transferred to Thomas Nelson publishers. Thompson International, Routledge's holding company, was, in the parlance of the day, "letting Routledge go." Arden, of course, remained safe in its multinational home, not least because of Thompson's awareness of the series' potential in the emerging market of educational e-commerce.

In some ways, this turbulence in the upper reaches of the global publishing business seems both unsurprising and, for the tenured scholars who work in its primary production, irrelevant. We have become attuned to a certain knowingness about the commodification of culture, including and perhaps especially in the case of Shakespeare.

Moreover, as the publishers' move shows, different versions, editions, and packaging of the bard rise and fall, but the primary product, the plays themselves, the works of Shakespeare, have once again survived and are set fair to continue, not for an age but for all time.

A critique of this process seems, at this point in the millennial market-place, almost passé. As long ago as 1984, Frederic Jameson was reminding us that, according to the cultural logic of late capitalism,

161

Aesthetic production today has become integrated into commodity production generally: the frantic economic urgency of producing fresh waves of ever more novel-seeming goods (from clothing to airplanes), at ever greater rates of turnover, now assigns an increasingly essential structural function and position to aesthetic innovation and experimentation. Such economic necessities then find recognition in the institutional support of all kinds available for the newer art, from foundations and grants to museums and other forms of patronage. ("Postmodernism" 56)

Many scholars since have offered corroborating accounts of the assimilation of Shakespeare into cultural tourism or the appropriation of Shakespeare as cultural icon into the marketing practices of multinational companies.[1] However, this increased awareness of the material conditions in which Shakespeare is reproduced cannot in itself provide a satisfactory account of the cultural impact of that process. For example, Chin-tao Wu observed that in 1991 Nomura Securities, the world's largest stockbroking company, sponsored a European tour of the Royal National Theatre production of *Richard III* and *King Lear.* Nomura's cultural initiative apparently gained them access to Vaclav Havel, the playwright and president of Czechoslovakia, and subsequently won "important commissions from the Czech and Hungarian governments" (Wu 51). Wu's critique of this action elides a view about the relations between Shakespeare and commerce with an account of Nomura's role in "one of the largest financial scandals since the war" (52). As in Alan Sinfield's account of the use of Shakespeare in marketing the Royal Ordnance or Wu's own story of Philip Morris's million-dollar donation to the Metropolitan Museum's *Origins of Impressionism* exhibition (49–51), the critique depends upon an ethical view taken about guns or smoking or dodgy banks. Critiques of corporate patronage depend on assumptions about the innate corruption of money. They evade both an analysis of the appropriation and control of labor in cultural production and the evocation of endless desire involved in cultural consumption.

This ethical critique is harder to articulate when the sponsoring agency is less clearly associated with the more dangerously exploitative forms of capitalism.[2] In those cases, it is harder to identify the negative impact of commerce on Shakespeare. Individual instances of commercially sponsored production are, as Jameson remarked, merely

added to the dossier as yet another space in which something like the postmodern "great transformation" can be read. ("Marxism" 40)

There remains, as a result, a fundamental gap between general accounts of cultural production and the interpretative process of accounting for the forms and impact of particular cultural products.

One way of closing this gap is to recognize that in the world of corporate sponsorship, a Shakespeare play becomes the occasion for a marketing event that brings together sponsors and customers. There is often, as a result, an almost comic disjunction between the work of art chosen for sponsorship and the product being marketed. (It is hard to imagine Shakespeare plays less supportive of the aims of Nomura Securities than *Richard III* or *King Lear.*) The Shakespeare play, regardless of its explicit content, stands in for values that the sponsoring group wishes to attach to its product. This dynamic relationship between the brand name of Shakespeare and the cultural capital associated with his works is quite candidly acknowledged by the business sponsors and their agents. Discussing Nomura's sponsorship of the Royal National Tour, Colin Tweedy, director general of the UK Association of Business Sponsors of the Arts (ABSA), announced:

If you are a Japanese business trying to break into Europe, you want to do everything as "unJapanese" as you can. What could fit the bill better than staging Shakespearean English theatre. (Wu 51–52)

Leaving aside Tweedy's somewhat crass Orientalism, his comment reiterates and triumphantly assimilates the critical work of those who showed how "Shakespeare" in the late twentieth century had become a marketable icon of Englishness. As England, like more and more nation-states, is marginalized by the structures of global capital, Shakespeare not only represents Englishness but also *substitutes* for legitimating national identity, which then itself becomes marketable.

It is this *substitution effect* which seems to me most worthy of note. It is part of a process in which the moment-by-moment experience of a Shakespeare play is replaced by a hermeneutic possibility which is, in Jameson's words, "taken as a clue or a symptom for some vaster reality which replaces it as its ultimate truth" ("Postmodernism" 59). That hermeneutic potential can then stand in for the relations of production and consumption, between the sponsor's product and the audience. The association between Shakespeare and "Englishness" or the invention of the human or the supreme poetic account of the human spirit—meanings generated in part by critical discourse—can then be assimilated into the circulation of the value system of the sponsoring agents.

The "substitution effect" of commodified Shakespeare operates regardless of the style of the production. Shakespeare can stand in for heritage and the continuity of Englishness but it can also, in more avant-garde adaptation, stand in more generally for values of innovation and renewal. Chin-tao Wu quotes the executive vice president of Philip Morris enthusing about avant-garde art:

There is a key element in this "new art" which has its counterpart in the business world. That element is innovation—without which it would be impossible for progress to be made in any segment in society. (31)

Avant-garde form and radical critique, for all their temporary power to astound the bourgeoisie, can be appropriated by commerce. This is not only because of the intrinsic power of the market to determine the means of production and consumption but also because the market creates the conditions in which the hermeneutic potential of particular works can be extrapolated from the works themselves and circulated in commodified form.

If we are to understand rather than merely illustrate this process, we need to return to history. The aim of this return is not merely to reiterate the commonplace that Shakespeare and early modern drama were themselves located and implicated in emergent relations of cultural production. Even less is it to claim an easy analogy between early modern market relations and those of the highly developed capitalism of the twenty-first century.[3] It is rather to reflect upon the ways in and the extent to which market relations inflected the hermeneutic potential of early modern plays in order better to understand their position in the millennial market.[4]

The connection between the market and the hermeneutic potential of drama is a complex one, and it is easily short-circuited. One such short circuit occurs when we connect motifs of commercialization articulated in the plays and the real economic relations in which plays were produced.[5] The early modern dramatists, who participated in and offered a critique of the commercialization of theater, recognized that the muses had turned to merchants,[6] and their plays both celebrated and lamented the liberating and oppressive consequences of economic change and its social effects. However, the very continuity of those recurrent and long-lived tropes from medieval complaint and Juvenalian satire indicates the familiar dissonance between changing modes of production and the discourses of their articulation.[7]

Drawing attention to the absence of direct connections between plays and the economics of play production is not to deny the historicist emphasis on the shared social discourses of plays and other forms of cultural production. It would be reductive to suggest that playwrights sold their artistic birthright for a mess of commercial pottage.[8] The process of commercialization of theater involved a more mediated process of negotiation among playwrights, audiences, theatrical financiers, and other cultural officials, a process which ultimately involved separating out the plays from their social formation.[9]

Traces of this process can be found in the prologues and addresses to the reader which surround the production of early modern drama. In those prologues, the dramatists' intellectual engagement with the purpose of playing was most clearly implicated in their new economic relationship with their audience. The success of commercial theater in its constant negotiation with the civil authorities depended upon turning a potentially unruly crowd into an audience. The dramatists used their prologues in part to appease the regulating authorities' insistence on civil behavior, but the terms in which they did so also turned their audience into appropriately behaved consumers. They taught their audience to value plays as separate objects, connected to themselves by taste and discrimination rather than by religious faith or membership of a guild or an Inn of court.[10]

That conception of a play as a cultural object distinct from its audience also protected the playwrights from the commercial threat of censorship. As Richard Dutton (178) and Janet Clare (155–76) have observed, recurrent censorship scandals offer evidence of the extent to which the delicate balance between commercial companies and touchy court officials could be disrupted by an insistence on the particularity of reference in individual performances. The commercial process of turning participants into consumers involved insisting on the more generalized pleasures of playgoing, eliding the content of the play and the occasion of playing into a desired acquisition of fashionable good taste and aesthetic judgment.

The multilayered irony of Jonson's induction to *Bartholomew Fair,* for example, mocks a reductive commercialism that would equate judgment to seat price. It nevertheless constructs the conditions for appreciating the new play in its insistence on the importance of novelty and the distinction between this play and those of rival playwrights. The particularity which was to be awarded to this play could not, however, extend to topical meaning. The scrivener, drawing up his contract with the audience, is contemptuous of the "politic picklock of the scene, so solemnly ridiculous as to search out who was meant by the ginger-bread woman, who by the hobby-horse-man, who by the costermonger, nay who by their wares" (Jonson 11.133–35).

Jonson had a right to be touchy on this subject since the cloth-eared literal-mindedness of an unsophisticated Scot had already landed him in jail. By 1613, however, when Jonson was instructing his audience on the right reception for a play at the Hope, *Eastward Ho,* which had seemed so subversive in 1605, was under new management and was revived at court with no comment beyond the payment of the standard ten-pound fee.[11]

The successful court revival of *Eastward Ho* is only one instance of the way that plays could be separated from the occasion of their performance in order to be handled as exchangeable commodities. The company that effected the transaction was engaged at the same moment in the conflict with Henslowe, its financier, precisely over the ownership of its playbooks. Playbooks had become part of the commercial capital of a playing company, subject to commercial negotiations. Their significance did not depend on the moment of production but was available for revival where even their form could be adapted to new needs for new theatrical considerations.

When the King's Men acquired *The Malcontent* for their repertory, they cheekily announced their coup in the induction to the play. They also revealed that they had made "additions" to the play "only as your sallet to your greate feast, to entertaine a little more time, and to abridge the not received custome of musicke in our Theatre." The King's Men's defiant celebration of their right to perform a play from another company's stock is similarly placed in the context of a discussion of appropriate relations between the producers and consumers of art. The actors' induction discussion distances their performance from any instrumental relationship to the audience, claiming that it is "neither Satyre nor Morall, but the meane passage of a historie" (A3v). Moreover, the Burbage figure explicitly contrasts the players' own robust artistic independence to the constraining relations imposed by patronage:

Sir, you are like a Patron that presenting a poore scholler to a benefice, inioynes him not to raile against any thing that standes within compass of his Patrons follie: Why should not we inioy the antient freedome of poesie? (A4r)

Sly, the troublesome spectator, had asserted that "any man that hath wit may censure (if he sit in the twelve-penny roome)" (A4r). Burbage, for his part, insisted that the new commercial relations of consumption offered no such rights.

These negotiations over proper behavior in the theater were repeated in a number of inductions, prologues, and epilogues; they show the dramatists' concerted intellectual engagement with ensuring a response for their plays which would free them from particular, localized, and potentially dangerous meaning. In the process, the dramatists both assured their own freedom from censorship and connected the discourses of artistic and commercial liberty. The effect was, once again, to empty out particular meaning, separating the commercial relations of theater from the hermeneutics of particular theatrical events.

Discussions of the development of this commodified relationship between plays and their audiences is often tinged with an anticonsumerist nostalgia. However, it is worth contrasting the commercial repertory of the early modern theater with the masques and occasional drama of court entertainments. Those theatrical events, as scholars such as Martin Butler and James Knowles have painstakingly shown, spoke directly to the immediate concerns of their audience and even involved them formally in the action. However, where the repeatable, exchangeable, commodified, commercial plays are available for further negotiated revival in later markets, those traces of earlier, more unified relations of cultural interaction remain, in Greenblatt's resonant phrase, "dead on arrival" (7). This observation is not made in order merely to reverse the values implied in the anticonsumerist critique. It is rather to suggest that those values must also be subjected to historical analysis and their role in the process of commodification more fully understood.

The early modern negotiation between the "antient freedom of poesie" and the emergent commercial relations of production and consumption became the subject of a new discourse of value in the early twentieth century. Discussion of the audience for Shakespeare's theater and the original circumstances of production of his plays was deployed as often to inform cultural debate about theater as it was to provide information about its economic history. Chambers's account of the Actor's Economics, for example, provided invaluable information about the relations between playwrights, acting companies, and their financiers, but it also established the originating opposition between the collaborative ethos of Shakespeare's company and the hack-writer stable of Philip Henslowe (Chambers 348-88).[12] However, as William Ingram reminds us (31-35), E. K. Chambers was writing in the context of the early-twentieth-century economic history. In so far as Chambers does, intermittently, concern himself with larger questions of economics (and Ingram's dismissive reference to his preoccupation with "book keeping" is a little unfair [33]), he echoes the terms of that economic historical discussion. For example, he describes Henslowe, quite unself-consciously, as "a capitalist." In doing so, he explicitly strips the question of production of its ethical dimension, stating baldly: "Whether Henslowe was a good or a bad man seems to me a matter of indifference. He was a capitalist" (Chambers 368). However, he immediately goes on to blur the distinction between the economic and the ethical:

And my object is to indicate the disadvantages under which a company in the hands of a capitalist lay, in respect of independence and stability. Organized upon a legal basis which made an act of association between the members of less importance than individual contracts . . . with the capitalist, they were at his mercy if, for purposes of his own, he chose to use his powers under those contracts to bring about their dissolution. (Chambers 368)

Chambers is ostensibly discussing a set of economic relations, but ethical questions are clearly not excluded. Behind the modern economic discourse of capitalism and contract lay the ethical language and concepts which emerged equally from economic history, in particular the economic history of Tawney's *Tudor Economic Documents*. Those documents, like the ethical accounts of theater which Chambers himself printed in his sections on "Documents of Criticism" and "Documents of Control," situated economic activity in a clear ethical framework. The discourses of the "Documents of Control" invoke ethical considerations as they describe the relative wealth of players in relation to the neglected poor and the socially distorting effects of idleness.

   The primacy of the ethical over the economic found in Chambers's account of theatrical production is even more evident in accounts of consumption. In their discussions of the audience for the early modern stage, Alfred Harbage and Louis Wright used economic data—the cost of entrance to the playhouse—to define the different audiences for early modern theaters. There are obvious historical problems with the basis of their economic data: most of the evidence about the costs of attending the theater come from literary texts where the symbolic value of the money specified, its definition of class and status, is more significant than its exchange value. It is impossible to estimate the substitution effect of the cost of theater or apply rational choice theory for the consumption of commodities when the diversity and range of wealth in the audience and the wages of most categories of the early modern worker involved varying amounts of payment in kind so that any ratio of prices and wages is immediately flawed. For Wright and Harbage, however, economic data served primarily as the authenticating underpinning of a discussion about the value of theater in which they polarized the coherent organic community of Shakespeare's original spectators against the alienated, divided mass consumers of commercial entertainment.

Francis Mulhern has written tellingly about the early-twentieth-century "cultural competition" in which economics was the loser in the "struggle for rights to a synoptic explanation" in the domain of culture (312). Shakespeare and early modern drama were used in that struggle partly because of Shakespeare's high cultural status but also because of the eloquent articulation of the struggle over value found in early modern texts. Lear on the heath, Timon's disquisition on glittering gold, Portia's invocation of the quality of mercy all spoke of values which transcended the commercial. Their location in an imagined moment of economic change both linked the economic with the aesthetic and separated them into contrasting value systems. For modernist artists and intellectuals, facing their own crisis of value, Shakespeare became the locus and legitimation of their own creative experiments. Their struggle over the meaning of Shakespeare took the form of repudiating old meanings couched in a dead language and moribund theatrical forms and in the process, they created a meaning for Shakespeare which was articulated in abstract aesthetic terms.

Edward Gordon Craig, for example, struggling to find an appropriate aesthetic form for his production of *Macbeth,* emphasized the play's insubstantial mystery, describing it in terms that beg the question of precise theatrical realization:

It is just those figures which seldom shape themselves more definitely than a cloud's shadow, that give the play its mysterious beauty, its splendour, its depth and immensity, and in which lies its primary tragic element. (Sheren 45)

Craig was enough of a theater practitioner to know that something must appear on the stage, but the examples he chose did not refer to the language or narrative of Shakespeare's play; they offer, instead, iconic theatrical moments. In his discussion of the witches in *Macbeth,* for example, he evokes moments which have no part in the text:

We should see them . . . offering the woman a crown for her husband, flattering her beyond measure, whispering to her of her superior force, of her superior intellect; whispering to him of his bravery. (Sheren 45)

Craig's desire, in effect, to rewrite Shakespeare in modernist style, to reduce the textuality of the play to abstract images, shows him grappling with the gaps between text, performance, and meaning. As a theater practitioner, he turns the textuality of the play into abstract images whose ethical meaning depends upon a prior "interpretation" by the director or designer of the action as the play of sex and power.

These innovations of modernist theater practice—the ability to communicate the essence of a Shakespeare play from its narrative, untrammeled by particular ordering of words or traditional theatrical images—seemed to liberate Shakespeare to become the bearer of all the meanings of modernity. However, these innovations were, in the early twentieth century, constrained by the commercial realities of theatrical production. Craig's theatrical career was dogged by conflict with directors whose crass philistinism, as Craig saw it, deformed his scenic designs in the interests of successful commerce. The opposition between artistic vision and theatrical realization was summed up when Craig exhibited his designs for *Macbeth* to coincide with the opening of Beerbohm Tree's 1911 production of the play. Tree had been persuaded to reject Craig's designs by his chief scene painter, Joseph Harker, on the grounds that they would not be realizable onstage. They could excite the imagination as freestanding works of art but could not survive the material demands of performance.

This tension within modernist theater production continued throughout the twentieth century. On the one hand, Shakespeare was used to legitimate an anticonsumerist, autonomous domain for the aesthetic. On the other, the move toward abstraction in design and interpretation stripped the Shakespeare play of its textual specificity and historical particularity, turning it into an empty vessel which could be filled with any meaning which particular markets required. The activity of assigning meaning to the text was thus completely separated from the material conditions of its production and consumption. It was constructed as an unmediated communication from the imagination of the director to the collective imagination of the audience. Peter Brook, for example, describes his restless, eclectic search for new theatrical styles in terms of a theatrical experience whose satisfying sense of authenticity will transcend the language of Shakespeare's plays, allowing an almost mystical communication between performance and audience, a union of past and present unmediated by institutions or the material circumstances of particular performance events:

> The Shakespearean theatre speaks simultaneously in performance to everyone, it is "all things to all men," not in general, but at the moment when it's being played, in actual performance. It does so by reconciling a mystery, because it is simultaneously the most esoteric theatre that we know in a living language, and the most popular theatre. (Williams 144)

The artistic innovation of Brook's work, together with his use of "nontheatrical" venues, create a powerful illusion of unalienated experience, a seamless communication between performer and audience which is immensely satisfying for the spectators who are privileged to experience it.

This invocation of individual interpretation, the mystery of communication from the imagination of the director to the collective imagination of the audience, is one of the enduring legacies of modernism. It turned the repeatable text of early modern commercial theater into a set of abstract motifs, valued for their aesthetic power and discursively separated from the economic realities of the contemporary conditions of cultural production.

In the post–World War II period, theater, and especially Shakespearean theater, was rescued from the constraints of commercial production by increasingly generous state subsidy. So deeply embedded was the ideological opposition between the aesthetic and the commercial that the subsidizing agencies exercised what in the United Kingdom is called the "arm's-length principle" that disavowed any explicit connection between funding and production.

This sense that the modernist theater production of Shakespeare will communicate directly with its audience occludes the real relations of theatrical production; it also occludes the class relations which benefited most from dependence on the state. Francis Mulhern has indicated how one effect of the high-minded aesthetic of the early-twentieth-century Scrutiny group was "to mediate the introduction of a new, mainly petit bourgeois and self-consciously provincial social layer into the national intelligentsia" (23). Similarly, after World War II, the audience who enjoyed the unmediated appreciation of the mystery of Shakespeare was able to do so precisely because the economic costs of the production, like the economic costs of railroads or education, was both discursively and actually separated from its aesthetic appreciation.

A further effect of state funding in the post–World War II period was that the technical and commercial setbacks that had inhibited the realization of Craig's theatrical vision were solved for the most prestigious companies by an ability to draw on a global market of theatrical and design talent which could more than compete with the aesthetic pleasures of technologized entertainment such as television and film. In doing so, they reproduced the technical and organizational features originally developed to increase the profits of commercial companies. Fund-raising and marketing became important parts of theater organizations, along with a specialization of functions such as design and production.

This aspect of the commercialization of theater has made international theater significantly more expensive to produce and has widened the gap between the aesthetic and cultural impact of international Shakespeare companies and other versions of Shakespeare. That aesthetic and cultural impact depends, as with other forms of commodity production, on a marketable meaning—an innovative "take" on the play which transcends mere repetition. The separation of the discourses of economics and aesthetics occludes their actual interdependence and allows the production's hermeneutic potential to float free as the commodified object of consumption.

Anthony Sher's account of the production of *Titus Andronicus* he and Greg Doran mounted at the Market Theater in Johannesburg in 1995 illustrates the point. Sher's return to his native South Africa after the end of apartheid was both emotionally and politically significant. The Market theater in Johannesburg had been the venue where some of the most important oppositional theater of the apartheid regime, including the work of Athol Fugard, had been staged. Sher himself was returning from exile, a motif he picked up for Titus's triumphant return at the beginning of the play. The production was informed by interviews with a number of different groups in Johannesburg, and it emphasized the themes of battle fatigue and atavistic violence. For Sher and Doran, these themes had an especial resonance in the Johannesburg of 1995 where the play's "wilderness of tigers" was reconfigured as "a harsh urban jungle, like Jo'burg" (156).

The resonances between the venue, the play, and the moment of political change seemed to offer the potential to reunite meaning to event, to rediscover a unity which had been lost in the commercial theater. The production, however, was dogged with organizational problems, from an inexplicable funding hoax, which almost foiled the whole venture, to the day-to-day frustrations of working in the Market Theater, which for all its political and historical associations had no supporting infrastructure of publicity and marketing, front of house, and production facilities (Sher and Doran 154). The thematic coherence which Sher and Doran so eloquently describe was undermined at every stage by the material constraints of finding props and costumes and marketing the play to an audience un-accustomed to the new international style of modern-dress productions, unaccustomed indeed to theatergoing itself.

The production was a thematic success, especially with the English critics who had flown out to see it, but its aesthetic pleasure could only be connected to its political circumstances in the most generalized and abstract terms. The aesthetics and politics belonged to a discourse of criticism that had no purchase on the material conditions of its production. Further attempts to extend the production into the global market for theater were similarly separate from the aesthetics of the play. It was reproduced at a theater festival in Spain, and there were plans for a U.S. tour. Those plans also reveal the lack of fit between the thematics and the material conditions of production:

A big American foundation was prepared to put up the necessary money for the tour on two conditions: first, that the Market use the opportunity for a big fund-raising gala (to help secure their finances), and second, that this gala be organised by those members of the Market trustees who had wealthy American friends. Unfortunately the trustees in question declined—for reasons which were never made clear. As a result the revival was cancelled. America never saw the show, the Market lost a huge fund-raising opportunity and alternative employment for the autumn had to be sought by twenty three South African actors, musicians and stage managers. (Sher and Doran 301–02)

There was no apparent thematic connection between the American foundation's action and the production. Indeed, the foundation was intent on securing the Market theater's financial future. The event could be seen as the efforts of a global organization to secure an audience for theater in the new South Africa, much as other global organizations were engaged in developing consumer culture in the precarious and unstable new nation.

The case of the South African *Titus* reveals some of the currents which circulate around Shakespeare production in the millennial market. Sher and Doran's spin-off book about the production shows how it was informed by a late modernist aesthetic which assumed that Shakespearean revivals could speak to a contemporary condition if the setting and design could be made to deliver an abstracted meaning, rearticulated by both the original language of the play and its potential immediate analogies. The commercial realities of producing a play, however, depended on quite separate considerations to do with the expense of realizing the show and the inadequacies of the organizational infrastructure of the then South African economy.

This mismatch between the means of cultural production and the meanings which it generates is evident across a whole range of millennial Shakespeare production. The connections between a theater event and its hermeneutic significance have to be insisted upon by establishing abstracted analogies which will generate meaning within the experience of the play. Those analogies are made possible by the styles of modernism— the use of modern dress, which insists on contemporary relevance, and the unlocalized settings, which release the play from time, place, and narrative in order to insist on abstract connections.

A recent adaptation of *Macbeth* by the two-person fringe company Volcano illustrates the point. The production used video footage and various styles of music from operatic arias to 1950s ballads to signal its avant-garde position, reinforced by the fringe venues in which it toured. It used a collage of speeches from the play, offering an inchoate evocation of the supernatural evil that informed the overpowering sexuality of the relationship between Macbeth and his lady. The juxtaposition of scenes made no concession to narrative coherence or the pleasures of suspense, offering instead a random display of raw passion linking sexual feelings to the horrific violence enacted upon a life-size doll which was connected with both Macduff's son and the lost child of Lady Macbeth's infanticidal fantasy. The video footage cut across the action with repeated images of stairs leading down to a cellar, evoking the house in Gloucester which had been the scene of the terrible story of child abuse and multiple murders enacted by Fred and Rosemary West, recently convicted at Winchester Crown court.

By making an apparently random link between the Macbeths' sexual passion and the explosive cocktail of sex and violence which overflowed from the Wests' case, the production stripped both stories of their narrative and social particularity. Both *Macbeth* and the West case were subsumed into a generalized and abstracted enactment of sadomasochism. As the lights came up and the audience left the theater, the sound system played the sentimental 1950s song, "That Old Black Magic Called Love." The witty finale teased the audience by offering an apparent summary meaning of the events of the play but one whose sentimental style was manifestly at odds with the horrors which had been both enacted and invoked.

The juxtaposition of the Macbeth, the Wests, and the maudlin clichés of romance seemed at one and the same time both factitious and profound: it could be admired as a political statement about the equal implication of both high and commercial culture in legitimating violent heterosexuality, or it could be deplored as an empty universalizing which occludes the historical and social particularity of sexual violence. The process of connection and the sophistication with which it was made depended entirely on the intellectual predisposition of the individual audience member.

Given its small scale, public funding, touring, and fringe-venue status, the Volcano *Macbeth* is unlikely to become one of the canonical productions of Shakespeare performance studies. However, the relationships it established between the Shakespeare text, the performance event, and the production of meaning seem to me characteristic of the reproduction of Shakespeare in the millennial market. The hermeneutic potential the Volcano *Macbeth* offered was only one pleasure among the many which the production could afford. It took its place alongside sexual voyeurism or the pleasure of recognizing this line or that music. Shakespeare was thus commodified not only as a discrete product, the Shakespeare text, but as a spectrum of pleasures which can be reconstructed in a variety of formats. The familiarity of the plays' narratives allows them to be attached to an infinite range of contemporary events; the resonant eloquence of Shakespeare's poetry allows it to extend, through imagery, beyond the narrative to a more generalized evocation of universal ideas about sex or violence or the supernatural or the horror of war. In the process, random features of modern life can be captured and given significance—if not meaning—by their connection with the high cultural status of Shakespeare.

Macbeth has been variously used in recent years as an image which can
extend the significance of gang warfare on a Birmingham housing estate
(in a schools TV production), the continuing ethnic conflict in the Balkans
in the recent Sher and Doran production at Stratford, or, for that matter,
the destruction of the Australian aborigine in the Footsbarn production
from 1992.[13] The play can no longer speak of the politics of witchcraft and
kingship and so has become, in the words of one reviewer, "a tragedy of
fathers and sons, brothers and weird sisters, mothers and babes crawling
between a Shakespearean heaven and hell."[14] The pleasure of a Shakespeare
play, in other words, stands in and substitutes for an economic or a social
or a historical analysis of these modern events. Faced with the puzzling or
terrifying or absurd phenomena of modernity, we can reach for the security
of the telling Shakespeare quotation or narrative analogy. Shakespeare is
used to stand in for an ethical engagement with the modern world: the
ethical and the aesthetic are elided, but the economics of their production
are invisible.

The relationship between this elision and the resulting occlusion of
the economic is a complex one. Shakespeare, as we have seen, is most
commonly produced in developed economies in varying combinations of
corporate marketing and state-funded cultural subsidy. Attempts to make
a distinction between the products of those funding methods seem to me
ill-founded: publicly funded companies seek supplementary funding from
corporate finance, and a change of sponsorship seldom makes a direct
impact on the style or interpretative design of a particular production. The
hermeneutic pleasures of Shakespeare, on the other hand, are produced
not by the play production itself but by the process of consumption by a
particular fragment of the audience. This fragment consists of journalist
and academic critics. Their position in the commercial world is increasingly
marginalized and proletarianized as education, along with other forms of
cultural production, becomes increasingly subject to the disciplines of
the market. This group may not equate exactly to the lower-middle-class
contributors to Scrutiny, but its members are similar to them in their efforts
to locate themselves outside of the locus of the market, in control of the
meanings which that market merely buys and sells. However, that notion of
a location outside of commerce, the haven in a heartless world, is itself part
of the legitimizing ideology of commerce. The tension between commerce
and art is, in the millennial cultural market, not only compromised but
materially insignificant.

The continuing vitality of this tension lies in its ability to produce the desired objectives of the culture as a whole, the objectives of growth and innovation which will fuel the millennial market. Those who generate the abstracted meanings of Shakespeare make Shakespeare speak of race, class, and gender, the emergence of nationhood, or the destruction of the environment. They act as "cultural brokers" (to use Paul Gilroy's term), maintaining the presence of Shakespeare through new readings and critical controversy, using teaching and writing to add value to and ensure its continuing validity in the millennial market.

That process of cultural broking has, however, in recent years itself been contested in and subject to the market. Recent film versions of Shakespeare, Baz Luhrmann's *Romeo + Juliet* and the Stoppard-Madden *Shakespeare in Love,* are both informed by and demand to be read in terms of critical abstractions such as gender and power. These hermeneutic possibilities, however, are themselves part of the pleasurably witty play of images which ensure the films' artistic as well as economic success. In Luhrmann's film, the tattered posters for Shakespeare plays on the city walls, the empty shell of the Globe theater's proscenium arch on the beach, the Shakespearean costumes of the masked ball all defy the disapproval of critics by offering them the seductive pleasure of recognizing references assumed not to be available to the teenage audience. The fragmented nature of the postmodern audience is both acknowledged and then made whole by the sheer range of diverse pleasures the film has to offer. The same defiance of academic criticism is also evident in Tom Stoppard's script for *Shakespeare in Love.* Because of superior technology and finance, the film can create a simulacrum of historical authenticity far more satisfying than anything dreamed of by modernist theater directors. Film techniques can literalize poetic metaphors in visual form, and the techniques of montage and crosscutting can juxtapose powerful images in ways only gestured at in Craig's tottering screens. The images of the teeming muddy streets of Elizabethan London in *Shakespeare in Love* draw, to be sure, on cinematic conventions, [15] but the researched detail of costumes and props together with the use of "real" Elizabethan country houses for some settings provide a spectrum of pleasures it seems churlish to deconstruct. Moreover, once again, that deconstruction is preempted by the knowing references to Shakespeare's father's dunghill, to the death of Christopher Marlowe, to the youth of John Webster, and even, in passing, to John Taylor the Water poet. By knowing as much as, if not

more than, the critic, the film leaves the discourse of analysis limping
lamely behind it.

The construction of the artist as superior to and transcending the critic,
which was always implied in modernism, is most fully articulated in Al
Pacino's film *Looking for Richard*. There the street interviews with ordinary people, that cut across the rehearsal for a production in the fake
medieval Cloisters of the Metropolitan Museum, insist on an immediate,
accessible popular art. Shakespeare is easily subsumed into and substituted
by the generalized account of power play, which equates the high-culture
Shakespeare with the familiar commercial versions of the mafia conflict
seen in such cultural products as *The Godfather* but equally in the settings
for Jonathan Miller's controversial version of *Rigoletto*. High art has no
point of purchase in a culture that has rejected its elitism and assimilated
it to the most banal images of commercialized entertainment. Pacino's
complete rejection of the brokerage of high culture is made explicit in his
treatment of the English theater directors and even more so in his travestied
image of scholarship, represented by two distinguished Oxford University
academics. Even though he is using real directors and academics, the style
and aesthetic economy of Pacino's film render them icons of a rejected high
culture, at odds with the egalitarian, New World ethos of his production.
These real figures become commodified simulacra, part of the circulation
of images by which Pacino valorizes his version of Shakespeare.

The economic viability of these films is assured by their use of Hollywood
stars, and the populist colloquialism of their cinematic style mitigates the
unfamiliarity of the Shakespearean language, giving it all the decorative
charm of "heritage" marketing.[16] To a large extent, the ethical concerns of
modernist Shakespeare have disappeared or have been assimilated within
a teenage morality of true love and fair play. They stand at the end of a
historical process of commodification in which the plays were released
from their originating moment of production to become reproducible
aesthetic commodities able to take on any meaning the changed conditions
of production required. Cultural brokers in the academy and the culture
industries have assisted in the reassignment of significance to those products, which then assures their continued reproducibility.

Coda

It is impossible to conclude this account of the processes of commodification as they apply to Shakespeare with any call to action. Indeed,

my opening and final remarks about the commodification of intellectual activity itself suggest that literary criticism and cultural studies are all too easily appropriated to create new cultural products within the millennial market. As Perry Anderson reminded us in the editorial to his millennium edition of the restructured *New Left Review,* "For the first time since the Reformation there are no longer any significant oppositions—that is systematic rival outlooks—within the thought world of the West" (17). His equally trenchant account of the cultural scene in the same editorial, notes among other things, the mutual caricature of high and low forms of culture "as obverse forms of kitsch" (20). In the face of these features of the millennial moment—and his account of them is far more complex than I can record here—Anderson calls for "an uncompromising realism" (14), a refusal either to celebrate or merely console oneself in the face of the dominance of capitalism. In the perhaps now barren and certainly compromised field of Shakespeare studies, this uncompromising realism will certainly involve looking behind the current commodified versions of the commercial bard to a real understanding of the role of the early modern and the millennial market.

Notes

1. See, for example, Bristol; Kennedy.

2. For a subtle account of the relationship between radical theater and a conservative state sponsorship, see Armstrong.

3. The cultural sources and cultural power of that analogy are discussed later in the chapter.

4. I am grateful to the anonymous reviewer of the draft version of this piece for making me articulate this position more clearly.

5. See my discussion of this in McLuskie, "Shopping Complex."

6. See Dekker.

7. Theodore B. Leinwand has recently offered a subtle and persuasive "interpretive inventory of the responses to socioeconomically induced stress." In my review of his book, I suggest that this account illustrates the abstracting effect of economic discourse on the diversity of early modern dramatic form. See Leinwand; McLuskie, rev.

8. Compare Yachnin.

9. I have described this process in more detail in McLuskie, "Patronage."

10. I have discussed this more fully in McLuskie, *Dekker and Heywood* 6-9.

11. The stages in this process are more fully discussed in McLuskie, "Making and Buying."

12. See also Knutson.

13. See Cousin.

14. Publicity flyer for *Macbeth* as performed by Mark Rylance and Jane Horrocks at the Chichester Festival Theatre, 28 November-2 December 1995.

15. Compare the Pasolini *Canterbury Tales* or the film version of Natalie Davis's account of *The Return of Martin Guerre.*

16. Compare the success of the English shop Past Times and museum shops worldwide. Past Times and many museum shops also successfully market their wares through catalog and Internet sales for those who are unable to visit in person.

Works Cited

Anderson, Perry. "Renewals." *New Left Review* 2.1 (Jan.-Feb. 2000): 5-25.

Armstrong, Isobel. "Thatcher's Shakespeare." *Textual Practice* 3.1 (1989): 1-14.

Bristol, Michael D. *Big-Time Shakespeare.* London: Routledge, 1996.

Butler, Martin. "Entertaining the Palatine Prince: Plays on Foreign Affairs 1635-7." *Renaissance Historicism.* Ed. Arthur Kinney and Dan S. Collins. Amherst: University of Massachusetts Press, 1987. 265-92.

Chambers, E. K. *The Elizabethan Stage.* Vol. 1. Oxford: Clarendon, 1923.

Clare, Janet. "Historicism and the Question of Censorship in the Renaissance." *ELR* 27 (1997): 155-76.

Cousin, Geraldine. "Footsbarn: From a Tribal Macbeth to an Intercultural Dream." *NTQ* 33 (1993): 16-30.

Dekker, Thomas. "The Gull's Hornbook." *The Non-Dramatic Works.* Ed. A. B. Grosart. New York: Russell and Russell, 1963.

Dutton, Richard. *Mastering the Revels: The Regulation and Censorship of English Renaissance Drama.* Iowa City: University of Iowa Press, 1991.

Gilroy, Paul. *The Black Atlantic: Modernity and Double Consciousness.* London: Verso, 1993.

Greenblatt, Stephen. *Shakespearean Negotiations.* Berkeley: University of California Press, 1988.

Harbage, Alfred. *Shakespeare's Audience.* New York: Columbia University Press, 1941.

Ingram, William. *The Business of Playing: The Beginnings of the Adult Professional Theater in Elizabethan London.* Ithaca: Cornell University Press, 1992.

Jameson, Frederic. "Marxism and Postmodernism," *New Left Review* 176 (July-Aug. 1989): 31-45.

———. "Postmodernism, or The Cultural Logic of Late Capitalism," *New Left Review* 146 (July—Aug. 1984): 53-93.

Jonson, Ben. *Bartholomew Fair.* Ed. G. R. Hibbard. London: Ernest Benn, 1977.

Kennedy, Dennis. "Shakespeare and the Global Spectator." *Shakespeare Jahrbuch* 131 (1995): 50-64.

Knowles, James. "The Running Masque Recovered: A Masque for the Marquess of Buckingham (c. 1619-20)." *English Manuscript Studies* 8 (2000): 79-135.

Knutson, Rosalyn Lander. *The Repertory of Shakespeare's Playing Company 1594-1613.* Fayetteville: University of Arkansas Press, 1991.

Leinwand, Theodore B. *Theatre, Finance and Society in Early Modern England.* Cambridge: Cambridge University Press, 1999.

Looking for Richard. Dir. Al Pacino. Perf. Al Pacino, Kevin Spacey, Winona Ryder, and many others. Fox, 1996.

Marston, John. *The Malcontent. Augmented by Marston. With the Additions Played by the Kings Maiesties Servants.* London, 1604.

McLuskie, Kathleen E. *Dekker and Heywood: Professional Dramatists.* Basingstoke: Macmillan, 1995.

———. "Making and Buying: Ben Jonson and the Commercial Theatre Audience." *Refashioning Ben Jonson: Gender, Politics and the Jonsonian Canon.* Ed. Julie Sanders, Kate Chedzgoy, and Susan Wiseman. New York: St Martin's, 1998. 134–54.

———. "Patronage and the Economics of Theatre." *A New History of Early English Drama.* Ed. John Cox and David Kastan. New York: Columbia University Press, 1997. 423–41.

———. Rev. of *Theatre, Finance and Society in Early Modern England,* by Theodore B. Leinwand. *Shakespeare Quarterly* forthcoming.

———. "The Shopping Complex: Materiality and the Renaissance Theatre." *Textual and Theatrical Shakespeare: Questions of Evidence.* Ed. Edward Pechter. Iowa City: University of Iowa Press, 1996. 86–101.

Mulhern, Francis. *The Moment of "Scrutiny."* London: NLB, 1979.

Romeo + Juliet. Dir. Baz Luhrmann. Perf. Leonardo DiCaprio and Claire Danes. Fox, 1996.

Shakespeare in Love. Screenplay by Tom Stoppard and Marc Norman. Dir. John Madden. Perf. Gwyneth Paltrow, Joseph Fiennes, Geoffrey Rush, Colin Firth, Ben Affleck, and Judi Dench. Miramax, 1998.

Sher, Anthony, and Greg Doran. *Woza Shakespeare: Titus Andronicus in South Africa.* London: Methuen Drama, 1996.

Sheren, Paul. "Gordon Craig and Macbeth." *Theatre Quarterly* 1.3 (1971): 44–47.

Sinfield, Alan. *Fault Lines: The Politics of Dissident Reading.* Berkeley: University of California Press, 1991.

Tawney, R. H. *Tudor Economic Documents.* London: Longmans, 1924.

Williams, David. *Peter Brook: A Theatrical Casebook.* London: Methuen, 1988.

Wright, Louis B. *Middle-Class Culture in Elizabethan England.* Chapel Hill: University of North Carolina Press, 1935.

Wu, Chin-tao. "Embracing the Enterprise Culture: Art Institutions since the 1980s." *New Left Review* 230 (July–Aug. 1998): 28–57.

Yachnin, Paul. "The Powerless Theatre." *ELR* 21 (1991): 49–74.

Notes on Contributors

REBECCA ANN BACH, an associate professor of English at the University of Alabama at Birmingham, is the author of *Colonial Transformations: The Cultural Production of the New Atlantic World, 1580-1640*. She has published articles on early modern English drama and culture in journals such as *Textual Practice, SEL, Medieval and Renaissance Drama in England,* and *Journal of Narrative Theory* and in the essay collection *Race, Ethnicity, and Power in the Renaissance.*

DOUGLAS A. BROOKS is an assistant professor at Texas A&M University, where he teaches Renaissance literature. He is the author of *From Playhouse to Printing House: Drama and Authorship in Early Modern England* and the editor of the essay collection *Parenting and Printing in Early Modern England.* He is writing a book entitled *All the Kings' Printers: The Imprint of Royal Authority in Early Modern England, 1509-1649.*

AARON KITCH is a graduate student at the University of Chicago, where he is completing his dissertation on the intersection of printing and secular drama as fields of cultural production in early modern England.

LEAH S. MARCUS is Edwin Mims Professor of English at Vanderbilt University. She is the author of *Childhood and Cultural Despair: A Theme and Variations in Seventeenth-Century Literature; The Politics of Mirth: Jonson, Herrick, Milton, Marvell, and the Defense of Old Holiday Pastimes;*

Puzzling Shakespeare: Local Reading and Its Discontents; and *Unediting the Renaissance: Shakespeare, Marlowe, Milton* and coeditor of *Elizabeth I: Collected Works.*

JAMES J. MARINO is a doctoral student in English at Stanford University. He is writing a dissertation on early modern dramas as intellectual property.

KATHLEEN E. MCLUSKIE is the deputy vice-chancellor and a professor of English at the University of Southampton. She has published widely on early modern drama and is editing *Macbeth* for Arden 3.

STEVEN R. MENTZ is an assistant professor of English at Iona College in New Rochelle, New York. He has published articles on the publication history of Sidney's *Arcadia* and on other works of Elizabethan fiction. "Wearing Greene" is part of a larger study on the evolution of romance in early modern fiction and drama.

RANDALL NAKAYAMA is an associate professor of English at San Francisco State University. He edited and wrote the introduction for *The Life and Death of Mistress Mary Frith, Alias Moll Cutpurse.* His articles include "Domesticating Mr. Orton" in *Theatre Journal,* "The Sartorial Hermaphrodite" in *ANQ,* and "'I Know She Is a Courtesan by Her Attire': Clothing and Identity in *The Jew of Malta*" in *Collected Essays from the Fourth International Conference.*